Debates in Computing and ICT Education

Debates in Computing and ICT Education explores the major issues teachers of computing encounter in the classroom. Written by expert contributors and aimed at both pre-service and in-service teachers, the book provides an authoritative review of issues as diverse as:

- approaches to teaching computing
- the importance of teaching online ethics and digital literacy in an online world
- technology, inclusivity and the 'digital divide'
- the increasing gender disparity in computing education
- technology as a tool to augment cognition.

With the aim of stimulating critical thinking and enabling readers to form their own personal philosophy of teaching computing, this book provides a comprehensive grounding in the issues central to discussion and debate in teaching and learning with computers. It encourages critical reflection and aims to stimulate both novice and experienced teachers in thinking more deeply about their practice, encouraging them to link research and evidence to what they have observed in schools.

It is also designed to support the in-depth work required to achieve master's level credits on PGCE courses. Succinct chapters fully supported by pedagogical features mean you can dip in and out of this book as time allows – ideal for reflective practice and enhancing your professional thinking.

Sarah Younie is Professor in Education, Innovation and Technology at De Montfort University, UK.

Pete Bradshaw is a tutor and doctoral supervisor at the Open University, UK.

Debates in Subject Teaching Series

www.routledge.com/Debates-in-Subject-Teaching/book-series/DIST
Series edited by: Susan Capel, Jon Davison, James Arthur, John Moss

The **Debates in Subject Teaching Series** is a sequel to the popular **Issues in Subject Teaching Series**, originally published by Routledge between 1999 and 2003. Each title presents high-quality material, specially commissioned to stimulate teachers engaged in initial training, continuing professional development and master's level study to think more deeply about their practice and link research and evidence to what they have observed in schools. By providing up-to-date, comprehensive coverage, the titles in the **Debates in Subject Teaching Series** support teachers in reaching their own informed judgements, enabling them to discuss and argue their point of view with deeper theoretical knowledge and understanding.

Titles in the series

Debates in Mathematics Education
Edited by Dawn Leslie and Heather Mendick

Debates in Modern Languages Education
Edited by Patricia Driscoll, Ernesto Macaro and Ann Swarbrick

Debates in Music Teaching
Edited by Chris Philpott and Gary Spruce

Debates in Physical Education
Edited by Susan Capel and Margaret Whitehead

Debates in Religious Education
Edited by L. Philip Barnes

Debates in Science Education
Edited by Matt Watts

Debates in Computing and ICT Education
Edited by Sarah Younie and Pete Bradshaw

Debates in Computing and ICT Education

Edited by Sarah Younie and
Pete Bradshaw

Routledge
Taylor & Francis Group

LONDON AND NEW YORK

First published 2018
by Routledge
2 Park Square, Milton Park, Abingdon, Oxon OX14 4RN

and by Routledge
711 Third Avenue, New York, NY 10017

Routledge is an imprint of the Taylor & Francis Group, an informa business

British Library Cataloguing in Publication Data
A catalogue record for this book is available from the British Library

Library of Congress Cataloging in Publication Data
A catalog record for this book has been requested

ISBN: 978-1-138-89176-0 (hbk)
ISBN: 978-1-138-89178-4 (pbk)
ISBN: 978-1-315-70950-5 (ebk)

Typeset in Galliard
by Swales & Willis Ltd, Exeter, Devon, UK

Contents

Introduction to the series   vii
General introduction   ix
SARAH YOUNIE AND PETE BRADSHAW
Notes on contributors   xvi

PART I
Curriculum developments   1

1 What can technology actually do?   3
   CHRIS SHELTON

2 Computer studies, information technology, ICT and
   now computing   14
   JOHN WOOLLARD

3 The impact of teachers' perspectives on the development
   of computing as a subject   27
   JAN BARNES AND STEVE KENNEWELL

4 Assessment of Computing and ICT at 16: What are
   the perceptions of learners?   43
   PETE BRADSHAW

5 How female friendly is the new computing curriculum?   52
   REENA PAU

6 Towards tomorrow's successful digital citizens:
   Providing the critical opportunities to change mindsets   63
   CHRISTINA PRESTON, MOIRA SAVAGE, MALCOLM PAYTON
   AND ANTHONY BARNETT

PART II
Whole school learning environments   79

  7 Learning spaces: exploring physical and virtual
     pedagogical principles   81
     CHRISTINA PRESTON, ALLISON ALLEN AND RICHARD ALLEN

  8 Using Web 2.0 technologies to enhance learning
     and teaching   97
     LEON CYCH, LAWRENCE WILLIAMS AND SARAH YOUNIE

  9 Understanding online ethics and digital identities   114
     PETE BRADSHAW AND SARAH YOUNIE

 10 Computational thinking and creativity in the
     secondary curriculum   137
     MOIRA SAVAGE AND ANDREW CSIZMADIA

 11 Bring your own device?   153
     PAUL HYNES AND SARAH YOUNIE

 12 Technology and inclusion   167
     CHRIS SHELTON

PART III
Classroom applications   179

 13 Debates in the use of tablets in secondary classrooms   181
     JON AUDAIN, EMMA GOTO AND TIM DALTON

 14 Does Facebook have a place in the school classroom?
     Exploring risks and opportunities   195
     ANGELOS KONSTANTINIDIS

 15 Using video for assessment practices inside classrooms   209
     CHRIS DANN AND TONY RICHARDSON

 16 Developing reflective practice in the classroom using ICT   223
     HELEN BOULTON

     Index   234

Introduction to the series

This book, *Debates in Computing and ICT Education*, is one of a series of books entitled *Debates in Subject Teaching*. The series has been designed to engage with a wide range of debates related to subject teaching. Unquestionably, debates vary among the subjects but may include, for example, issues that:

- impact on initial teacher education in the subject
- are addressed in the classroom through the teaching of the subject
- are related to the content of the subject and its definition
- are related to subject pedagogy
- are connected with the relationship between the subject and broader educational aims and objectives in society, and the philosophy and sociology of education
- are related to the development of the subject and its future in the twenty-first century.

Consequently, each book presents key debates that subject teachers should understand, reflect on and engage in as part of their professional development. Chapters have been designed to highlight major questions and to consider the evidence from research and practice in order to find possible answers. Some subject books or chapters offer at least one solution or a view of the ways forward, whereas others provide alternative views and leave readers to identify their own solution or view of the ways forward. The editors expect readers will want to pursue the issues raised, and so chapters include questions for further debate and suggestions for further reading. Debates covered in the series will provide the basis for discussion in university subject seminars or as topics for assignments or classroom research. The books have been written for all those with a professional interest in their subject, and, in particular, student teachers learning to teach the subject in secondary or primary school; newly qualified teachers; teachers undertaking study at master's level; teachers with a subject coordination or leadership role and those preparing for such responsibility; as well as mentors, university tutors, CPD organisers and advisers of the aforementioned groups.

Books in the series have a cross-phase dimension, because the editors believe that it is important for teachers in the primary, secondary and post-16 phases to look at subject teaching holistically, particularly in order to provide for continuity and progression but also to increase their understanding of how children and young people learn. The balance of chapters that have a cross-phase relevance varies according to the issues relevant to different subjects. However, no matter where the emphasis is, the authors have drawn out the relevance of their topic to the whole of each book's intended audience.

Because of the range of the series, both in terms of the issues covered and its cross-phase concern, each book is an edited collection. Editors have commissioned new writing from experts on particular issues, who, collectively, represent many different perspectives on subject teaching. Readers should not expect a book in this series to cover the entire range of debates relevant to the subject, or to offer a completely unified view of subject teaching, or that every debate will be dealt with discretely, or that all aspects of a debate will be covered. Part of what each book in this series offers to readers is the opportunity to explore the interrelationships between positions in debates and, indeed, among the debates themselves, by identifying the overlapping concerns and competing arguments that are woven through the text.

The editors are aware that many initiatives in subject teaching continue to originate from the centre, and that teachers have decreasing control of subject content, pedagogy and assessment strategies. The editors strongly believe that for teaching to remain properly a vocation and a profession, teachers must be invited to be part of a creative and critical dialogue about subject teaching and should be encouraged to reflect, criticise, problem-solve and innovate. This series is intended to provide teachers with a stimulus for democratic involvement in the development of the discourse of subject teaching.

Susan Capel, June 2017

General introduction

Sarah Younie and Pete Bradshaw

This book is being published at a critical time for the subject of computing and ICT (information and communications technology). Changes in 2014 to the national curriculum in England have seen the introduction of computer science as a core subject for inclusion in the English Baccalaureate (EBacc) set of qualifications at GCSE – the high-stakes qualification in schools at 16+. While this has promoted the subject in schools (the EBacc provides one of the key reporting metrics for schools), this change has been accompanied by the disapplication of ICT at GCSE. In other words, ICT is no longer a subject in the national curriculum, and GCSE qualifications in it will not be offered.

The CREST Report (Dallaway, 2016) argues that this scrapping of ICT, albeit with an enhanced position for computer science, was 'a mistake' and that the education system would be best served with qualifications to allow for two subjects: the more specialised computer science and the more generalised ICT. Contributors to the report from teachers, awarding bodies (examination boards) and industry groups argued that there is a substantial difference in emphasis between the two subjects. They saw that computer science focuses on how the computer and related devices work and on programming, while ICT focuses on how to use technology for business and employment purposes. This can be expressed as the difference between teaching pupils how computers work and teaching pupils how to use computers, analogous to teaching a car mechanic how the engine works and a driver how to drive. The seminal and now historic moment came in January 2012 when the then Secretary of State for Education for the UK Government announced the disapplication of ICT from the English national curriculum and started these most recent and important changes in the history of the subject. It is against this momentous backdrop that this book is published. We refer to 'computing and ICT' throughout this book to cover the 'subject' unless a specific qualification is being discussed.

With a wide array of issues relating to the teaching of computing and ICT and teaching with technology, and the curriculum changes outlined above, this book considers key debates that teachers and schools will need to understand, reflect on and engage in. The chapters examine what major questions we should be considering and explore the evidence from research and practice, particularly with respect to the role of the teacher and use of computing technologies for pedagogic practice. Through consideration of the key issues and debates, we aim to provide an enriched understanding of the subject and how the broader issues of computing and ICT impact beyond the classroom to the whole school and into the home, wider community and contemporary society. Thus, for example, we consider digital citizenship and online identities – of learners and teachers. As technologies permeate more areas of our lives, personally and professionally, so we can expect the need for considered debate and reflection.

The specific debates included are those most topical and relevant to teaching computing and ICT, and are considered in relation to development in the teaching of the subject, which may also include mentoring and/or subject leadership, too. More broadly, the book also considers the impact and affordances of computing technologies on whole school issues, which include the learning environment and pedagogic practice across the curriculum. Each debate is explored through providing commentaries and, where it exists, through reference to relevant research, which will enable deeper examination of the issues in more depth, through further reading.

Computing and ICT is a complex area, because it is both a discrete curriculum subject, with clearly defined content and a set of skills, which can be used across the curriculum to enhance the learning and teaching of all subjects and which digitally literate learners need to develop for effective engagement in their learning and to become fully reflective and active citizens. Further, there are debates about how teachers can engage with technology to enhance their classroom practice and their professional development.

Underpinning all the debates considered in the book is the tension between the perceived transformational affordances of digital technologies for learning versus the costs of the technology. This may explain why bring your own device (BYOD) has gained more traction in recent years and is a theme debated across a number of chapters.

The book is organised into three sections although there is, perhaps, an arbitrary element to this, given that the issues and debates cut across contexts.

The first section (Part I) considers the computing and ICT curricula and the changes that these have undergone since their inception and, in particular, since 1990 (DES/WO, 1990). The implications of these changes are considered from both teachers' and learners' perspectives.

The second section (Part II) focuses more broadly on the learning environment across the school and how technology can be used to enhance pedagogic practice across subjects. This will involve an examination of computing and ICT in relation to whole school learning environments and the impact of computing technology on teachers' practice and learners' engagement. This section focuses on debates concerning cross-curricular issues and whole school debates with technology, including how a school manages access to technology resources.

The final section (Part III) addresses issues focused inside the classroom and explores those debates concerning technology applications that teachers have appropriated to enhance learning.

Part I Curriculum developments

The first section of the book considers a central debate that concerns the relationship between computer science as a discrete subject and the affordances of computer technologies, which form a set of cross-curricular skills that can be applied to the learning and teaching of all subjects. The tension between subject knowledge and transferable skills also highlights a further debate, not only about the status of the subject and its wider applicability, but about even the very terms we use to debate these issues.

A reoccurring theme that runs through a number of chapters in this first section pertain to the changes in the curriculum and the debates surrounding the scope of the specialist subject of computer science. A key part of this debate, with the new computing and ICT curriculum, is an emergent fear that it is overly focused on programming, or coding, and that the need for digital literacy, e-safety and basic ICT skills may fall victim to the dominance of computer science. Thus, we consider whether the rush to code means that teaching digital citizenship will suffer due to the demands of the computer science aspect of the new curriculum. This in turn raises questions about whether the new curriculum will meet the needs of employers and those in further/higher education and the IT industry who were instrumental in the demand for the changes to the curriculum (Royal Society, 2012). A concern noted in the CREST Report (Dallaway, 2016) identifies that the numbers of students entered for ICT were three times higher than those currently registered for computer science GCSE. While this is a fluid situation, there is a great concern that the percentage of learners progressing with computing after Key Stage 3 (age 14) is significantly lower than it was when ICT was part of the national curriculum. Also of concern is that ICT GCSE has historically had a more or less equal gender balance, with approximately equivalent numbers of boys and girls taking the qualification, whereas computer science tends to attract significantly more boys, with schools reporting 85% male intakes (Dallaway, 2016).

In the first chapter, Shelton discusses the debates around what digital technology can actually do for education. These debates centre around both positive and negative claims about the impact of the use of ICT on pupils' learning and, in turn, lead to disputes about whether schools should make more or less use of technology. A feature of these debates is the positive claims that state ICT can raise GCSE results, lighten teacher workload and make learning more engaging, and in short, that technology can transform education for the better in some way. The other side of the debate, however, claims that using technology distracts from real learning, that investments in new gadgets are wasteful uses of the limited money in school budgets, or that technology just does not work in the way it was supposed to.

In Chapter 2, Woollard begins by asking: is it ICT, computing or IT? Given that the subject's name and status has changed over the last 25 years and the fact its usage is still contested, we need to understand the debate over terminology. This very question concerning the terms leads Woollard to focus on the contemporary computer science curriculum and understanding the changes and debates over the previous three decades. Woollard also raises an important related debate concerning the balance between content knowledge, with respect to computer science as a discrete subject, and ICT competencies as a set of cross-curricular skills applied to the teaching and learning of all subjects.

The next chapter aptly follows the previous one, continuing the debate concerning subject content by looking at the development of policy and practice in the computing curriculum. Kennewell and Barnes, in Chapter 3, examine the debates on curriculum policy by investigating the introduction of a new computing curriculum from the perspective of ICT teachers and discussing the development of appropriate pedagogical practices. They show how activity systems can be used to characterise variations in perceptions of the subject and compare approaches to teaching across three case study schools.

The different views of ICT and computing as a subject are next considered from the learner's perspective in the following chapter by Bradshaw. He explores learners' perceptions of ICT, arguably a somewhat neglected area regarding research, and in particular, their views on assessment in the subject. Chapter 4 reports on findings from primary research undertaken by the author with 16-year-old secondary school learners to ascertain their perceptions of the subject, its utility and what it is that makes for 'being good at ICT/computing'. Giving voice to learners is considered and opens a key debate concerning the value of computing and ICT as perceived by learners.

Following the focus on learners' perceptions, Pau examines issues of gender and why it is that so few girls study computer science. In Chapter 5, she debates the issue of girls in computing, from a UK and an international perspective, and considers the poor 'take up' of the subject by girls in compulsory education. In England, recent developments in the national curriculum have led to a change in emphasis to include more aspects of computer science, and this has been associated with reduced numbers of girls opting to take the subject. The challenge with the renewed emphasis on computer programming in schools is to explore the opportunities to rethink how we engage girls in computer science.

In Chapter 6, Barnett, Payton, Preston and Savage explore the area of digital citizenship and the development of digital literacy skills. The authors examine the debate concerning the shift in the curriculum and the issues about whether the 'softer' aspects of digital literacy might be downgraded by a concentration on computer science and especially coding at the expense of developing broader digital citizenship skills that are needed in today's contemporary culture and for future employment.

Part II Whole school learning environments

The second part of the book focuses more broadly on whole school learning environments and how technology can be used to enhance pedagogy across the curriculum. The chapters here focus on the challenges facing schools as they engage with and develop technology for pedagogic purposes, and provides a critical overview of the debates concerning the use of technologies for teaching. For technologies which have a contested track record in classroom application, teachers will find a helpful synopsis of the potential uses and the important debates surrounding mobile devices. A number of chapters provide a comprehensive account of the new opportunities these developments present and an examination of the essential issues concerning the use of computing technologies for teachers' practice.

This will include an examination of BYOD approaches, which are pertinent given the increased availability and use of mobile devices. Cross-curricular themes are examined that relate to the uses of technology such as inclusion, creativity and ethical considerations. Issues of ethics are heightened when using devices from home or through a flipped classroom model, with respect to pupils using personal technologies for their learning in and out of school.

An exploration of the issues concerning the development of mobile devices and how these are configured to support learning, both in school and out, is a key theme of this section of the book. Looking at the BYOD/BYOT (bring your own technology) debates, a range of authors examine issues regarding access out of school and how e-safety is ensured, and the implications of 'cloud technologies' for learners storing data. The pedagogical debates around the place of programming and the extent to which ICT and computing foster creativity are also discussed.

The section starts with and discusses the importance of learning spaces. In Chapter 7, Preston, Allen and Allen consider the debates about where and how learning should occur and how technology allows us to think differently about learning spaces, for example, through the use of a flipped classroom, which has gained much attention in recent years.

The authors argue that a flipped classroom can change the relationship between teachers and pupils, and this is discussed through the examination of different strategies for changing pedagogy. The chapter takes a case study approach through comparing three different schools to illustrate the potential of pupils' own devices to facilitate greater control of their learning agenda and the impact on pupils' learning habits. While these projects are still in progress, a number of questions have been raised that will help other schools considering these debates plan for the future. The chapter debates which strategies are most effective.

In Chapter 8, Cych, Williams and Younie explore Web 2.0 technologies and how these can be used across subjects to enhance. Specifically, the authors explore how Web 2.0 tools can be used to create a social constructivist learning environment that links multiple pedagogical contexts. The aim of such technologies is to stimulate learner engagement and to examine how to deploy Web 2.0 technologies effectively in the classroom.

In Chapter 9, Bradshaw and Younie discuss teachers' professional need to develop a thorough understanding of online ethics and digital identities for both learners and for ourselves as teachers. Arguably, this is a debate no school, teacher or parent can afford to ignore. It is a nuanced debate about both promoting and protecting digital identities and is examined through a careful consideration of both sides of the debate.

In Chapter 10, Csizmadia and Savage investigate computational thinking and creativity, and explore whether computational thinking opposes, or complements, creativity. Further, the authors invite us to consider whether computational thinking is in itself creative. By referring back to the new national curriculum in England, initial reactions from teachers of 'where have all the creative bits gone' and listening to how teachers envisaged creativity, this chapter outlines the tensions and key issues concerning computing and creativity.

In Chapter 11, Hynes and Younie continue the debate about BYOD. At the core of this debate is that learners are taking responsibility for the purchase, maintenance, training, insurance and eventual replacing of the technology they use for learning both within and outside school, rather than the school.

This debate considers the arguments for why schools would choose to opt for a BYOD scheme, and this is followed by a critical examination of the issues that cover classroom management and how some teachers make the transition easily, with phrases like 'screens down', which replaces the more traditional 'pens down', whereas other teachers find it more difficult and need to gain confidence at their own pace. As new devices appear so do new functions and new apps raising the issues of schools and teachers needing to know what is available and how to exploit it, and, crucially, its impact on learning. Arguably, there is still a lack of a replicable model for BYOD so, as a whole school technology strategy, this needs to be carefully thought through. Linked to this is the observed parental negativity concerning the use of mobile devices in schools and how schools can cope with such resistance. Finally, the chapter considers the issues that BYOD raises concerning inclusion and ensuring parity of access to technology.

Shelton, in Chapter 12, picks up this debate concerning technology and inclusion. He distinguishes between narrow conceptions of inclusion and broader understandings that see inclusion as an approach to education based on inclusive values (including equity, participation, compassion and respect for diversity), and in adopting this broader view, Shelton is concerned with how we can ensure the inclusion of all learners through technology.

Part III Classroom applications

This section discusses the implications resulting from the use of technology inside the classroom and the issues for teachers' professional practice. This includes how teachers are facing the challenge of integrating technology-based pedagogic tools into their practice. The section also discusses a range of issues arising from the use of technologies such as social media.

In Chapter 13, Audain, Goto and Dalton debate the use of tablet technology in the classroom. Specifically, they look at how the use of tablets can change teachers' pedagogy and the impact this has on learning design and on issues of classroom management. The process of using tablets in the classroom can be fraught with issues about their use: how they support learning and the operational debates surrounding their systems and daily maintenance. This is a complementary chapter to the BYOD by Hynes and Younie, as it draws on different research to address the issues and therefore deepens the debate on mobile devices for learning.

In Chapter 14, Konstantinidis examines the use of social media in the classroom, for example Facebook, and considers in this debate the issues for and against its use. Given the popularity of social media among pupils, this raises an interesting conundrum with respect to teachers' pedagogical appropriation of this tool as a way of engaging pupils in their learning. Most teachers eschew adding learners as friends on Facebook or stay away from social media altogether, yet there are voices arguing for a different and constructive approach to social media use for learning and communicating with learners. What are the potential motivational and learning benefits for both teachers and learners using social media? What is more, how should teachers proceed in such practices? This chapter will examine these important issues and the debate surrounding the use of social media in the classroom.

In Chapter 15, Boulton highlights the debates and controversies concerning developing reflective practice in the classroom and the use of technology to support teachers' reflective practice. By providing an overview of the place of reflective practice for teachers' professional development, she debates whether technologies are able to advance current practice. In particular, she explores how technologies can provide a virtual space for reflection, alongside the collection of authentic multimedia evidence, which can be shared online and thereby enhance teachers' professional development.

In Chapter 16, Dann and Richardson debate the place of video assessment use in classrooms for learning. They argue that the increase in mobile video-enabled technologies has the potential to meaningfully alter assessment practices. Given this, arguments for and against the use of video for classroom assessment will be examined. The authors debate the ethics of using video in classrooms, alongside the power of video evidence to support pupil learning through providing an effective form of feedback, as well as storage implications for the video assessment evidence.

References

Dallaway, E. (2016) *GCSE reform: a new dawn for computer science*. GB, CREST. Available from: http://www.crest-approved.org/wp-content/uploads/CREST-GCSE-Reform-June-2016.pdf

DES/WO. (1990) *Technology in the national curriculum*. London: Department for Education and Science-Welsh Office.

Royal Society. (2012) *Shut down or restart*. London: Royal Society.

Contributors

Allison Allen is Director of Outstream Consulting and has held several governance roles, as an academy trust governor, Trustee of Naace, LGfL and Senior Fellow of MirandaNet. She is joint author of several publications and leads on digital safeguarding including the national Self Review Framework and school accreditation. Allison has worked at senior level within the education sector, specialising in using education technology to enhance the life chances of children, supporting the moral imperative to develop learners who have the higher thinking skills and confidence that sustains effective, safe and innovative creation and use of technology.

Richard Allen Richard is a Specialist in Education Transformation and Learning Services. He has a background of business management working with blue-chip companies in international hi-tech industries, as a business school senior lecturer, as a teacher trainer and as a consultant to government, local authorities, schools and business. He served on the Board of Management of Naace and has written, delivered and assessed university courses from foundation degree to MBA level, and his research interests include the application of virtual reality.

Jon Audain is Senior Lecturer in ICT/Computing and Music for Primary ITE at the University of Winchester, UK and an Apple Distinguished Educator (ADE). He is a Fellow of the College of Teaching and a Fellow of the Royal Society for the Encouragement of Arts, Manufacturers and Commerce (FRSA).

Jan Barnes is a Senior Lecturer and Researcher at the University of Wales Trinity Saint David. Her research interests are in digital technology and its relationship to pedagogy, and the development of cultural historical activity theory as an analytical in tool in education. Other research interests include perceptions and practice of initial teacher education and the growing use emergent technology in education. Jan has presented her work at both national and international conferences.

Anthony Barnett is a Senior Lecturer at University of Worcester. He teaches on a range of modules including ICT and learning theory, and critical issues in ICT and education. His research interests include asynchronous discussion thread patterns. He co-authored *Digital Literacy for Primary Teachers* and *Technology Enhanced Learning in the Early Years*. His other interests include innovative approaches to educational research.

Helen Boulton is Associate Professor at Nottingham Trent University and a National Teaching Fellow. Dr Boulton is Chair of the National Subject Association ITTE (Information Technology in Teacher Education). Dr Boulton's research is focused on emerging pedagogy for new technologies in learning and teaching, and building communities of practice to support professional development. Dr Boulton's work is published nationally and internationally.

Pete Bradshaw worked as a teacher of Computing and ICT in schools for over 20 years and in higher education for another 15. He currently works for The Open University, teaching on the master's programme and tutoring teachers taking the Doctor in Education qualification. His specialisms there include school organisation, leadership, management and assessment. He has been a chief examiner for ICT and was formerly a board member of Computing At School.

Andrew Csizmadia is Senior Lecturer in Computer Science Education at Newman University Birmingham, where he trains new computing teachers. He has supported in-service teachers in the transition from ICT to computer science through coordinating regional and national computing projects. Andrew was a member of the CAS Computational Thinking Working Group and a co-author of *Computational Thinking: A Guide for Teachers*, and is a member of the CAS Assessment Group. Currently, Andrew is the Secretary for the national subject association ITTE and is the Academic Lead and Senior Assessor for the British Computer Society's Certificate in Computer Science Teaching, which is an accreditation scheme for in-service computing teachers.

Leon Cych taught in London schools for 23 years. In that time, he became a Primary IT and Computing specialist. For the last 14 years, he has been an Educational Consultant who documents grass roots teacher activity through video and video streaming. He has worked for the BBC, BECTA, NESTA, ResearchED and Northern Rocks. He currently co-hosts the UK education podcast *theEDfiles*.

Chris Dann is an Adjunct Lecturer at the University of the Sunshine Coast, where he led the work-integrated unit responsible for the placement and management of approximately 1,000 students each year. In 2009, he led the writing of a four-year undergraduate degree in pre-service primary teacher education while completing a master's degree in internationalisation of pre-service teacher education. He was a principal and administrator in schools for 18 years before moving to the higher education sector. He has been innovating in assessment for over 25 years and is now completing his doctoral study on the use of mobile devices in formative assessment of learners in schools.

Tim Dalton is a Product Manager at Smoothwall, an internet security and safeguarding company providing technology and advice to the education sector. He works with teaching staff and students to understand their needs, and with development teams to build products that support them. Previously, Tim spent 10 years at Wildern School leading on new technologies and providing IT consultancy to many schools across the UK. He recently completed an MSc Digital Education with University of Edinburgh focusing on the impact of 1:1 computer deployments.

Emma Goto is a Senior Lecturer in Teacher Development at the University of Winchester. Emma previously worked as a school teacher and as a Local Authority Funded Advanced Skills Teacher (AST) for ICT. She has undertaken research in the fields of learning technology and computing. Emma undertakes consultation and development work with teachers, schools and other organisations. She has contributed to a range of publications, including writing the text for several of the BBC *Bitesize Computing* guides.

Paul Hynes is Vice Principal at George Spencer Academy in Nottingham where his responsibilities include whole school learning technologies, timetable, data and the curriculum. Paul has always been passionate about using ICT to help with the learning of students and following his role as an assistant head teacher in charge of ICT developments, Paul went on to join the Specialist Schools and Academies Trust (SSAT) in September 2003 as the subject leader for ICT with responsibility for technology colleges. Paul worked on various projects including e-mentoring, driving New Technologies, Leading Edge and Future Schools programmes and then onto his role as Vice Principal.

Steve Kennewell is a Visiting Professor of Education at Cardiff Metropolitan University, having retired from Swansea Metropolitan University in 2011. He has been involved in computer education for over 40 years as a secondary teacher, teacher educator and researcher. During this time, he has authored, edited and contributed to many books concerning the teaching of computing and ICT and about the use of ICT in teaching and learning. For several years, he was editor-in-chief of ITTE's international journal *Technology, Pedagogy and Education,* which he now co-edits with Sarah Younie.

Angelos Konstantinidis is a Computer Science Teacher in Greek state schools and associate teacher in the distance learning master's programme Digital Technologies for Language Teaching at the University of Nottingham. He has been actively involved in numerous international school projects that foster the integration of digital technologies in learning activities. In collaboration with fellow educators, he started in 2012 an initiative called ICT4ALL (http://ict4all.gr/) with the triple aim to support teachers in developing digital competences for lifelong learning, help them to strengthen their knowledge of how to use digital technologies in their daily teaching practice and promote openness of educational practices.

Reena Pau is a Researcher focused on gender and STEM. Reena visits schools to run motivational sessions and full-day programmes as the Electronics and Computer Science (ECS) department's Outreach Officer from the University of Southampton. As part of her PhD, Reena explored factors which influence how female students perceive electronics and computing careers at different ages. Her research was with 11- to 19-year-olds as a computing workshop coordinator for the Technocamps project and later as a freelance diversity consultant.

Malcolm Payton has spent all his life in education, working as a teacher, executive head, local authority director of education and a professional advisor to government education departments. For the last 10 years, Malcolm has provided consultancy, supporting education departments across the world. His work often touches on leadership and the use of technology, but the main focus is building local capacity so that teachers and education systems can become self-aware and self-improving.

Christina Preston is Associate Professor at the Institute for Education Futures at De Montfort University, and founded the MirandaNet Fellowship (mirandanet.ac.uk) in 1992. This professional organisation focuses on innovation in education and has become a global thought leader, with over 1,000 members in 80 countries. Knowledge sharing and managing the change process is at the core of MirandaNet's philosophy and research.

Tony Richardson is currently completing his PhD at the University of the Sunshine Coast, Queensland, Australia. Tony is a former teacher with the Queensland Department of Education, Australia. During the past seven years, Tony has worked at The University of the Sunshine Coast as a Lecturer and International Consultant. Tony has an interest in ICT that focuses on the use of data to assist in helping teachers and preservice teachers engage in diminishing their 'gaps-in-knowledge'. A book, co-authored by Chris Dann, Bev Dann and Shirley O'Neill on this topic, is currently being prepared for publication.

Moira Savage is a Senior Lecturer in Education at the University of Worcester leading on computing in primary education. Previously to this post, Moira had worked in several schools as subject leader for information and communication technology. Moira has considerable expertise in developing and promoting technology enhanced learning in both early years and primary phase and was a member of the Department for Education National Curriculum Group for Computing and an elected member of ITTE. Moira regularly publishes and presents at conferences on computing and technology enhanced learning.

Chris Shelton is Head of the Primary PGCE at the University of Chichester Institute of Education where he teaches on a range of modules related to ICT, computing and professional studies. Prior to this, he worked in primary schools across key stages 1 and 2 and was a school ICT co-ordinator. Chris has a range of research interests relating to technology, computing and digital literacy in schools and universities and his recent work has explored teacher beliefs and knowledge about technology and the pedagogy of teaching computing.

Lawrence Williams is an experienced classroom practitioner, who currently teaches Literacy, ICT and Computing on ITE courses at universities and colleges in London and abroad. He is both a Senior MirandaNet Fellow and Ambassador, and has officially represented the UK on behalf of the DfES and Becta at international conferences. His interests are in literacy, creative uses of ICT, cross-curricular teaching and learning, and international collaborations, on which he has published widely. He has received many national and international awards, including a National Teaching Award for the "Most Creative use of ICT in Secondary Schools", and the 2012 "Naace ICT Impact Award: Life Long Achievement".

John Woollard is a Senior Teaching Fellow in Southampton Education School, University of Southampton. John is the Computing At School coordinator for the CAS Tenderfoot CPD project, chair of the CAS Assessment Working Group and Assessor for the BCS Certificate for Computer Science Teachers. Following a teaching career as a mainstream special needs teacher, he has taught computing from infants all the way through to postgraduate level. He has been involved in EU- and UK-based research projects and published three books on learning theory and pedagogy. John was a member of the Royal Society advisory group that authored the "Shut down or restart?" report in 2012, which underpinned some of the new Computing curriculum.

Sarah Younie is a Professor in Education, Innovation and Technology at De Montfort University and the Co-director for the Institute for Education Futures at the University. She is the Editor-in-Chief for the Journal of *Technology, Pedagogy and Education*. Sarah has been involved in international and national teaching and research on educational technologies for over 25 years, including for UNESCO, EU and UK government agencies, including DfE, Becta, BBC, HEA and JISC. In her previous role as UK chair of the National Subject Association of IT in Teacher Education (ITTE), she conducted national research, including submitting evidence for the Parliamentary Select Committee inquiry into education.

Part I

Curriculum developments

Chapter 1

What can technology actually do?

Chris Shelton

Introduction

This chapter considers the debates around what digital technology can actually do for education. These centre around positive and negative claims for the impact of ICT on pupils which, in turn, lead to disputes about whether schools should make more or less use of technology for learning. A feature of these debates is that they can seem rather repetitive, because as new technologies become available, very similar arguments are used to make the case for or against their use as were used to debate the use of older technologies. So, repeatedly we hear different claims being made for ways in which the latest technologies can help or hinder schools, teachers and pupils. Sometimes we hear positive claims that they will raise GCSE results, lighten teacher workload, make learning more fun, and so on, and in short, that technology will *transform* education for the better in some way. At other times, we hear negative claims: that time using technology distracts from real learning, that investments in new gadgets are wasteful uses of the limited money in school budgets, or that technology just doesn't work in the way it is supposed to.

This chapter summarises these debates and introduces some of the different ways that we can think about what technology might do for education. In turn, these different ways of thinking about technology have led to further debates that we will also consider, concerning how we should understand the relationship between technology and society.

The chapter starts by looking at some of the assumptions that underpin the contrasting claims for technology and suggests some alternative ways of thinking about these. Then we will discuss the concept of 'affordance' and how this can help teachers to identify where technology will be useful for them. In the final part of the chapter, we will consider the social and political aspects of technology use and the debates about how these might shape how technology is used in education.

Claims and counterclaims for the effect of technology

You do not have to look very far to find examples of the promises that have been made for technology. In fact, claims for technology's potential to improve education can be traced back to the first half of the 20th century when first educational radio, then film and then television were expected to change schools and schooling dramatically. Today the technologies may have changed but the promises are similar, that new technology will improve the quality of pupils' learning and, simultaneously, save time or money. The most obvious places to find such messages are in the advertisements created by technology companies. For example, while later adverts are much more nuanced, the first marketing campaign aimed at introducing the Apple iPad to educational markets was full of ambitious claims, including that the iPad will "transform" learning and that it holds "all the world's learning in it" (Apple, 2011).

Sometimes these marketing claims are made without foundation but sometimes they are supported by evidence collected in schools (e.g. Apple, 2014).

However, despite the large investments in new technologies made by schools, local authorities and governments, and the dedicated work of many pioneering teachers, it has long been argued that educational technology has not transformed teaching and learning in the way that many had anticipated (e.g. Cuban, 1986, 2001; Oppenheimer, 1997; Selwyn, 1999). For Cuban (2001), the claims that digital technology will transform teaching are merely 'hype' and he points to the lack of impact of previous technologies as an indicator that the latest innovations will not live up to their promises. Others go further and suggest that not only are some of the claims made for technology just myths, but also that this is due to a "technopositivist ideology" of compulsive enthusiasm for technology (Njenga and Fourie, 2010, p. 200).

While these responses suggest that the benefits of technology promised by some will not be delivered on, another argument suggests that technology will actually make things worse. Thus, Oppenheimer (2003) claims that far from transforming our schools for the better, technology has had a negative effect on learning through distracting pupils and diverting time and money from other more productive activities. In turn, this is reflected in newspapers and online news sites that regularly print stories such as "Too much technology 'could lower school results'" (BBC, 2015).

Such claims are sometimes described as 'booster' or 'doomster' accounts of technology (e.g. Bigum, 1998) and have tended to have a high profile in debates about technology. However, although these claims present opposite sides of an argument, they have one thing in common: both sides of the debates described above assume that technology will make a difference to education. They assume that technology effects a change of some kind to schools or pupils. However, as we shall see, it is not at all clear that any technology can actually do this.

Technological determinism

Given that we can easily find arguments that technology has had a positive impact on education and opposing arguments that technology has had a negative effect on education, it might be tempting to discount both sides of the debate.

However, these claims cannot just be ignored because they continue to be promoted and reappear in different forms with every new technology. Underlying the argument that technology has the potential to transform education is the assumption that technology can cause change, that it can determine what happens in the social world, in this case, in education. This idea is called 'technological determinism'.

A consequence of having a 'technological determinist' view is that if you believe that technology causes change, you would expect it to work consistently. While this is a useful assumption to promote for those marketing a technology ("it worked here so it will work for you"), it raises the question of how to explain why technology has not had the impact that was expected.

One approach to explaining the lack of impact of technology in education has been to identify factors that might militate against the successful use of technology. As technology has been promoted as a solution to perceived problems or as a force for change, when that change has not appeared, this may be attributed to 'barriers' to its progress. Such 'barriers' are well documented in research in schools; for example, Bingimlas' (2009) literature review identifies a number of barriers and categorises these as 'school-level' or 'teacher-level' barriers. School-level barriers are said to be "lack of time", "lack of effective training", "lack of accessibility" and "lack of technical support" (p. 239), while teacher-level factors are identified as "lack of teacher confidence", "lack of teacher competence" and "resistance to change and negative attitudes" (p. 237). Bingimlas further acknowledges the complex relationships between these factors.

However, while each of these 'barriers' will clearly affect how a technology is used (or not used), the implication of this discourse is that if the barriers can be overcome, then technology will be able to do what was promised. At its worst, this can lead to teachers or schools being blamed for obstructing progress. But this view of technology as an agent of change has frequently been challenged (e.g. Oliver, 2011) for suggesting that technology has the power to cause social change (in this case educational 'transformation'). Others have argued that technology itself does nothing – it will only be once individuals adopt the technology that any change will happen and that this change will depend on what they choose to do with the technology.

Social determinism or instrumentalism – is technology just a tool?

While technological determinist arguments are common (particular from those promoting a particular device or software), an alternative view of technology is that it has no inherent effect (either positive or negative) on education, and any educational changes are entirely due to what the user does with that technology. This is the opposite view to technological determinism and is more commonly held amongst teachers. It is often expressed by the phrase "technology is just a tool" and implies that technology is neutral and can be used in whatever way the user (in this case, the teacher or student) wishes. This can be described as a 'social determinist' or 'instrumentalist' view where the social context determines the impact of the technology (Feenberg, 2002).

The social determinist view provides one way of explaining the variation in impact of technology in education. If the technology is a neutral tool, then any educational impact depends on how well the user adopts the new technology, and poor use will lead to little or no measurable impact on learning. As Feenberg has noted, "Education is not a pill, and relationships between cause and effect are notoriously difficult to establish" (Feenberg, 2009, p. viii).

This is confirmed in the Education Endowment Foundation's meta-analysis reviewing the impact of digital technology on learning (Higgins et al., 2012) which notes that although research linking technology and attainments has tended to find "consistent but small positive associations with educational outcomes", this does not imply a causal link between technology and learning. They suggest that "it seems probable that more effective schools and teachers are more likely to use digital technologies more effectively than other schools." (p. 3). The report concludes that is not *whether* technology is used but *how* technology is used that makes a difference to learning.

A similar conclusion might be drawn from the 2015 OECD study, 'Students, Computers and Learning'. On publication, this study was reported widely as suggesting that technology was ineffective, for example: "Computers 'do not improve' pupil results, says OECD" (BBC, 2015) and "Overexposure to computers and the Internet causes educational outcomes to drop, study finds" (Wall Street Journal, 2015). Indeed, the report showed "no appreciable improvements in student achievement" in countries that had invested heavily in ICT. However, the conclusions of the reports' authors are more nuanced, and one explanation suggested was that "we have not yet become good enough at the kind of pedagogies that make the most of technology" (p. 3).

However, while these studies provide evidence that the way in which technology used is of crucial importance, they do not suggest that technology is a 'neutral tool'. In fact, several challenges have been put forward to dispute this view of technology as 'neutral'. One is that this places "far too much faith in people's abilities to exercise foresight and restraint" (Burbules and Callister, 2000, p. 9) and that it ignores the unintended consequences of using technology. In his book *Why Things Bite Back: Technology and the Revenge of Unintended Consequences*, Edward Tenner (1996) provides copious examples from medicine, sport, the workplace and the environment of times when the introduction of technology led to unexpected 'revenge effects'. In these cases, well-meaning actions had unpredictable consequences; for example, uses of technology intended to reduce workload had the effect of increasing it.

A second problem for both technological determinist and instrumentalist views are that they 'reify' technology by considering 'technology' to be a "single material thing with a homogeneous, undifferentiated character" (Chandler, 1995, p. 4). In fact, technology is not a single thing but rather a term for a wide range of different devices and software. Some technologies, for example the digital projector, have been widely adopted in a range of educational settings, while others, such as virtual reality, have proved far less pervasive. It would be hard to justify a claim that both these technologies have had the same effect on education or that they can be used in equivalent ways. If not all technologies are the same, then they cannot be entirely neutral – they must need to be used in different ways to get the most out of them.

Affordances

This term was coined by a psychologist, James Gibson, in 1979 to refer to the possibilities for action available to an individual in a particular environment: "The *affordances* of the environment are what it *offers* the animal, what it *provides* or *furnishes*, either for good or ill" (p. 127, emphasis author's own).

The concept was later applied to the design of computer interfaces by Donald Norman. However, he used the term slightly differently: "[T]he term *affordance* refers to the perceived and actual properties of the thing, primarily those fundamental properties that determine just how the thing could possibly be used" (Norman, 1998, p. 9, emphasis author's own).

It is worth noting that in the original definition of Gibson, the existence of the affordance has nothing to do with whether or not the animal (or computer user) perceives it to be there, but in Norman's definition the perception of what the technology offers is also important. (In later work, Norman (1999, p. 38) referred to this as "perceived affordance"). In computer interfaces, these depend on both the design of the interface and also the experience and knowledge of the user.

Since these original definitions, the term has been adopted by educational technologists as a way of thinking about what a technology 'affords' or provides to the user (e.g. Kennewell, 2008). For example, a teacher using an interactive whiteboard might write notes on the board in response to their class. The whiteboard affords the possibility of a space for them to collate the responses. However, they don't have to do this. If the class had a set of tablets, they might ask pupils to write responses together on a shared document. Although the teacher chooses which tool to use and how they will use it, the different affordances of the technologies available constrain or enable their choices.

Thinking about affordances in this way suggests that if technology is a tool, it is not a *neutral* tool – it has an influence even if we don't immediately notice it. If this is correct, then understanding the affordances of a particular technology might help the user to use the technology in the most effective way. Thus, several authors have suggested lists of affordances that might be used to describe the technologies that are used for educational purposes. Kennewell (2001) provides a definition of affordance that is more straightforward to apply in education. He defines affordances as "the attributes of the setting which provide potential for action" (p. 106).

Kennewell (2001) refers to a list of six features of technology published in 1998 as part of the Teacher Training Agency curriculum for teacher training:

- speed;
- automaticity;
- capacity;
- range;
- provisionality;
- interactivity.

(TTA, 1998, Section A1)

This list of affordances provides a useful tool for teachers who wish to evaluate what a particular technology might do to support pupils' learning. By considering what the affordances of the technology might be, the teacher can identify ways of making use of that affordance in their lessons. For example, the "provisionality" of an electronic document (the fact that it can be easily changed and updated) means that students can redraft and improve their work without needing to start again on a blank page.

Kennewell (2001) also notes that as well as considering positive 'potential for actions', it is vital that we also consider any potential 'constraints' to action that a technology might afford for the user. These constraints are not necessarily something to be avoided, though. They might support learning, for example, by reducing the complexity of a task.

Others authors have suggested a wider range of affordances; for example, Conole and Dyke (2004) suggest:

- accessibility;
- speed of change;
- diversity;
- communication and collaboration;
- reflection;
- multi-modal and non-linear;
- risk;
- fragility and uncertainty;
- immediacy;
- monopolisation;
- surveillance.

However, the use of the concept of affordance to analyse the potential for technology to be used in education is not without its critics. Oliver (2005) criticises Conole and Dyke's list for using affordance in several different ways: some of the items in the list are features of the technology (e.g. multi-modal and non-linear), some are of the user (e.g. reflection) and some relate to their mutual relationship (e.g. immediacy). Oliver concludes that the concept of affordance is too ambiguous and has limited value, although others (e.g. Hammond, 2010) have found analysing affordances to be a very useful way to think about how technology relates to teaching and learning.

The social and political aspects of technology

While the concept of affordance offers us a tool to understand the non-neutral nature of technology, it could be suggested that this is just a slightly more sophisticated form of social determinism that merely replaces the idea of technology as 'just a tool' with a concept of technology as a 'non-neutral' tool. While this helps to explain why different technologies might be used in different ways and have different effects, it does not entirely address the earlier concerns because it still assumes that the user of the technology has absolute control over their choices about how to use technology.

In contrast, it can be argued that many of the uses of technology that we find in schools are not just the result of the decisions of a particular teacher on a particular day but are actually happening within a much wider political and ideological context (Monahan, 2005). The use of digital technology in education is therefore "not a matter of specific choices, but a constellation of changes, some active, some passive, some intentional, some only evident in hindsight" (Burbules and Callister, 2000, p. 1).

There are many alternative ways of understanding the relationship between technology and society (for several examples, see Selwyn, 2012). A way of understanding how technology and society interact that attempts to avoid the problems of determinism can be found in theories of the 'social shaping of technology' (Williams and Edge, 1996). These consider how the creation and use of technology are shaped by a range of different organisational, political, economic and cultural factors. As MacKenzie and Wajcman argue, "The social shaping of technology is, in almost all the cases we know of, a process in which there is no single dominant shaping force" (1999, p. 28). Rather, they argue that multiple factors work to shape how technological artefacts develop and are used. Such theories also consider how at the same time that society shapes technology, technologies can also shape aspects of society, for example, how technologies have impacted conceptions of gender (Cockburn and Ormrod, 1993).

One influential account of technology and society is Pinch and Bijker's (1987) account of the Social Construction of Technology (SCOT). According to SCOT, technological artefacts are not developed in a linear way but through a process of variation and selection. Although with hindsight it may appear that a particular technology developed cumulatively with each new advance building on the last, SCOT suggests that this is incorrect. Instead, through analysing case studies of the development of devices such as the bicycle, it suggests that at each stage of development, multiple variations are possible which could lead in different directions. However, different social groups view the variations in particular ways and influence which variations are continued and which are abandoned. The theory thus highlights the importance of different social groups and how some variations of technology could be ignored because those groups who would most value that variation are excluded from any influence.

However, the SCOT approach has been criticised for being unable to fully account for the political aspects of technology. Winner (1993) noted that SCOT focussed on how technologies were developed rather than how they were used in the present and how uses of technology embody existing power relationships in society. For Winner, technologies are "inherently political" (Winner, 1980, p. 123) and have consequences. They can be designed to allow or restrict the opportunities of groups, or be more compatible with particular social purposes. In order to take account of these political influences, Feenberg (2002) proposed that a 'critical' theory of technology is needed. For Feenberg, technology structures the world regardless of the intentions of the user and that "choosing our technology . . . shapes our future choices" (p. 14). As he sees the values of a social system 'installed' in the design of procedures and machines, he views technology as a scene of social struggle. In education, these political struggles can be seen in political debates about the curriculum (what should be taught and what should be omitted), assessment (what and how pupils are assessed) and pedagogy (how pupils are taught and learning is organised). Choices about technology can reinforce decisions about all three of these areas and also restrict different approaches. For example, schools may find future curriculum choices are limited by the technologies available to be used or find that the technologies they have do not always match the teaching approaches they wish to use. Conversely, teachers may feel forced to use a particular approach or teach a particular topic because of the resources available.

Considering the political aspects of our uses of technologies demonstrates the complexities of the educational consequences of our use of technology. It also raises questions of power: who chooses which technologies are used and who influences what technologies are available?

Social shaping theories of technology and critical theories of technology highlight the need to look more broadly at the different contexts in which technology is used. If we are to understand how educational outcomes relate to uses of technology then we need to consider not just the immediate context of teacher, learner and technology but also the institutional context of the school and the wider cultural, social, economic and political context (Selwyn, 2010). Such work tends to provide a much more nuanced discussion of the reasons for the success or failure of technology in education; for example, Lynch and Redpath (2014) discuss the introduction of iPads in the early years and note the conflicts that arose between early years policy, context and curriculum; institutional practices and teacher intentions to use technology.

Conclusion

This chapter began by presenting some of the claims that have been made for the effect technology has on education. As we have seen, both the claims that technology can have a positive effect on education and those that claim a negative impact on learning are based on a misplaced assumption of determinism – that technology causes social change. However, the alternative view that ICT is 'just a neutral tool' to be used in whatever way the teacher wishes is also inadequate for explaining the impact of technology on learning because it fails to acknowledge the differences between technologies and underestimates the influence of social factors on technology use.

Debates will continue to be had about the potential impact of particular technologies and about what methods of using technology might be the most effective. While there is no consensus regarding how technologies are shaped by and shape society, it is clear that important social and political factors matter, and that issues of power should not be ignored.

Although some of the ideas in this chapter have been relatively abstract, they are also very practical concepts that we can use to analyse and critique the claims and the technologies that we are presented with. When faced with competing claims for technology, paying attention to what the technology affords, how it might be used and the context in which it will be used will go some way towards finding out what the possible outcomes of that use might be.

References

Apple (2011) *iPad in education – learning with iPads*. Available from: https://www.you tube.com/watch?v=dtQRMD_IHOI [Accessed July 2016].

Apple (2014) *iPad in education results*. Available from: http://images.apple.com/ education/docs/ipad-in-education-results.pdf [Accessed July 2016].

BBC (2015) *Too much technology 'could lower school results'* Available from: http://www. bbc.co.uk/news/education-34252598 [Accessed July 2016].

Bigum, C. (1998) Solutions in search of educational problems: Speaking for computers in schools. *Educational Policy*, 12(5), pp. 586–601.

Bingimlas, K.A. (2009) Barriers to the successful integration of ICT in teaching and learning environments: a review of the literature, *Eurasia Journal of Mathematics, Science & Technology Education*, 5(3), pp. 235–245.

Burbules, N.C., and Callister Jr, T.A. (2000) *Watch IT: the risks and promises of information technologies for education*. Boulder: Westview Press.

Chandler, D. (1995) *Technological or media determinism*. Available from: http://www. aber.ac.uk/media/Documents/tecdet/tecdet.htm [Accessed: February 2014].

Cockburn, C., and Ormrod, S. (1993) *Gender and technology in the making*. London: SAGE.

Conole, G., and Dyke, M. (2004) What are the affordances of information and communication and technologies. *ALT-J Research in Learning Technology*, 12(2), pp. 113–124.

Cuban, L. (1986) *Teachers and machines: The classroom use of technology since 1920*. New York: Teachers College Press.

Cuban, L. (2001) *Oversold and underused: computers in the classroom*. Cambridge: Harvard University Press.

Feenberg, A. (2002) *Transforming technology: A critical theory revisited*. Oxford: Oxford University Press.

Feenberg A. (2009) Foreword. In: N. Friesen, ed. *Re-thinking e-learning research: foundations, methods, and practices* (Vol. 333). New York: Peter Lang.

Gibson, J. (1986) *The ecological approach to visual perception*. New York: Lawrence Erlbaum Associates.

Hammond, M. (2010) What is an affordance and can it help us understand the use of ICT in education? *Education and Information Technology* 15, pp. 205–217

Higgins, S., Xiao, Z., and Katsipataki, M. (2012) *The impact of digital technology on learning: a summary for the education endowment foundation*. Durham, UK: Education Endowment Foundation and Durham University.

Kennewell, S., (2001) Using affordances and constraints to evaluate the use of information and communications technology in teaching and learning. *Journal of Information Technology for Teacher Education*, 10(1&2), pp. 101–116.

Kennewell, S., Tanner, H., Jones, S., and Beauchamp, G. (2008) Analysing the use of interactive technology to implement interactive teaching. *Journal of Computer Assisted Learning*, 24(1), pp. 61–73.

Lynch, J., and Redpath, T. (2014) Smart technologies in early years literacy education: a meta-narrative of paradigmatic tensions in iPad use in an Australian preparatory classroom. *Journal of Early Childhood Literacy* 14, pp. 147–174

MacKenzie, D., and Wajcman, J. (1999) *The social shaping of technology*. London: Open University Press.

Monahan, T. (2005) Just another tool? IT pedagogy and the commodification of education. *The Urban Review*, 36(4), pp. 271–292.

Njenga, J.K., and Fourie, L.C.H. (2010) The myths about e-learning in higher education. *British Journal of Educational Technology*, 41(2), pp. 199–212.

Norman, D. (1998) *The psychology of everyday things*. New York: Basic Books.

Norman, D.A. (1999). Affordance, conventions, and design. *Interactions*, 6(3) pp. 38–43.

OECD (2015) *Students, computers and learning: making the connection*, OECD Publishing, Paris. Available from: http://dx.doi.org/10.1787/9789264239555-en [Accessed August 2017].

Oliver, M. (2005) The problem with affordance. *E–Learning*, 2(4) pp. 402–413.

Oliver, M. (2011) Technological determinism in educational technology research: some alternative ways of thinking about the relationship between learning and technology. *Journal of Computer Assisted Learning*, 27(5), pp. 373–384.

Oppenheimer, T. (1997). The computer delusion. *The Atlantic Monthly*, 280(1), 45–62.

Oppenheimer, T. (2003) *The flickering mind: the false promise of technology in the classroom, and how learning can be saved*. New York: Random House.

Pinch, T.J., and Bijker, W.E. (1987) The social construction of facts and artifacts. *In:* W.E. Bijker, T.P. Hughes, T. Pinch, eds. *The social construction of technological systems: New directions in the sociology and history of technology*. Cambridge: MIT press.

Selwyn, N. (1999) Why the computer is not dominating schools: a failure of policy or a failure of practice? *Cambridge Journal of Education*, 29(1), pp. 77–91.

Selwyn, N. (2010) Looking beyond learning: notes towards the critical study of educational technology. *Journal of Computer Assisted Learning*, 26(1), pp. 65–73.

Selwyn, N. (2012) Making sense of young people, education and digital technology: the role of sociological theory. *Oxford Review of Education*, 38(1) pp. 81–96

Tenner, E. (1996) *Why things bite back: technology and the revenge of unintended consequences*. London: Fourth Estate.

Teacher Training Agency (TTA) (1998) *Initial teacher training national curriculum for the use of information and communications technology in subject teaching*. London: DfEE

Wall Street Journal (2015) *Technology in classrooms doesn't always boost education results, OECD says*. Available from: http://www.wsj.com/articles/technology-in-classrooms-doesnt-always-boost-education-results-oecd-says-1442343420 [Accessed July 2016].

Williams, R., and Edge, D. (1996) The social shaping of technology. *Research Policy*, 25(6), pp. 865–899.

Winner, L. (1980) Do artifacts have politics? *Daedalus Vol 109 No. 1*, p. 121–136.

Winner, L. (1993) Upon opening the black box and finding it empty: social constructivism and the philosophy of technology. *Science, Technology and Human Values*, 18(3), pp. 362–378.

Chapter 2

Computer studies, information technology, ICT and now computing

John Woollard

In January 2012, the then Secretary of State for Education for the UK Government announced the disapplication of the English national curriculum for ICT (Information and Communication Technology) and thus started the most recent and important change in the nature of teaching learners how to use computers and teaching them how computers work (Gove, 2012). The national curriculum for Computing was implemented in September 2014. The name has changed, but is what we're teaching going to be better?

A brief history of computers in education

The history of teaching computing in UK schools began in the mid-1970s with GCE (A and O level) examination courses in computer studies for pupils aged 14 to 18 years. These focussed on the mechanics of the technology, the past and current developments, some computer programming and, to a large extent, the commercial applications of computing. Computer-assisted learning (CAL) was developed by enthusiastic teachers with a computer interest and knowledge, and focussed on rote skills training, closed questioning and programming (BASIC). The justification included the value of motivation, immediate feedback (behaviourism), Piaget's cognitive development (constructivism) and Papert's constructionism through LOGO (Papert, 1980; Abelson, 1982). The next phase saw the introduction of generic software: word processing, spreadsheets, painting programs and database management. The emphasis lay in using computers to support other activities through curriculum-specific and -focussed tasks.

The arrival of the windows-based computers saw the take-up of authoring and multimedia technologies (Acorn Computers, 1993). Learning was seen to be through activity and synthesis (Bloom's taxonomy, 1956) of material to support learning. The national curriculum saw the rationale for a balanced use of computing in five strands (communicating, handling, controlling, monitoring and measuring) and continues as the four aspects within the knowledge, skills and understanding of the pre-disapplication of the ICT national curriculum. The 1990s saw the model of cross-curricular delivery being promoted and also, in contrast, a return to the rote learning and closed answers of integrated learning systems (Wood, 1998).

In 1997, the Stevenson Report (Independent ICT in School Commission, 1997) aimed for "basic confidence and competence" regarding both teachers and pupils and pleas for stability in policy.

The national curriculum for England then required that all subjects should include ICT (QCA, 1999). The National Grid for Learning, and, later, the Key Stage 3 Strategy for ICT Capability (DfES, 2002), saw a renewed focus on computer suites in primary and specialist teaching in secondary education (Kennewell et al., 2003), but issues of teacher attitude remained factors in the effective use of ICT across the curriculum (Williams et al., 1998) and in communication with pupils (Cunningham and Harris, 2003). In the autumn of 2004, we saw the re-emergence of ICT across the curriculum (ICTAC) as part of the Secondary Strategy (DfES, 2006). The e-Learning Strategy (DfES, 2004) and the developments in VLEs (virtual learning environments) and MLEs (managed learning environments), and a renewed interest in the principles of pedagogy (Conole et al., 2004) and assessment (Bull and McKenna, 2004) in the form of computer-assisted assessment (CAA), came under scrutiny.

In 2008, a meeting of academics, industrialists and teachers started a grass-roots organisation called CNG Computing Next Generation, later to become Computing At School (CAS, 2010). The Royal Society (2012) report "Shut down or restart?" and comments by industrial leaders such as Google's Eric Schmidt (2011) prompted a rebuke for the teaching of ICT (Gove, 2012) and the re-introduction of computer science into schools through a revised curriculum, which also included digital literacy and information technology under the curriculum name Computing. The new focus is away from IT with most of the "Pupils should be taught to:" statements being computer science. This chapter discusses the challenges and opportunities that those changes present to curriculum designers and the teachers of computing.

Computing – how is it different from ICT?

In 2012, the blueprint for the 2014 national curriculum was first articulated (CAS, 2012) and gives a fuller picture of the motivations behind its content.

> Computing is the study of principles and practices that underpin an understanding and modelling of computation, and of their application in the development of computer systems. At its heart lies the notion of computational thinking: a mode of thought that goes well beyond software and hardware, and that provides a framework within which to reason about systems and problems. This mode of thinking is supported and complemented by a substantial body of theoretical and practical knowledge, and by a set of powerful techniques for analysing, modelling and solving problems.
>
> Computing is deeply concerned with how computers and computer systems work, and how they are designed and programmed. Pupils studying computing gain insight into computational systems of all kinds, whether or

not they include computers. Computational thinking influences fields such as biology, chemistry, linguistics, psychology, economics and statistics. It allows us to solve problems, design systems and understand the power and limits of human and machine intelligence. It is a skill that empowers, and that all students should be aware of and have some competence in. Furthermore, pupils who can think computationally are better able to conceptualise and understand computer-based technology, and so are better equipped to function in modern society.

Computing is a practical subject, where invention and resourcefulness are encouraged. Pupils are expected to apply the academic principles they have learned to the understanding of real-world systems, and to the creation of purposeful artefacts. This combination of principles, practice, and invention makes it an extraordinarily useful and an intensely creative subject, suffused with excitement, both visceral ("it works!") and intellectual ("that is so beautiful").

(CAS, 2012, np)

This viewpoint of the curriculum prevailed in the subsequent years. Computer science is the dominating factor of the Computing curriculum with the other aspects identified in the Royal Society report (2012), digital literacy and information technology, taking smaller parts.

Computing is a new subject – can ICT teachers teach it?

Some issues emerge from the fact that computing is a subject within its own right with a set of principles, theories and practices that focus on computer programming and computational thinking. The implementation of the ICT curriculum was based on a broad framework of design, investigation, communication, analysis and control but was often limited to office-type software, development of media and exploration of web-based resources. For many, ICT was seen as an important literacy that served other aspects of the curriculum and provides essential lifelong skills for pupils living in a world dominated by information technology. Subsequently, many very proficient ICT teachers have become disenfranchised by the introduction of the new curriculum. Many teachers believe they do not have skills or they do not have the motivation to teach computational processes, especially programming, algorithm and abstraction.

Previously, the teaching of ICT in schools was suffering through difficulties of recruitment and low staffing levels, and thus required non-specialists to take ICT classes. This is exacerbated by the fact that in changing to computing, it is now no longer a subject that can be covered by non-specialists and that many of the specialist (ICT) teachers cannot, or do not wish to, teach computing because of the computer science and computer programming elements. An emergent fear is that we do not have the capacity to teach computing to everyone.

Learning to program is difficult – so why are we doing it?

A series of truisms introduces the next issue associated with computing. "Learning to program is difficult. Teaching someone else to program is more difficult. Teaching 30 people at the same time how to program is extremely difficult."

We have a developing pedagogy associated with teaching computer programming, but it is far from being complete, or widely understood or even agreed upon. Within the teaching of computing, for example, teaching algorithms, we have a history of less than 50 years and we have been teaching programming to learners under 14 years old for just 20 years. Many of the strategies of teaching aspects of computing are yet to be proven and reach the status of accepted subject pedagogy. Some of the strategies borrowed from other subject areas are perhaps better understood and appreciated. And, as with all subjects, the teaching of computing is highly dependent upon the teaching styles of the teachers.

In the national curriculum, there is an element of expectation that all learners must learn how to write computer programs. For example, in Key Stage 2 (ages 7 to 11), all pupils should be taught to "design, write and debug programs that accomplish specific goals, including controlling or simulating physical systems". There appears to be a "rush to code", however, associated with this changing curriculum. Many commercial and educational establishments are exploiting the interest and hype of enabling 4-year-olds to program including: hour of code (hourofcode.com); code week (codeweek.eu); year of code (yearofcode.org); coding competitions and code jams (code.google.com/codejam) and the BBC coding strategy (www.bbc.co.uk/learning/overview/about/digitalliteracy.shtml).

This coding hype is generating a number of issues with teachers new to computing, especially those in the primary sector. Some are perhaps conflating the idea of computing with the idea of computer programming. Many people think that computer programming is at the heart of computing when in fact it is better to think that computational thinking lies at the heart of the subject. The opening sentence of the national curriculum states that a "high quality computing education equips pupils to use computational thinking and creativity to understand and change the world" (DfE, 2013). This focus on computational thinking gives the opportunity for ICT teachers less confident or motivated in programming to engage with computing and computer science. It is also providing the opportunity for a lot more unplugged activities (CSUnplugged, 2015; CS4FN, 2015).

The CPK of coding – are we ready to teach computer programming?

CPK, content pedagogic knowledge (Shulman, 1986), is not the knowledge of a subject but the knowledge of how to teach that subject. The important step is for teachers to go beyond "knowing". "Those who can, do. Those who understand, teach" (Shulman, 1986, p. 4). The pedagogy associated with teaching computer programming has come under rigorous scrutiny in the further education and higher education sectors (Bennedsen et al., 2008; Cooper et al., 2003; Dann et al., 2012; Dijkstra, 1972; DuBoulay, 1989; Guzdial; 2004, Kölling, 1999; Mannila; 2007, Means, 1988; Soloway; 1993). Key Stage 3 and 4 teachers can learn much from their analyses. The issues include cognitive ability, the gender divide, didactic approaches, visualising object-orientated approaches and left-brainedness and teaching strategies matched to learning styles. The contrasting approaches are: synthesis versus analysis; exploration versus didactic and product versus process orientation. For many, computer programming is a way of illustrating and exercising the principles and understanding of computer science including abstraction, decomposition, algorithm and logical reasoning in general – programming is the vehicle for learning computational thinking.

Working in Key Stage 3 and 4, Mara Saeli identifies the importance of a deep subject knowledge and deep pedagogical knowledge (Saeli et al., 2010). The teacher merely knowing how to program is not sufficient; there must also be the ability to teach programming, taking into account previous level of knowledge, background and experiences. Perhaps the challenge facing many teachers is that they will have to teach programming that is, enable the learners to gain the skills and understanding of programming without themselves knowing how to program? Certainly, we need to make teachers feel comfortable working in an area where the learner's skills, experience and perhaps understanding is greater than that of the teacher and that we simply provide the learning opportunities for pupils to develop further? However, this latter approach places even more importance upon the teacher having the pedagogic content knowledge. They must fully appreciate why we are teaching programming and why we use particular strategies and resources for teaching programming.

Researching pedagogy and computing – how do we know what is best?

Much of the pedagogy of the long-established subjects of mathematics and science has been mandated or justified through the rigorous research associated with the approaches used. The issue related to research and educational computing is that there are varying and contrasting areas of interest. There is a large body of research associated with the use of technology to support learning, and over recent times, this has dominated the research activity. The focus has included: office-type software, for example spreadsheets to model; learning with media by adopting a constructionist approach and learning through exploration, data collection and the World Wide Web. In parallel to this has been the exploitation and evaluation of the technologies. Since the 1980s it was light pens and concept keyboards to enable access; the mouse and graphical interface enfranchising many; the interactive whiteboard; class response systems; the developments in mobile technologies and of late, the application of collaborative and social media approaches.

This research activity has detracted attention and funding away from researching how we teach "how the technology works". Consequently, the pedagogy associated with teaching *with* technology is much stronger than our understanding of how to teach *about* technology. So, our teaching of computing has a weak underpinning, and it is not clear which approaches are better than others. The affordances of different approaches to teach about technology, programming and computational thinking are yet to be clearly defined.

Computational thinking – are we ready to teach "thought processes"?

Computational thinking sits at the heart of the national curriculum program of study for computing. The scope of computational thinking is described in the first aim – "understand and apply the fundamental principles and concepts of computer science, including abstraction, logic, algorithms and data representation" (DfE, 2013, p. 188). Computational thinking was first coined by Jeannette Wing in 2006, but prior to that, Seymour Papert and colleagues established that working with computers through programming environments could develop specific and important cognitive skills. Papert's theory of constructionism shares Piaget's constructivist ideas where learning is seen as "building knowledge structures" irrespective of the circumstances of the learning and where the learner is consciously engaged in constructing a public entity, whether it's castles of sand on the beach or a theory of the universe (Papert and Harel, 1991). This is reflected in two parts of the computing curriculum: build through computer programming and "undertake creative projects that involve selecting, using, and combining multiple applications, preferably across a range of devices" (DfE, 2013, p. 206).

Jeanette Wing defined computational thinking as including "a range of mental tools that reflect the breadth of the field of Computer Science" (Wing, 2006, p. 33). Computational thinking is the way that humans think about solving problems. It is the "thought processes" we use to transform a difficult problem into one that can be solved more easily. The Royal Society identifies computational thinking in an even broader sense as "the process of recognising aspects of computation in the world that surrounds us, and applying tools and techniques from Computer Science to understand and reason about both natural and artificial systems and processes" (Royal Society, 2012, p. 29); it is a way of thinking about computing (Guzdial, 2004) and representing problems as information processes and representing solutions as algorithms (Denning, 2011).

Previous developments in pedagogy have focussed upon thinking skills (DfEE, 1999; DfES, 2002; Wickens, 2007) as underpinning areas of the curriculum. "Thinking Hats", based on de Bono's work (de Bono, 2000; de Bono, 2007), is a popular approach in which pupils are encouraged to think about the way they think. The Computing curriculum is now challenging pupils to think using particular strategies for solving problems and understanding situations. However, computational thinking is itself in danger of becoming a "buzz word" in the teaching of computing. Teachers acknowledge the need to teach computational thinking but may struggle with the various and conflicting interpretations of its nature. This may be the result of debate by individuals and groups (Computer Science Teachers Association (CSTA), 2011; Henderson et al., 2007; Lu et al., 2009; Naughton, 2012; Wing, 2006; Wing, 2008; Yadav et al., 2011) concerning what is and is not computational thinking. Some of these definitions are broad and overlap other subjects (Bundy, 2007; CSTA, 2011). The paper "Computational thinking in the national curriculum: A guide for teachers" (CAS, 2015) endeavours to establish a framework that helps teachers establish for themselves a working model of computational thinking. The Barefoot interpretation has been promoted for primary phase pupils and describes the six aspects of computational thinking with the five approaches that pupils take when problem solving.

The concepts are logical reasoning, algorithmic approaches, decomposition (identifying component parts), pattern identification, abstract (removing unnecessary detail) and evaluation. The approaches are tinkering, creating, debugging, persevering and collaborating. By understanding these concepts and promoting these approaches, teachers can add value to the computer programming activities. Instead of the learning being about how to program a computer, which is a fairly idiosyncratic and short-lived skill set, they will be learning how to approach problems and complex situations and then understand them in a rationalised, logical and systematic way. In this way, we are ready to teach thought processes.

Computer programming for all – is the argument persuasive?

Computers are now instrumental to our society, and the need for learners to attain a form of "digital literacy" is now generally accepted. This is currently interpreted as the need to be able to use standard applications such as office-type software within a windows environment interface, proficiently. However, the use of computers is changing rapidly. There are now as many mechanisms for social communication as there are office tools. As this connectivity expands to every aspect of our lives, the ability to exercise control over the information becomes crucial. Controlling information is one of the fundamental skills of programming. If learners master this skill, they will be able to engage successfully, not just with today's applications, but also with uses of technology that have yet to be devised. Academic support for this comes from Church and Whitten (2009) and Blackwell's Attention Investment (1999).

Programming offers the ability to create new uses for computers. Whereas a competence in office-type software allows the production of new documents, programming allows the creation of new behaviours, rather than just the consumption of behaviours provided for us by others. Computer programming is carried out by many people and it can be a hobby, pastime, leisure pursuit, interest, diversion, relaxation and so on. For our learners, it could be a way of enabling them to "enjoy and achieve" – an aim of the Every Child Matters agenda (TSO, 2003).

As Malone (1980, p. 79) concludes:

> In some senses, computer programming itself is one of the best computer games of all. In the 'computer programming game', there are obvious goals and it's easy to generate more. The 'player' gets frequent performance feedback (that is, in fact, often tantalisingly misleading about the nearness of the goal). The game can be played at many different difficulty levels, and there are many levels of goals available, both in terms of the finished product (whether it works, how fast it works, how much space it requires, etc.) and in terms of the process of reaching it (how long it takes to program, etc.). Self-esteem is crucially involved in the game, and there is probably the occasional emotional or fantasy aspects involved in controlling so completely, yet often so ineffectively, the behaviour of this responsive entity. Finally the process of debugging a program is perhaps unmatched in its ability to raise expectations about how the program will work, only to have the expectations surprisingly disappointed in ways that reveal the true underlying structure of the program.

Computer programming is also a vocational pursuit and may enable our pupils to "achieve economic well-being", another aim of Every Child Matters (TSO, 2003). Pupils discovering their proficiency in handling syntax, algorithm, logic and analysis may find they can enter an industry in which those skills are highly valued. It is argued that teaching every child how computers work and how to make them work develops their mental capacity (computational thinking), their leisure activities and their potential vocational opportunities.

Will the new curriculum meet the needs of learners and those in further/higher education and the employers who demanded the change?

The new curriculum arose out of discussions and actions of CAS. The curriculum for ICT was a concern of educationalists and industrialists that we were not encouraging enough learners with the knowledge, understanding and motivation to pursue computer science academically and vocationally. The cause of the reduction in numbers studying computer science and the problems of recruitment into employment was seen to stem from the Key Stage 3 curriculum that associated computing with office-type software (and not creativity through programming or understanding how computers work). It was supposed that those with an aptitude or motivation to pursue computer science were demotivated by ICT and then later never considered specialising in "ICT" associated subjects. Those happy with the ICT curriculum were quickly disillusioned with the post-16 courses that required a high level of mathematical and logical reasoning and were not happy with the programming elements. It was in this context that the new computing curriculum was designed and introduced.

We can be sure that through the changes to the national curriculum, all learners in state schools will experience some form of computing teaching. However, because of recent education reforms in the UK, many schools are exempt from teaching the national curriculum. The statutory requirement lies only on those schools remaining under local authority control. Also, the reforms in a curriculum need not necessarily transform into changes in attitudes, activities or opportunities. The factors causing the gender divide, whereby girls consistently out-perform boys yet boys dominate the computing options and opportunities, might not have been addressed. The continuing fall in the UK of numbers of learners wanting to pursue computer science into post-16 and then university might not change, because those computer and programming savvy young people might continue to experience poor, uninspiring, skills-based teaching of those parts of the curriculum most easily accessible by the non-specialist or inexperienced computing teachers. Changing the curriculum does not necessarily change those features of the teaching of ICT that caused the decline in the numbers pursuing computer science to higher education and vocations.

The observation that "many pupils are not inspired by what they are taught and gain nothing beyond basic digital literacy skills" (Royal Society, 2012, p. 5) might become in the near future, "many pupils are not inspired by what they are taught and gain nothing beyond basic coding skills". Changing the curriculum does not change the observation that there is a "shortage of teachers who are able to teach beyond basic digital literacy" or "a lack of continuing professional development for teachers of Computing" or "features of school infrastructure inhibit effective teaching of Computing" (Royal Society, 2012, p. 5). Many of the qualifications associated with ICT did not appear to provide what employers and higher education were looking for. Are we convinced that the developed content of the new GCSEs are addressing employers' needs or are simply reflecting a moving down the age range of the same computing concepts of the previous GCE specifications. The continued popularity of vocational and other skills-based courses suggests that the concern of "an unwieldy catalogue of often poorly understood qualifications which are mostly variations on IT literacy" continues.

And finally, could we have missed the point?

The 2014 national curriculum is lauded as inspirational and instrumental in bringing computational thinking to the fore in the education of all learners. Gerard Berry from College de France and Carlos Ghezzi, President of Informatics Europe, both noted the value of the new curriculum (CAS, 2014). This change "will only serve to positively impact children in England and their futures". Rachel Swidenbank, head of Codecademy, acknowledged the fact that the UK is the first G20 country to formally recognise the importance of teaching children computing (Computer World UK, 2014) and the declaration that "even if you are not a big fan of Mr Gove, the inclusion of computing in the new curriculum could well prove to be his lasting legacy for the children of this country, not to mention the economy" (Telegraph, 2014).

However, should we be celebrating? An analysis of the national curriculum document quickly reveals that it is very thin on ensuring that learners have a rounded and contextualised understanding of the values of technology. We should be lamenting the failure of ALL the subjects of the national curriculum to embrace the opportunities of technology in the teaching of their subject. Is it the case that they have abdicated all responsibilities of their subject to teach the skills, knowledge and understanding of technology and its role within their curriculum and in the world associated with their curriculum?

Technology and information technology is fully integrated into and pervasive across all our lives, and a national curriculum for the 21st century should have reflected that integration and pervasiveness. Instead, the subject has become siloed. It is taught in Computing and it is taught nowhere else. The use of technology to support the subject teaching across the whole of the curriculum is limited to music and Key Stage 1 design and technology. In both cases, it states "where appropriate", as if teachers might be tempted to use technology "inappropriately". The national curriculum does nothing to enhance society's use and exploitation of technology, or to promote its value in lifelong learning, citizenship or community action. As a result of this short-sightedness, will we be producing a generation of young people with no formal understanding of the values and affordances of the technology in much of their education and their lives? Perhaps the next challenge is to ensure all subjects of our pupils' education fully recognise, celebrate and integrate an understanding of the role of technology and information technology.

References

Abelson, H., 1982. *Apple logo.* BYTE/McGraw Hill.

Acorn Computers, 1993. *The horizon project.* Hampshire Microtechnology Centre.

Bennedsen, J., Caspersen, M.E., and Kölling, M., 2008. *Reflections on the teaching of programming: methods and implementations.* Springer.

Blackwell, A.F., 1999. *First steps in programming: a rationale for attention investment models.* DOI: 10.1109/HCC.2002.1046334. Source: CiteSeer.

Bloom, B.S., 1956. *Taxonomy of educational objectives: the classification of educational goals. Handbook 1: Cognitive domain.* New York: David McKay Co. Inc.

Bull, J., and McKenna, C., 2004. *Blueprint for computer-assisted assessment.* London: Routledge Falmer.

Bundy, A., 2007. Computational thinking is pervasive. *Journal of Scientific and Practical Computing,* 1, 67–69.

CAS, 2010. Available from: http://www.computingatschool.org.uk [Accessed July 2017].

CAS, 2012. Computing science: a curriculum for schools. Computing At School. Available from: http://www.computingatschool.org.uk/data/uploads/ComputingCurric.pdf [Accessed 9 March 2015].

CAS, 2014. *Best practice in education award.* Computing At School. Available from: http://www.computingatschool.org.uk/index.php?id=best-practice-in-education-award-2014 [Accessed 9 March 2015].

CAS, 2015. *Computational thinking in the national curriculum: a guide for teachers.* Computing At School. Available from: http://www.computingatschool.org.uk/data/uploads/CT_Framework.pdf [Accessed 9 March 2015].

Church, L., and Whitten, A., 2009. *Generative usability: security and user centered design beyond the appliance.* New Security Paradigms Workshop, Oxford.

Computer World UK, 2014. *Coding in British schools: a review of the first term.* Available from: http://www.computerworlduk.com/in-depth/careers/3595505/coding-in-british-schools-a-review-of-the-first-term [Accessed 9 March 2015].

Conole, G., Dyke, M., Oliver, M., and Seale, J., 2004. Mapping pedagogy and tools for effective learning design. *Computers and Education,* 43, pp.17–33.

Cooper, S., Dann, W., and Pausch, R., 2003. Teaching objects-first in introductory computer science. In *Proceedings of the 34th SIGSE technical symposium on computer science education,* pp. 191–195.

CS4FN, 2015. *Computer science for fun.* Queen Mary, University of London Available from: http://www.cs4fn.org [Accessed 9 March 2015].

CSTA, 2011. *K–12 Computer science standards.* New York, Association for Computer Machinery.

CSUnplugged, 2015. *Computer science without a computer.* Available from: http://csunplugged.org/ [Accessed 9 March 2015].

Cunningham, M., and Harris, S., 2003. *The ever-open classroom: using ICT to enhance communication and learning.* National Foundation for Educational Research. Available from: http://www.nfer.ac.uk/research [Accessed 9 March 2015].

Dann, W., Cooper, S., and Pausch, R., 2012. *Learning to program with Alice.* Prentice Hall.

de Bono, E., 2000. *6 thinking hats (revised).* London: Penguin.

de Bono, E., 2007. *How to have creative ideas.* London: Vermillion.

Denning, P.J., 2011. Ubiquity symposium: what have we said about computation?: Closing statement. *Ubiquity,* 2011 (April), 1–7. doi:10.1145/1967045.1967046

DfE, 2013. *National curriculum in England: computing programmes of study.* London: Department for Education

DfES, 2002. *Framework for teaching ICT Capability.* London: Department for Education and Skills.

DfES, 2004. *Progress towards a unified e-learning strategy.* London: Teaching Strategy Unit, Department for Education and Skills. Available from: http://www.dfes.gov.uk/elearningstrategy [Accessed 15 May 2004].

DfES, 2006. *Secondary national strategy.* London: Department for Education and Skills.

Dijkstra, E.W., 1972. Notes on structured programming. *In:* O.J. Dahl, E.W. Dijkstra and C.A.R. Hoare, eds. *Structured programming.* London and New York: Academic Press, pp. 1–82.

DuBoulay, B., 1989. Some difficulties of learning to program. *In:* E. Soloway and J.C. Spohrer, eds. *Studying the novice programmer.* London: Lawrence Erlbaum Associates, *pp.* 283–299.

Gove, M., 2012. *Speech.* Available from: http://www.education.gov.uk/inthenews/speeches/a00201868/michael-gove-speech-at-the-bett-show-2012 [Accessed 9 March 2015].

Guzdial, M., 2004. Programming environments for novices. In: S. Fincher and M. Petre, eds. *Computer science education research.* Lisse, The Netherlands: Taylor and Francis, pp. 127–153.

Henderson, P.B., Cortina, T.J., and Wing, J.M., 2007. Computational thinking. *Proceedings of the 38th SIGCSE technical symposium on computer science education.* Covington, Kentucky, USA: Association for Computer Machinery.

Independent ICT in School Commission, 1997. *Stevenson report.* Available from: http://rubble.ultralab.anglia.ac.uk/stevenson/ICTUK [Accessed 15 May 2004].

Kennewell, S., Parkinson, J., and Tanner, H., 2003. *Learning to teach ICT in the secondary school.* London: Routledge Falmer.

Kölling, M., 1999. The problem of teaching object-oriented programming, Part I: Languages. *Journal of Object-Oriented Programming,* 11, pp. 8–15.

Lu, J.J., and Fletcher, G.H.L., 2009. Thinking about computational thinking. *In: Proceedings of the 40th ACM Technical Symposium on Computer Science Education,* Chattanooga, TN, USA. New York: Association for Computer Machinery, pp. 260–264.

Malone, T.W., 1980. *What makes things fun to learn? A study of intrinsically motivating computer games. Technical report.* Palo Alto, CA: Xerox Palo Alto Research Center.

Mannila, L., 2007. Novices' progress in introductory programming courses. *Informatics in Education,* 61, pp. 139–152.

Means, W.H., 1988. A content analysis of ten introduction to programming textbooks. *ACM SIGCSE Bulletin,* 201, pp. 283–287.

Naughton, J., 2012. Why all our kids should be taught how to code. *The Guardian* [Online]. Available from: http://www.theguardian.com/education/2012/mar/31/why-kids-should-be-taught-code [Accessed 01-04-2017].

Papert, S.A. 1980. *Mindstorms: children, computers, and powerful ideas.* Boston: Basic Books.

Papert, S.A., and Harel, I., 1991. *Constructionism.* New York: Ablex Publishing Corporation.

QCA, 1999. *The national curriculum programmes of study and attainment targets.* London: Her Majesty's Stationery Office.

Royal Society, 2012. *Shut down or restart?* Available from: http://royalsociety.org/education/policy/computing-in-schools/report [Accessed 9 March 2015].

Saeli, M., Perrenet, J.C., Jochems, W.M.G., and Zwaneveld, B., 2010. *Portray the pedagogical content knowledge of programming – the technical report.* Internal publication. Available from: http://alexandria.tue.nl/extra2/724491.pdf [Accessed 9 March 2015].

Schimdt, E., 2011. Available from: http://www.guardian.co.uk/technology/2011/aug/26/eric-schmidt-chairman-google-education [Accessed 9 March 2015].

Shulman, L.S., 1986. Those who understand: knowledge growth in teaching. *Educational Researcher,* 15, pp. 4–14.

Soloway, E., 1993. Should we teach students to program? *ACM Communications,* 3610, pp. 21–24.

Telegraph, 2014. *When pupils know more than teachers.* Available from: http://www.telegraph.co.uk/education/educationopinion/11354499/When-pupils-know-more-than-teachers.html [Accessed 9 March 2015].

TSO, 2003. *Every child matters.* London: HMSO.

Wickens, C., 2007. Creativity. *In:* S. Kennewell, A. Connell, A. Edwards, M. Hammond and C. Wickens, (eds.), *A practical guide to teaching ICT in the secondary school.* Oxford, UK: Routledge.

Williams, D., *et al.*, 1998. *Teachers' ICT skills and knowledge needs: final report to SOEID.* Available from: http://www.scotland.gov.uk/library/ict [Accessed 9 March 2015].

Wing, J., 2006. Computational thinking. *Communications of the Association for Computer Machinery*, 49, 3, pp. 33–35.

Wing, J., 2008. Computational thinking and thinking about computing. *Philosophical Transactions of The Royal Society A*, 366, pp. 3717–3725.

Wing, J.M., 2013. *Computational thinking.* Pittsburgh, Carnegie Mellon University

Wood, D., 1998. *The UK ILS Evaluations Final Report.* Coventry: Becta. Available from: http://www.becta.org.uk [Accessed 15 May 2004].

Yadav, A., *et al.*, 2011. Introducing computational thinking in education courses. *Proceedings of the 42nd ACM technical symposium on computer science education.* Dallas, TX, USA: Association for Computer Machinery.

Chapter 3

The impact of teachers' perspectives on the development of computing as a subject

Jan Barnes and Steve Kennewell

This chapter complements debates on matters of policy by investigating the reality of school settings: exploring the introduction of a new computing curriculum from the perspective of ICT teachers and discussing the development of appropriate pedagogical practices. We will discuss how the analysis of activity systems can be used to characterise variations in perceptions of the subject and compare approaches to teaching. We will highlight typical contradictions within the recent teaching of ICT in three case study schools in Wales, and discuss the implications of introducing computer science teaching and learning in these settings. The conclusions will be used to generate issues for discussion and investigation by teachers and education students.

Policy and practice

The rational model for policy making can be summarised as follows:

- Identify issue
- Identify possible solutions
- Choose best solution
- Implement policy
- Evaluate policy in practice.

(Bates et al., 2011, p. 39)

However, in practice policy making is often "a messy process" (Bates et al., 2011, p. 40) which is "unco-ordinated and contradictory" (Trowler, 2003, p. 35). The history of policy development in relation to ICT/computing as a subject in England and Wales demonstrates a clear example of this.

If we attempt to fit the events of the past 25 years to the rational model, we see that the originators of the national curriculum for IT (DES/WO, 1990) did indeed identify an 'issue', viz. that all young people should develop an 'IT capability' in order to participate actively and effectively in an increasingly digital world. However, only one solution was proposed: a scheme heavily influenced by the developments in business education. Furthermore, this curriculum was specified only at an outline level, leaving schools to make decisions on possible solutions and choose the one they perceived to be best. This was done in the cause of 'futureproofing' the curriculum against changes in the particular technologies available – with the added advantage to the government that they were not committing to providing expensive resources.

As for implementation, any curriculum specification is going to be mediated by cultural practices at school and classroom level; those involved in implementation bring their own values, beliefs, attitudes and behaviours. Policy which is imposed is often ignored, subverted or even resisted, and as Mee (2015) says:

> If we define 'the curriculum' as ... what is actually taught rather than what is defined by a programme of study then how that curriculum manifests itself in reality will not be shaped by 'the teacher' but by a range of forces which transcend the power of the teacher or even the school.

Changes in practice occur in response to a variety of factors at personal, organisational and policy level, and at classroom level, the curriculum may be better analysed in terms of actual learning activity than using documentation which merely sets out plans. Outcomes are rarely the same in different contexts; impacts are not always those intended. In the case of IT (subsequently ICT), there were multiple sources of variation of practice from the intended policy, leading to considerable differences in expectations of learning in different classrooms. This is reflected in the evaluation reports of the inspection bodies in England and Wales (e.g. Ofsted, 1997; Estyn, 2014).

Background to the ICT/computing curriculum 1989–2013

In order to understand the current situation and judge its likely evolution, a brief summary of how it came about will be helpful (see also Chapter 2). The initial specification for the national curriculum (NC) set out general requirements concerning what was to be taught and the learning expected at different levels. The attainment target named 'IT capability' was split into five 'strands of progression':

- Developing ideas and communicating information
- Handling information
- Modelling
- Measurement and control
- Applications and effects.

(NCC, 1990, C4)

The statutory orders were supplemented by non-statutory guidance which characterised IT capability as a "cross-curricular competence" (NCC, 1990, C4) that can enhance the learning process and thus should be integral to learning activities. It is very clearly stated that, whilst Design and Technology is a discrete subject in its own right, this is not the case for IT; rather it is inherently cross-curricular in nature.

This placed it in a unique and anomalous position within a curriculum based on formal domains of knowledge. Information Technology (IT) and later Information Communication Technology (ICT) grew into a subject in its own right, becoming part of the NC in both England and Wales in 1999, with ICT capability being linked to the discrete subject of ICT (DfEE, 1999). Whilst the same NC was statutory in both England and Wales, there were variations in the non-statutory guidance issued by the now devolved Welsh Government and in the focus of the reports by the different inspection bodies.

Kennewell et al. (2000) identified five components which characterised the notion of ICT capability:

- Routines such as using a mouse or double clicking on an application,
- Techniques such as adjusting margins to make text fit a page,
- Key concepts such as menu, file, database, spreadsheet, web site or hypertext link,
- Processes such as developing a presentation, seeking information, organising, analysing and presenting the results of a survey,
- Higher order skills and knowledge such as recognising when the use of ICT might be appropriate, planning how to approach a problem, making and testing hypotheses, monitoring progress in a task and evaluating the result, reflecting on the effect of using ICT in a particular situation.

All of these elements are employed when using ICT for a particular task; techniques are learned operations which require conscious thought, and routines are techniques which have been moved into an automatic response through practice. Processes are "multi-stage procedures for achieving specified goals" (Kennewell et al., 2000, p. 21), and key concepts underlie the selection of techniques when carrying out a process, for instance knowing that items in graphics are objects which can be selected and formatted (Gaskell, 2003). Higher order skills enable the ICT user to orchestrate all the other components whilst solving problems and creating artefacts.

The 2008 NC orders in Wales also included a wider appreciation of the place of ICT in society:

At Key Stage 3, learners should be given opportunities to build on the skills, knowledge and understanding acquired at Key Stage 2. They develop a growing awareness of the relevance and plausibility of information and begin to identify and question bias in sources. They should be taught to become increasingly independent in their use of safe and suitable information sources, both ICT and non-ICT; to use a range of ICT skills and resources to find, analyse, communicate, present and share information, whilst becoming more aware of the need to check the accuracy of their work; to consider the advantages and limitations of using ICT in their activities across a range of subjects thus becoming increasingly aware of the social, ethical, moral and economic effects of ICT in the wider society.

(DCELLS, 2008, p. 5)

The dilemma is that some schools have interpreted the guidance to mean that ICT provision should be supplied on a cross-curricular basis only. This approach has been particularly encouraged in Wales, through non-statutory guidance and inspection reports.

> The most popular model has discrete ICT skills lessons in Year 7 taught by specialist IT teachers and some cross-curricular work in a limited range of subjects. By Year 9, the discrete lessons have been replaced by cross-curricular work in a wide range of subject areas. For the majority of schools this is the more effective approach to the teaching and application of ICT skills.
>
> (Estyn, 2007)

However, it does mean that much of the teaching of ICT capability has become the responsibility of non-ICT specialists, or, if being taught by ICT specialists, it may have been constrained by the requirements of the subject providing the context for the ICT activity. The most recent Estyn thematic report on ICT at Key Stage (KS) 3 (Estyn, 2014) recognised this and made it clear that to be rated 'good' or better in ICT as a subject, secondary schools should provide regular discrete lessons throughout KS3. However, Estyn finds that "pupils do not generally apply the skills learned in discrete ICT lessons well in other subjects" (p. 15).

The KS3 ICT curriculum is vague in its nature when compared to the curriculum of other core subjects. This has its advantages but may have led to differences in teachers' perceptions of ICT capability. This variation in perception may lead to a difference in how ICT capability is taught, or at the very least to a difference in emphasis for certain aspects of the curriculum.

The 2002 revision of the ICT Orders in England set out requirements in a little more detail; however, despite the greater power, availability and familiarity of ICT resources, the demands were not increased. Indeed, the strands were renamed in more general language as

- finding things out
- developing ideas and making things happen
- exchanging and sharing information
- reviewing, modifying and evaluating work as it progresses.

(DfES, 2002)

Alongside these new statutory orders, a national strategy was developed for teaching ICT at KS3; this involved a framework for curriculum planning which specified how the subject could be taught at the level of individual lesson plans. Although not compulsory, the inspection body Ofsted used it as a benchmark for adequacy in their judgments of schools' provision.

Neither of these schemes were adopted in Wales, which in 2008 split the subject into two distinct contributory parts; that of finding and analysing information and of creating and communicating information (DCELLS, 2008). It further states that

Schools should choose material that will

- provide a meaningful, relevant and motivating curriculum for their learners
- meet the specific needs of their learners and further their all-round development.

(DCELLS, 2008, p. 5)

To enable this, teachers will need to have an in-depth understanding of the elements, but the guidelines for the teaching of ICT in Wales have been vague and teachers have interpreted the teaching requirements of the subject in a variety of ways.

Influences affecting the learning of ICT/computing

Wood and Webb (2002) suggest that the generic nature and lack of specificity in the subject has meant that the curriculum has lasted well, but it has also meant that many teachers are unsure in their perceptions of ICT capability. Any variation in the teaching of ICT at KS3 will also have an effect on achievement at this level and pupils' perception of their learning.

Furthermore, ICT is also a tool for learning: specialists in other subjects will utilise ICT capability to further pupils' learning in their own disciplines.

Kennewell et al. (2000) suggest that there needs to be a gap between learners' current knowledge and the intended learning, and that the gap must be small enough to be bridged through cognitive effort and the support provided by the teacher, peers, and other resources.

Consequently, it is the responsibility of the teacher to design tasks related to the learning objectives and assist the learners in achieving the task goals, perhaps by the setting of differentiated tasks that will have a 'learning gap' appropriate to the learning objectives and ability of the learners. This will rely on the specific subject knowledge of the teacher and their perceptions of what is required to develop ICT capability (Webb, 2002).

Our observations of ICT teaching in many schools over several years suggested that there was a wide variation in pedagogical practice, and that this reflected not just different pedagogical beliefs but different perceptions about the nature of the subject. Furthermore, classroom practices were dependent on whole school factors as well as the individual teacher's perceptions, and in order to probe the effects of teacher perceptions, a research study was needed to examine the ICT classroom as an activity setting from a number of perspectives.

Investigating the teaching of ICT

Activity theory is a form of research and theorising which is based upon work carried out by the cultural historical school of Russian psychology (Engeström et al., 1999; Engeström, 2007). Over the years, this method of research and analysis has been refined by contemporary researchers and theorists, particularly Engeström.

It was the work of Engeström (2001) which was used to establish a possible analytical framework for this study. Cultural Historical Activity Theory (CHAT) allows the researcher to pay particular attention not only to the specific object of activity under research, which for the purposes of this study is the development of ICT capability, but also the Vygotskian focus of 'mediation and discourse' (Daniels et al., 2010).

This study is proposing to evaluate and analyse the perceptions of educators in the development of ICT and to examine their personal constructs in teaching the subject. The cultural and belief systems are going to have a strong influence. The use of CHAT within educational research has become increasingly popular over the last 30 years (Roth and Lee, 2007). When applying CHAT to the teaching of ICT/computing within the classroom in particular, the object of the activity is the pupils' learning. CHAT is particularly appropriate for studies such as this where the focus is on change in the activity.

The proposition of activity theory is that human activity consists of much more than mere action, but is a socially situated phenomenon. It is a theory or framework that examines practice, but situates that practice within an environment, which also examines the process and the purpose of that practice (Daniels et al., 2010). In doing this, it attempts to account for the complexity of real-time activity, investigating factors that influence the activity such as the beliefs and perceptions of those central to the activity. Engeström et al. (1999) further believe that activity theory has much to contribute to research as it allows for analysis of the micro, meso and macro environs in which the activity exists. Webb (2010) argues that our increasing understanding of cognition and metacognition has led to the need for researchers to develop more complex models of analysis, involving aspects of influence such as the environment in which learning is to take place. There is a need to recognise multiple dimensions of influence that may impact the practice of the teacher from a personal perspective, school perspective and national perspective. These dimensions of influence and their impact on education and individual teachers are likely to bring about change. Engeström (2007) also discusses variances within the settings and describes these as being deviations within the scripts of the setting, coining them as disturbances or *contradictions*. These contradictions are not necessarily conflicts, but characterise tensions which may exist historically and have built up over time, for example, changes within the ICT policy within a school or subtle changes in pedagogy with the advancement of technology.

It is the contradiction within the initial activity setting which will highlight a need for change, and the adjustment to this contradiction will bring about the transformation which is essentially the point of this form of analysis. An example of this may be a change in curriculum which demands a change in pedagogy to bring about new learning. The object of both activity settings is the learning taking place; however, with the introduction of new curriculum, the way in which that learning is developed may need to change. By comparing the two activity settings, before and after that change, a contradiction between the two will be identified.

CHAT, and in particular the activity triangle of Figure 3.1 (Engeström, 2001; Roth and Lee, 2007; Daniels et al., 2010), helps to analyse relationships and networks within related activity systems. Any change and alteration of an aspect of one system, whether it be part of the tools, rules, roles, individuals or outcomes, are likely to affect another part of the system or systems.

The primary focus for analysis is the object (or motive) which leads to the outcome of activity, with a secondary focus on the tools or operations that bring about that outcome (Jonassen and Rohrer-Murphy, 1999). The application of this to this study leads to the following:

Individuals and groups

The individuals and groups whose viewpoints are adopted are known as the subject in the standard activity theory triangle (Murphy and Rodriguez-Manzanares, 2008). The main viewpoints will be those of the teacher and the pupils. The beliefs and perceptions of the teachers will be particularly important, but the pupils' attitudes to learning will also play a key role.

Objects and outcomes

The object is the purpose of the activity, which is transformed by the other elements or mediating factors to produce the outcome. The main object for the classroom is learning, which is a process of change and has a complex relationship with the activity. Learning should not be confused with the pupil's completion of

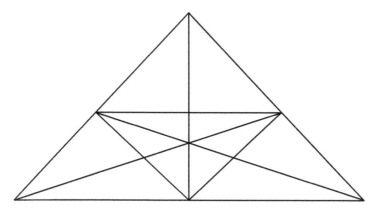

Figure 3.1 Activity triangle (Engeström, 2001; Roth and Lee, 2007; Daniels et al., 2010).

a set task, as this is a different kind of action. However, it has often been observed that completion of a set task is the only object for pupils (Kennewell, 2010).

Tools and artefacts

In a learning environment within the classroom, tools and artefacts include the curriculum and also the method in which this is achieved, for example, the plans and schemes put into place to facilitate the teaching of ICT at KS3. They also include the software and hardware used to support the teaching, together with the strategies used to bring about the learning process. These tools can be external ones, such as the national curriculum, but also may be symbolic and include the language which takes part in the transformation process of the object into an outcome (Murphy and Rodriguez-Manzanares, 2008).

Community and organisational structures

These factors include the class, school or indeed structures at a national level. One of the strong influences here is likely to be the culture that exists within the department or school concerning teaching and learning – for teachers and for pupils.

Roles and division of labour

This factor concerns who participates and what their level of participation is in producing the outcome. In education, the outcome is the learning, in this case the development of ICT capability. In this context, we would be interested in the roles taken in bringing about that goal, which would include any individuals such as the teacher and support assistants together with the pupils themselves. This is not just about participation in the objects of the activity setting, but also and importantly, the division of power within the activity setting's community. This can include the senior management within a school, and in turn, the government policies which drive the organisation and process of the learning activity.

Rules and codes of behaviour

These may include the attitude of all the participants to ICT and how this links to the culture of the organisation, for example, where ICT is perceived as a tool to assist learning on a cross-curricular basis or where it is afforded a higher level of status within the curriculum of the school. This also concerns pedagogical practices. However, from the pupils' perspective, the rules and behaviours associated with their everyday use of ICT in society are likely to impact upon the classroom setting.

Research study

In order to investigate perceptions of ICT capability, case studies were built using interviews, observation and teacher reflection.

An initial interview with each individual participating teacher was conducted at the start of the data collection process. The aim of this was to ascertain the teacher's personal constructs of ICT capability. Questions were posed regarding their personal beliefs regarding the nature of ICT capability and how this was dealt with in Wales. The interview also attempted to address issues such as the changes taking place in England at the time, the issue of motivation amongst pupils, especially the drop in motivation between KS2 and KS4, and to what extent ICT capability could be developed on a cross-curricular basis. All these questions would enable analysis to discern a number of factors relating to how they defined ICT capability, what its role was within the curriculum and how they thought it might or should change given the changes being discussed in England. By analysing how they felt the concept of ICT capability should change, there would be an indication of how they perceived the development of ICT capability and those applications or tools which might be required to develop ICT capability as an entity.

The chief question concerning the teacher's perceptions cannot be answered by interview alone; however, because part of the research question was whether the activity in the classroom during the development of ICT capability matched teachers' personal constructs of ICT capability, observations of classroom practice were also employed as a means of data collection. This involved observation of specific lessons where the teachers used the development strategy highlighted within their interviews in teaching ICT capability. The teacher was encouraged to discuss this as part of a post-observation reflective dialogue, to establish the teacher's reflective thoughts on the observed lesson, how it related to the development of ICT capability according to the personal constructs and beliefs of the teacher and how it may be adapted or improved for the next observation.

A final interview was conducted to explore whether there had been any changes in the teacher's personal constructs of ICT capability over the period or any changes in their strategies for the development of ICT capability. The teachers were also asked to reflect and evaluate the use of their chosen teaching strategy in the development of ICT capability.

By comparing the information gathered from both the interview and the observations, any contradictions which may have arisen between the teachers' personal constructs and their practice may be identified through themes and activity setting analysis. The CHAT framework helped us to do this in a rigorous and objective way.

Case study schools

School A was a large 11–18 comprehensive school with one specialist ICT teacher. To provide all pupils with a combination of specialist teaching and practical activity, for one week per year a whole year group worked on ICT through a series of 'masterclasses' lasting between 1 hour and 1.5 hours each morning throughout a week, followed up by workshops in ability-based groups for the rest of the day. The masterclasses were given to the whole cohort as a lead lecture by the ICT specialist; this was followed up with workshops by the specialist ICT teacher (for the most able class) and a number of non-specialist teachers with an interest in technology (for the other classes). There were no discrete ICT lessons for KS3 other than those given in this format once a year.

School B was a medium-sized 11–16 mixed comprehensive school. The school afforded a degree of status to the subject of ICT similar to other comparable subjects in that ICT was taught for the equivalent of 1 hour per week throughout KS3 by specialist ICT teachers, assisted by a non-specialist teacher who had some expertise in the subject. The department had designed a system of facilitation to attempt to encourage the pupils to take control of their own learning. This format moved away from the more traditional four-phase lesson structure and used a lesson structure more suited to facilitating coursework at KS4.

The teacher gave a very short recap, outlined a problem and directed the pupils to the tools to solve that problem. The aim was to enable the pupils to develop their metacognitive skills in solving the set problem. This problem was likely to include the exploration of given software and the selection and utilisation of particular tools of the software in order to solve that problem. The software techniques were not demonstrated, but there were a number of worksheets, help guides and demonstration movies which were stored on the school's virtual learning environment.

The pupils were directed to and reminded of the location of these resources, and encouraged to use them in their exploration of the software under investigation. The aim of this strategy was to enable the more able pupils to take greater control of their own learning and to use their metacognitive skills to construct knowledge. This also allowed time and opportunity for the teacher to support those pupils who were less able to manage their learning.

School C was a small 11–16 mixed comprehensive. At the time of analysis, ICT capability was developed through discrete weekly lessons for all KS3 pupils, with the scheme of work being designed by the two specialist ICT teachers within the department, and assistance for the teaching of the subject being drawn from an additional non-specialist ICT teacher. One of the strategies within the ICT department involved the use of a 'buddy' system, together with a 'learning ladder'. This was designed to try to empower the pupils to take a degree of control of their own learning and to utilise peer teaching systematically. Having designed their own success criteria for a task, the ladder had a series of steps which were designed to bring about the successful completion of the task. The buddy system came into operation when a pupil was finding difficulty with an aspect of the task; pupils were arranged in pairs and when seeking help, a pupil first asked their partner. If this 'buddy' were unable to help, the pupil would go on to ask another neighbour before ultimately asking the teacher.

Findings

The case studies and cross-case analysis revealed a continuum concerning perception of ICT capability, with variation concerning the nature of the skills being emphasised by the teacher. At one end of the scale was a focus on use of techniques and at the other end a focus on problem solving and evaluation.

The teachers were initially in agreement in including the higher order metacognitive skills as part of their explanation of their understanding of ICT capability. This is in line with the ethos of the national curriculum for Wales (ACCAC, 2008) which clearly refers to the use of 'thinking skills' within the learning of the subject, whilst Kennewell describes ICT capability as being a non-linear process involving the development of "routines, techniques, key concepts, processes and higher order skills" (Kennewell et al., 2003, p. 7). However, after a cycle of observation, reflection, further observation and a final interview, the perception of the teacher in School A changed to match the classroom practice, describing the skills which had previously been associated with metacognition as now being "synonymous" with the application tools. Thus, this moved the teacher's perception along the continuum to a tools-based subject, which corresponded more with the support of other subjects rather than one with its own conceptual framework. Furthermore, the subject was not held in high status within the school community, as it was not afforded regular discrete lessons within the curriculum. However, rather than solving the problem of a contradiction between practice and perception, there was now a contradiction between their practice/perception and the expectations set out in the national curriculum orders.

Schools B and C did not demonstrate contradictions between their perceptions of ICT capability and their classroom practice. Both defined ICT capability as having not only the tools-based component, where there was a need to be able to operate a variety of software applications, but also highlighted the need to be able to use higher order skills to be able to discuss the subject, using the language and terminology of the subject, and to use the software applications in an appropriate and effective way to solve problems. Where differences did emerge, it was in the way they interpreted the national curriculum and in particular the possible inclusion of computer science concepts and programming. School B felt that the proposed changes did not go far enough and that there was a need to teach aspects of hardware and computer and network engineering, whilst School C felt that the curriculum did not require change at all but that those teaching the ICT curriculum needed to be more innovative and motivational in their approach to the development of ICT capability.

The teaching strategies observed involved the use of quite different *pedagogical tools*. In the case of School A, the main pedagogical tool was the masterclass, which, on observation, emerged as a way of allowing the specialist ICT teacher to demonstrate the use of the software application to all the students within a year group at one time within a lecture theatre type environment. This was then followed up by workshops allowing different ability groups opportunities to engage with the task and achieve the outcomes required. This pedagogical tool was designed to focus on development of the techniques associated with application software.

In School B, the main strategy was one of facilitation by the teacher, allowing pupils the discretion to use prepared pedagogical tools, viz. movies and help sheets, in order to develop the knowledge of the software techniques and then to explore the best way in which those tools could be used. Further, part of that task was to prepare a form of help guide for their peers. They were able to develop their metacognitive skills in deciding the most appropriate form that this help would take. It may have been through the production of an on-screen video, showing their peers how to use a particular tool in a particular scenario to gain best effect, or it may have been the production of the word-based help guide. Either way, the pupils were required to evaluate the work they were carrying out, and to reproduce the method used and explain why. The one pitfall observed with this pedagogical tool was that it relied heavily on the individual motivation of the pupils, their mindfulness and their desire to learn.

Finally, the main teaching strategy used in School C involved systematic peer assistance, whereby when the pupils required help or assistance they were able to discuss their dilemma first with their partner then a member of their team, and finally if they were not available, their teacher. This allowed the pupils who were struggling to articulate their problem, which required the use of higher order skills to discern exactly where their quandary existed, and for those pupils assisting to articulate how that problem could be solved. Another pedagogical tool was that of discussion, and this was used throughout the classroom practice. It was present when discussing the learning objectives and when the pupils were enabled to develop their own success criteria for any subsequent task. This assisted them to both articulate and solve the problem, and in doing so, use their metacognitive skills to break down the problem and find ways to bring about its solution.

Thus, this examination of the practice in the three case studies highlighted another continuum, concerning teaching strategy. At one end is School A, where ICT was perceived as a subject which was a cross-curricular tool or aid for other discrete subjects, developed through a series of tasks with only superficial opportunities for evaluation or the use of higher order skills. At the other end of this continuum lies School B, where the development of ICT capability was one of a facilitation of learning by the teacher. The pupils had control over their own learning and were using their higher order metacognitive skills to define their learning and how they were going to solve the problem in hand. Lying within this continuum is School C, where ICT capability was developed using metacognitive skills, but with more scaffolding and teacher support. The scaffolding placed its practice between Schools A and B; however, the use of verbalisation in developing the learning ladders and the formulation of the success criteria by the pupils with varying degrees of guidance by the teacher pushes this school closer along the continuum to School B than School A.

Implications for the development of the computing curriculum

We have indicated that during the period of the research, changes were taking place in the national curriculum for England. A fundamental shift in policy-makers' perceptions of what all should be taught as future citizens came about through high-profile lobbying by representatives of worldwide ICT organisations (see Chapter 2) and the computer games industry (Livingstone and Hope, 2011). Powerful entrepreneurs were influential in arguing the need for 'excitement' and 'rigour' in the teaching of matters concerning computers, and enabled professional bodies in science (Royal Society, 2012), engineering (Royal Academy for Engineering, 2009) and computing (British Computer Society), together with the emergent association of interested teachers, Computing At School (CAS, 2012), to gain the highest level of political support for incorporating aspects of computer science in the statutory curriculum.

The Royal Society (2012) report *Shut Down or Restart* set out a proposal for the development of a curriculum for a broad subject, Computing, which was carefully argued in both economic and educational terms. This subject covered what was known as ICT in schools and IT in industry but organised under the titles Computer Science, IT and Digital Literacy. It stated that Computer Science was a 'rigorous academic discipline' and stressed the importance of 'computational thinking' and the teaching of algorithm design and coding. This led to detailed proposals for this new subject in the NC, with an explicit and demanding requirement for the study of programming. This aspect has been widely promoted under the popular title of 'coding', with an expectation that all pupils will be able to develop useful apps for their personal devices.

This change in the curriculum has not been formalised in Wales, but the influence of the shift in England has clearly been felt at government as well as teacher level. "We feel strongly that ICT has lost its meaning and become synonymous with word processing and spreadsheets" (The ICT Steering Group, 2013, p. 13), and a recent Estyn (2014) report suggests the inclusion of programming as an extension to the statutory curriculum requirements, albeit with an implication that this is primarily for the more able pupils. The Donaldson Review (Welsh Government, 2015) proposes that computer science should be introduced to a revised NC as a specific component within the Science and Technology Area of Learning and Experience.

It seems that the term 'ICT capability' has now been consigned to history, but the question remains as to what the educated citizen should be capable of in relation to digital technology, and what teaching should be provided by schools to achieve this educational goal. Our research suggests a number of aspects which will be problematic:

- Objects and outcomes: The current contradiction observed between a curriculum which specifies problem solving and higher order skills and teaching objectives based on software techniques may transfer directly into the programming aspect of the computing curriculum if the focus is on 'coding' per se.
- Pedagogical strategies and tools: There may be a contradiction between the self-directed and exploratory learning strategies and the 'rigorous' nature of computer science knowledge.

- Curriculum organisation: Finding the scheduled lesson time required for a demanding subject will be difficult for school management who are trying to meet a large number of demands on the timetable.
- Professional development: As well as needing greater understanding of the subject, particularly computer science, teachers may need to adapt their pedagogical strategy and develop new pedagogical tools.

There is much here to be considered for a future research agenda:

- What form will professional development take?
- How will the computing curriculum vary at national, school and classroom levels?
- How will pedagogy change as ICT becomes computing?
- Will non-specialist teachers be able to generate the "interest, excitement and creativity that even a modest mastery of the subject offers" (Royal Society, 2012)?
- What contradictions will arise and how will they be resolved?
- Will the new curriculum be successful in achieving educational and economic outcomes?

The work reported in this chapter is only a small contribution, but there is little other research concerning the teaching and learning of ICT/computing in the UK at present and we hope to stimulate further investigation.

Questions

1   Do you think that there is a contradiction between the concepts and methods of computer science and pedagogical strategies based on self-directed and exploratory learning?
2   How much variation is there in the teacher's perception of the subject and the pedagogical strategy in the different classes you have observed?
3   How important for a teacher of computing is their knowledge and perception concerning the curriculum requirements of the subject, compared with their knowledge and skill in using pedagogical strategies and tools?
4   Is the idea of 'capability' incompatible with the scientific rigour involved in the new subject?
5   Does Activity Theory provide useful tools for the analysis of curriculum and teaching?

Further reading

Computing At School. n.d. *Discussion forum*. Available from: http://community.computing atschool.org.uk/forums [Accessed 17 July 2017].
Daniels, H. 2008. *Vygotsky and research*. London: Routledge.

Kennewell, S., Parkinson, J., and Tanner, H. 2000. *Developing the ICT capable school.* London: Routledge Falmer.

Royal Society, 2012. *Shut down or restart.* London: Royal Society.

References

ACCAC, 2008. *Information technology in the national curriculum in Wales,* Cardiff: ACCAC.

Bates, J., Lewis, S., and Pickard, A., 2011. *Education policy, practice and the professional.* London: Continuum.

CAS, 2012. *Computing: a curriculum for schools, report of the Computing At School working party.* Available from: http://www.computingatschool.org.uk/ [Accessed 26th January 2012].

Daniels, H., *et al.,* 2010. *Activity theory in practice.* London: Routledge.

DCELLS, 2008. *Information and communication technology in the national curriculum for Wales.* Cardiff: Welsh Assembly Government.

DES/WO, 1990. *Technology in the national curriculum.* London: Department for Education and Science – Welsh Office.

DfEE, 1999. *Information and communication technology: the national curriculum for England.* London: Department for Education and Employment.

DfES, 2002. *Framework for teaching ICT capability: Years 7, 8 and 9,* London: Department for Education and Skills.

Engeström, Y., 2001. Expansive learning at work: toward an activity theoretical reconceptualization. *Journal of Education & Work,* 14(1), pp. 133–156.

Engeström, Y., 2007. Enriching the theory of expansive learning: lessons from journeys toward coconfiguration. *Mind, Culture and Activity,* 14(1–2), pp. 23–39.

Engeström, Y., Meittinen, R., and Punmaki, R.-L., 1999. *Perspectives on activity theory.* Cambridge: Cambridge University Press.

Estyn, 2007. *A review of information and communications technology provisions in schools and its impact on raising standards.* Cardiff, Estyn.

Estyn, 2014. *ICT at key stage 3: the impact of ICT on pupils' learning at key stage 3 in secondary schools.* Cardiff: Estyn

Gaskell, C., 2003. Capability or office fodder. *Teaching ICT,* Summer 2003, pp. 22–37.

The ICT Steering Group, 2013. *Report to the Welsh Government,* Cardiff, Welsh Government.

Jonassen, D.H., and Rohrer, M.L., 1999. Activity theory as a framework for designing constructivist learning environments. *Educational Technology Research and Development,* 47(1), pp. 61–79.

Kennewell, S., Parkinson, J., and Tanner, H., 2000. *Developing the ICT capable school.* London: Routledge Falmer.

Kennewell, S., Parkinson, J., and Tanner, H., 2003. *Learning to teach ICT in secondary school.* London: Routledge Falmer.

Kennewell, S., 2010. *Analysing the impact of information technology on activity and learning. In:* A. McDougall, J. Murnane, A. Jones, and N. Reynolds, eds. *Researching IT in education: theory, practice and future directions.* London: Routledge, pp. 112–120.

Livingstone, I., and Hope, A., 2011. *Next gen. Transforming the UK into the world's leading talent hub for the video games and visual effects industries.* London: Nesta.

Mee, A., 2015. Computer education: the new school curriculum misses the mark. Again. Available from: http://community.computingatschool.org.uk/forums/1/topics/3849#post_48864 [Accessed March 2016].

Murphy, E., and Rodriguez-Manzanares, M.A., 2008. Using activity theory and its principle of contradictions to guide research in educational technology. *Australasian Journal of Educational Technology*, 24(4), pp. 442–457.

NCC, 1990. *Non-statutory guidance: Information technology capability.* York: National Curriculum Council.

Ofsted, 1997. *Information technology – a commentary on inspection findings in English schools.* London: Office for Standards in Education.

Roth, W.M., and Lee, Y.-J., 2007. "Vygotsky's neglected legacy": cultural-historical activity theory. *Review of Educational Research*, 77(2), pp. 186–232.

Royal Academy of Engineering, 2009. *ICT for the UK's future*, London: Royal Academy of Engineering.

Royal Society, 2012. *Shut down or restart.* London: Royal Society.

Trowler, P., 2003. *Education policy.* London: Routledge

Webb, M., 2002. Pedagogical reasoning: issues and solutions for the teaching and learning of ICT in secondary schools. *Education and Information Technologies*, pp. Vol 7:3 pp. 237–255.

Webb, M., 2010. Models for exploring and characterising pedagogy within information technology. *In:* A. McDougal, J. Murnane, A. Jones, and N. Reynolds, eds. *Researching IT in education: theory, practice and future directions.* Abingdon: Routledge, pp. 91–112.

Welsh Government, 2015. *The review of assessment and the curriculum:* Cardiff, Welsh Government.

Wood, C., and Webb, A., 2002. *Teaching ICT,* 1 (3).

Chapter 4

Assessment of Computing and ICT at 16

What are the perceptions of learners?

Pete Bradshaw

As described elsewhere in this book, there has been and continues to be considerable debate as to the nature of the subject of computing and the related subject of ICT. In Chapter 2 from John Woollard, these issues are discussed and the relative merits of the subject domains considered. This has led to the dropping of ICT as an examined subject at 16 in England and corresponding changes to the curriculum that have favoured computational thinking, programming and understanding how computers work rather than their applications. Research into the views of learners regarding this change is relatively sparse.

This chapter draws on a study conducted between 2006 and 2011 that enquired into learner perceptions of Information and Communications Technology (ICT) and its assessment at age 16. This time period led into the change of the curriculum outlined above and the reintroduction of computing to the school curriculum. This chapter and the research on which it is based debates the views of learners and looks at questions of what qualities, knowledge and understanding they see as valuable for assessment at 16.

The prevailing orthodoxies amongst writers, commentators and educationalists prior to the curriculum change to computing were that the subject 'ICT' did not reflect the learning and use made by young people of technology. The voice of the learner, although often lauded in aspects of school democracy and in formative assessment, had not been heard in respect of the high-stakes assessment at the end of Key Stage (KS) 4 in schools in England. This research was a step in filling that void. It considered the views of learners aged 16 who were to take so-called 'high stakes' assessment, such as GCSE and other 'level 2' qualifications in ICT or similar. The overarching question was to what extent they saw the qualifications as being for the purposes they perceived.

Taking an interpretive phenomenological approach (Conroy, 2003; Smith and Osborn, 2003), three phases of empirical data collection were used, each building on the previous ones. To bring the learner perception and voice to the fore, a repertory grid analysis was initially used to elicit constructs of learning and assessment directly from the learners. This was followed by a questionnaire and semi-structured interviews across a sample of state-funded schools in England. The use of a multiple-phase data collection allowed phenomena to be distilled with successively more depth at each phase.

The study identified three phenomena that emerged as central to the learners' views. Firstly, learners identified ICT as a subject that was predominantly about their future lives. They equated what they were doing in school with their perceptions of the needs of future education, employment and as a tool for life. Secondly, they saw, in common with many commentators, creativity and ICT as being intrinsically linked. Thirdly, their views were dominated by the culture of the school in which they were studying. The institutional habitus gave an enculturation to their perceptions which coloured everything else (Bourdieu, 1984; Reay et al., 2001). Thus, they valued creative and open-ended activity in the use of technology, but only where that contributed to formal, in-school learning.

This chapter describes the research study and the findings from 2011, which was also the date that the then Secretary of State for Education, Michael Gove, delivered his speech to the Education World Forum, in which the changes to the ICT curriculum were first announced (Gove, 2011; Paige, 2011). Whilst originating from 2011, it can be argued that there is little reason to suggest that the research phenomena that emerged as significant for learners would not be similarly to the fore if the study were repeated. It is perhaps a deficit of the qualifications-dominated English education system that such views are not taken into account and learners are not allowed more freedom to express their learning with technology.

Discord between young people's use of technology and its assessment

The research was carried out in schools, with 16-year-old learners as respondents. It enquired into, and reported on, the views of those who were in the final year of ICT courses in KS4 (i.e. those that lead to assessment at age 16) at English secondary schools. Specifically, it reports on learners' perceptions of the subject and its assessment.

The initial stimuli for the research came from learners' and teachers' comments about ICT, supplemented by an unease the author had picked up whilst visiting schools and talking to trainee teachers about Oxford, Cambridge and RSA Examinations' national qualification in ICT, an increasingly popular option for ICT in schools (Vidal Rodeiro, 2010) and reportedly the fourth most popular qualification at 16 in England in 2009 (Paton, 2010). There was a concern, however, that passing it "look[ed] like a screenshot hoop-jumping exercise [with] endless amounts of 'evidence' seem[ing to be] the order of the day for all [ICT] qualifications" (Teacher, 2006).

A further issue was raised in a discussion on the Naace (national subject association for computers in education) online community's mailing list where it was reported that conversations with learners revealed that they do not appear to learn anything new in ICT at school. This discussion was summarised by Heppell (2007a) who contrasted the curriculum that was being experienced by learners in their everyday lives with that which was handed down through the formal education system. The difference, he claimed, was partially caused by the rate of change of technology. What might be considered to be essential for inclusion in school curricula today would be obsolete tomorrow and, worse, was very quickly seen to be irrelevant by learners, whose voice was not considered in the design of such curricula and its assessment (ibid.).

Three vignettes are provided here to illustrate what would appear to be a mismatch between the experience of learning about, and with, ICT in schools and learners' experience of learning, and use, of ICT out of schools. The first is from a national newspaper in England and the final two directly from learners.

Naughton (2007, p. 12), writing in *The Observer*, provided the first vignette:

> There's a surreal quality to it, conjuring up images of kids trudging into ICT classes and being taught how to use a mouse and click on hyperlinks; receiving instructions in the creation of documents using Microsoft Word and of spreadsheets using Excel; being taught how to create a toy database using Access and a cod Powerpoint presentation; and generally being bored out of their minds. Then the kids go home and log on to Bebo or MySpace to update their profiles, run half a dozen simultaneous instant messaging conversations, use Skype to make free phone calls, rip music from CDs they've borrowed from friends, twiddle their thumbs to send incomprehensible text messages, view silly videos on YouTube and ... to download episodes of [TV programmes]. When you ask them what they did at school, they grimace and say: 'We made a Powerpoint presentation, Dad'. Yuck!

It was interesting to note the plethora of names of pieces of software in these accounts. Even just a year later, many of them seemed outdated. By 2008 learners would, for example, probably have been using iPlayer or 4oD to watch missed television programmes, update profiles in Facebook, and post images on Flickr. This was evidence of the changing technological landscape, leading to a disparity between school curricula and assessment and learners' exposure to, and experience with, technology (McFarlane, 2001; Threlfall and Nelson, 2006; Heppell, 2007b). Whilst the use of different software does not imply different underlying learning, knowledge or skills, many of the things that Naughton (op. cit.) describes would have been impossible only a few years earlier. No software would have existed to make these tasks accessible to all but a few technological experts.

A second account was heard directly from a learner. Tellingly, he put assessment at the heart of ICT education:

> I find our education is based around assessment and therefore we are given what is required to pass these exams at the highest possible ability. We might even be given the syllabus of what is expected. Would it not be better to be given a greater depth of knowledge and a more true knowledge than just given what is required to pass exams?
>
> (Learner recorded by Millwood, 2008)

The final vignette, also from a learner, addressed this mismatch between assessment and what is done beyond school from another angle – that of the inadequacy of the examinations. Writing on a gaming forum, a 16-year-old said:

> ... just did [my] GCSE a few days ago and I am sure anyone else who did will agree it is shamefully and embarrassingly easy for GCSE.
>
> ('addonai', 2007)

This view that ICT assessment is too easy was echoed by the popular press (see, for example, *Daily Mail*, 2007).

Creativity, utility and learner voice

The research was carried out in three phases. Firstly, learners were asked to consider their uses of technology, both in school and out of school. This led to a prioritisation of what they saw as important. Secondly, these aspects were used alongside features from the existing qualification specifications in a survey to refine this prioritisation. Thirdly, learners were interviewed individually and in groups to develop a more in-depth understanding of their views and to triangulate with the earlier data collected. Throughout, the overarching objective of the research was to find out what learners considered to be important in the assessment of ICT and computing at 16.

The research found that learner perceptions of ICT and computing were largely focused on its utility and relevance for later life, for further education or for employment. This end justified almost any means of obtaining a qualification in ICT and computing. They saw that creative aspects of ICT use should be assessed although, when asked what should be added to a course, did not value things that were solely done at home. Their perceptions were dominated by the school and course they were following.

The prevailing orthodoxy as expressed anecdotally in the vignettes that initiated the research was that the ICT curriculum and its assessment are not fit for purpose in that they do not take account of the impact of technologies on young peoples' lives and learning. This is especially true in the informal contexts where a significant amount of technological use, and learning, takes place (Crook, 2008; Logicalis, 2009; Ofcom, 2011). Further, is it is argued that the assessment process is too conservative to take into account this wide-ranging and often creative understanding of ICT (Heppell, 2007b; Selwyn, 2011). There is a relationship between structural, institutional, social and personal factors and assessment systems, which affect motivation and autonomy. It is in motivation and autonomy that perception may be most visibly manifested (after Ecclestone and Pryor, 2003). The assessment system itself is both subject to concerns of validity and reliability (Wiliam, 2001). Its relationship to the agendas of learner voice (Ruddock et al., 2006; Walker and Logan, 2008) and personalisation is unclear (Underwood et al., 2008). In respect of this underlying knowledge landscape, this research has added to the field in three areas.

Firstly, and relating back to the vignettes in the prologue, learners taking ICT qualifications at 16 do not share the orthodox view of the assessment systems being unfit for purpose. They have high regard for their utility and for the skills they learn. They accept that what is in the specifications is of value and, in particular, cite its relevance for future life, employment or study. They do not talk explicitly about the underlying knowledge and understanding, however, focusing instead on the production of artefacts or solving problems. That is not to say that these are without cognitive endeavour, simply that learners do not articulate this in anything other than the vaguest terms. Tapscott's model (1998) of a system in which the learner is at the centre and the teacher as a facilitator to learning, supported by technology, is not one which is seen in KS4 ICT classes. The demands of the qualification are paramount and lead to 'working from a list' or 'teaching to the test'. This demand comes from the multiple high-stakes ways that the education system uses performance measures. Success in qualifications at 16 is the prime indicator of secondary school success in league tables. This overrides any needs of learners who, nevertheless, are accepting of what is and cannot see what might be. Their perceptions are heavily influenced by the school and they devalue ICT learnt outside of the course they are following.

Secondly, learners see technology very much as it is now, especially with relation to the content of an ICT course. Some technologies, such as games and mobile devices, are central to their lives outside of school but have not been adopted by the education system. Learners cannot articulate how these technologies might be included in assessment systems. They see little value in the learning they do with, and about, technology outside of school insofar as a qualification in ICT is concerned. This may be compounded by policies which restrict their use in schools as discussed elsewhere in this book. Participative and collaborative tools have been available to schools and learners for over ten years and the annual Horizon report (see for example Johnson et al., 2010) have been predicting their use in schools. They have, however, yet to be widely adopted for learning, let alone for assessment. Indeed the methods of assessment (examinations and coursework portfolios based on written reports of work) are so ingrained that it was not surprising that learners involved in this research were not cognisant of any possibility of use of technology in assessment. Whereas they use electronic devices for many aspects of learning, particularly out of school, similar uses for gaining qualifications are not on their agenda. Again, learners accept the status quo of the methods of assessment much as they accept the status quo of the curriculum.

Thirdly, learner voice is a key issue in education, but it has not entered the realm of engagement of learners in high-stakes assessments. Learners are involved and consulted at many stages in the learning process and in the life of the institution. They are not, however, involved in the design of assessment processes and qualifications at 16. Whilst they see that such assessment is germane for future education and employment, they do not see any scope for changes to curriculum, except for the desirability of more open-ended tasks. Projects have shown that learners are able to judge the work of others (Mcguire et al., 2004; Mitra and Dangwal, 2010) and this process of peer assessment was embedded in policy (DCSF, 2008, 2009) but it has not been applied to summative assessment. Mitra's self-regulating learning systems (2003) are entering the mainstream, but the analogous self-regulating assessment systems, if they exist, are not. Such a system would have activity and not specification as its starting point. Churches' digital taxonomy (2008) could be a tool for developing rigour in such a system with activities being judged according to such a framework. This would go some way to applying responses to socio-technological needs to the context of assessment (Facer, 2009), meeting calls for learner-centric assessment (Johnson et al., 2010) and promoting internal motivations for success in learners (Greenberg, cited in Gatto, 2005). It would also allow informal and non-formal learning to be considered alongside formal learning, addressing the debate outlined by the OECD (n.d.). Such an approach was seen in some qualifications, for example, the Certificate of Personal Effectiveness awards (ASDAN, 2008), but is not part of the mainstream. With the increased focus on 'tradition' and 'rigour' in GCSEs, however, this would seem unlikely to happen as end-of-course examinations become even more entrenched as the main vehicle for assessment.

Such systems prefer the assessment of formal learning over the informal and non-formal. Thus, what is learnt as a result of following the qualification specification and in 'lessons' in school becomes the dominant set of skills, knowledge and understanding. That which is learnt out of school or in incidental activities in school becomes relegated in the perceptions of learners. Whilst they may value creative aspects of technology use and understanding, they do not then see that they should be assessed.

An example from the research illustrates this apparent paradox. Learners were asked to consider learners they thought of as being good at ICT or computing. They were then asked to suggest things that these learners could do that supported this view of them being 'good learners'. Several responses were in the domain of problem solving with regard to hardware. Thus, someone who is considered good at ICT or computing might be someone who is able to repair non-functioning equipment, adjust settings to get optimum or desired performance or select devices to achieve particular aims. Such skills, and the underlying knowledge and understanding, is rarely part of specifications found in schools for pre-16 year olds. Thus, it is not assessed: it cannot be if it is not on the 'syllabus'.

Learners see this as valuable, linking it to one of the key aspects of the valued ICT and computing learning – that of creativity. On the other hand, however, when asked to suggest ways in which assessment might be changed, they do not see that this is an important thing to include in assessment. Indeed, they responded explicitly that it should not be. The reasons for this were unclear but, from other findings, it might be surmised that learners do not perceive that it could be part of the examination process because it is too far removed from the current model of examinations and coursework. Their views on the content and style of assessment are heavily moderated by the existing practice.

This leads us to the final issue for this debate into how learners perceive assessment of ICT and computing (and perhaps other subjects as well). There is a wealth of evidence into the disjunction between how learners use technology in school and how they use it out of school. This leads to the assumption that the informal learning in the use of technology is a significant factor in success in its use – to be a confident and competent user of electronic devices and applications requires more than what is learnt in school. When asked whether this learning is valuable, learners are able to give a number of examples of things that people they consider to be 'good at ICT/computing' can do. Learner voice in learning is considered to be important. It could be argued, therefore, that when designing assessment processes the views of learners should be taken into account. This research warns that these views are, however, so heavily influenced by the existing methods and content that they are not necessarily representative. To ascertain what learners' views are of assessment, it might be necessary to go back to the original questions posed to the learner respondents in this research and ask them 'What things can someone who is good at ICT and computing do, know and understand?'

Conclusion

The research described in this chapter showed that learners value creativity as part of the learning process and feel that it should be rewarded in assessment activity. On the other hand, there is variation in how they view this notion of creativity with some relating it to 'making' and some to 'problem solving'. Nevertheless, what is striking is that the assessment systems themselves, whilst on paper purporting to do just this – the project-marking schemes are about making things and identifying problems – projects tend to be quite heavily constrained by guidelines from awarding body and school teachers due to the high-stakes nature of the assessment. With creativity comes risk and risk is to be avoided in entering learners for qualifications.

A further dimension that emerges is the way in which learners are clearly able to recognise 'good work' or 'those who are good at computing' and perhaps the use of peer assessment of projects outside of the high-stakes qualification framework, for example in preparatory work or work that is not externally assessed, could help to inculcate the true nature of creativity in developing software solutions. Or, perhaps less likely, high-stakes assessment could be re-imagined to allow for more merit to be given for creativity acknowledging the risk. The link between computational thinking and creativity is explored in Chapter 10 by Savage and Csizmadia.

References

'addonai' (2007). Comment in the thread *Just got back from ICT GCSE*, 25 May 2007, 10.08 GMT [online]. Available from: http://uk.gamespot.com/pages/forums/show_msgs.php?topic_id=25648227&page=1 [Accessed 02/10/08].
ASDAN (2008). *CoPE: The Certificate of Personal Effectiveness: Standards 2008 for levels 1–3*. Bristol: ASDAN.

Bourdieu, P. (1984). *Distinction: a social critique of the judgement of taste*. London: Routledge.

Churches, A. (2008). Digital taxonomy [online]. Available from: http://edorigami.wiki spaces.com/Bloom's+Digital+Taxonomy [Accessed 18/6/10].

Crook, C. (2008). *Web 2.0 technologies for learning at KS3 and KS4: The current landscape*. Coventry: Becta.

Conroy, S. (2003). A pathway for interpretive phenomenology. *International Journal of Qualitative Methods*, 2(3), 36–62.

Daily Mail (2007). Qualification that 'an 11-year-old could pass' is worth four GCSEs in school league tables. *Daily Mail* [online], 19 May 2007. Available from: http://www. dailymail.co.uk/news/article-455813/Qualification-11-year-old-pass-worth-GCSEs-school-league-tables.html [Accessed 02/10/08].

DCSF (2008). *The assessment for learning strategy*. London: Department for Children, Schools and Families.

DCSF (2009). *Peer assessment*, London: Department of Children, Schools and Families.

Ecclestone, K., and Pryor, J. (2003). 'Learning careers' or 'assessment careers'? The impact of assessment systems on learning. *British Educational Research Journal*, 29(4), 471–488.

Facer, K. (2009). *Educational, social and technological futures: A report from the Beyond Current Horizons Programme*. Bristol: Futurelab.

Gatto, J. (2005). *Dumbing us down: the hidden curriculum of compulsory schooling*, (2nd edition). Gabriola Island, BC: New Society.

Gove, M. (2011). *Education for economic success*. Speech to the Education World Forum, 11 January 2011. Available from: http://dfe.gov.uk/inthenews/speeches/a0072274/ michael-gove-to-the-education-world-forum [Accessed 26/1/11].

Heppell, S. (2007a). *ICT as a tool for creativity*. E-mail on Naace mailing list, 16 July 2007, used with permission.

Heppell, S. (2007b). *Assessment and new technology: New straightjackets or new opportunities?* [online]. Available from: http://www.heppell.net/weblog/stephen/2007/01/29/ Assessmentandnewtechnologyne.html [Accessed 17/6/10].

Johnson, L., Smith, R., Levine, A., and Haywood, K. (2010). *2010 Horizon report: K-12 edition*. Austin, Texas: The New Media Consortium.

Logicalis (2009). *Realtime generation survey*. Slough: Logicalis.

McFarlane, A. (2001). Perspectives on the relationships between ICT and assessment. *Journal of Computer Assisted Learning*, 17, 227–234.

Mcguire, L., Roberts, G., and Moss M. (2004). *Final report to QCA on the eVIVa Project 2002–2004*. Chelmsford: Ultralab.

Millwood, R. (2008). *Simon, 15, England* [online]. Available from: http://www.future knowledge.org/youth-voice/simon-15-england [Accessed 14/10/08].

Mitra, S. (2003). Minimally invasive education: a progress report on the "hole-in-the-wall" experiments. *British Journal of Educational Technology*, 34(3), pp.367–371.

Mitra, S., and Dangwal, R. (2010). Limits to self-organising systems of learning – the Kalikuppam experiment. *British Journal of Educational Technology*, (41)5, 672–688.

Naughton, J. (2007). Welcome to IT class, children; log on and be bored stiff. *The Observer*, 7 January 2007, Business section, p. 12.

OECD (n.d.). *Recognition of mon-formal and informal learning*. Paris: Organisation for Economic Co-operation and Development [online]. Available from: http://www. oecd.org/document/25/0,3343,en_2649_39263238_37136921_1_1_1_37455,00. html [Accessed 18/12/06].

Ofcom (2011). *UK children's media literacy.* London: Ofcom.

Paige, J. (2011). Michael Gove pushes for return to more rigorous GCSE and A level exams. *The Guardian,* 18 June 2011, p. 18.

Paton, G. (2010). Learners flock to 'less demanding' ICT course. *Daily Telegraph,* 15 January 2010 [online]. Available from: http://www.telegraph.co.uk/education/educationnews/6998312/Learners-flock-to-less-demanding-ICT-course.html [Accessed 17/6/10].

Reay, D., David, M., and Ball, S. (2001). Making a difference? Institutional habituses and higher education choice. *Sociological Research Online,* 5(4).

Ruddock, J., Brown, N., and Hendy, L. (2006). *Personalised learning and learner voice: The East Sussex project.* London: Department for Education and Skills.

Selwyn, N. (2011). *Education and technology: Key issues and debates.* London: Continuum.

Smith, J., and Osborn, M. (2003). Interpretative phenomenological analysis. *In:* J. Smith, ed. *Qualitative psychology.* London: Sage, pp. 51–80.

Tapscott, D. (1998). *Growing up digital: The rise of the Net Generation.* New York: McGraw-Hill.

Teacher (2006). *OCR nationals.* Message posted on OCR ICT-GCSE message board, 5 December 2006, anonymised.

Threlfall, J., and Nelson, N. (2006). *A taxonomy of sources of difficulty in the assessment of ICT* [online]. Paper presented at the Association for Educational Assessment – Europe (AEA-E) Conference, 9–11 November 2006, Naples. Available from: http://www.aea-europe.net/userfiles/C3%20John%20Threlfall%20&%20Nick%20Nelson.pdf [Accessed April 12, 2007].

Underwood, J., et al. (2008). *Impact 2007: personalising learning with technology: final report.* Coventry: Becta.

Vidal Rodeiro, C. (2010). *Uptake of ICT and computing qualifications in schools in England 2007–2009 (statistics report series No. 25).* Cambridge: Cambridge Assessment.

Walker, L., and Logan, A. (2008). *Learner engagement: A review of learner voice initiatives across the UK's education sectors.* Bristol: National Endowment for Science, Technology and the Arts (NESTA) Futurelab.

Wiliam, D. (2001). Reliability, validity, and all that jazz. *Education 3–13,* 29(3), 9–13.

Chapter 5

How female friendly is the new computing curriculum?

Reena Pau

Computing is too important to be left to men.

(Karen Spark Jones, BCS, 2007)

The declining number of females taking computing is a cause for concern for those in education and the IT industry; a diverse workforce is necessary for there to be a creative balance. The reasons for this decline are varied and can be attributed to factors such as schooling, parental influences and the media. This chapter focuses upon the new computing curriculum and its influence in girls' decision-making. We discuss the history of female participation in computing, move on to discussing the statistics and then look at other factors impacting gender disparity in computing.

Computing in schools has had an unfavourable reputation and is said to be a factor in discouraging female learners from studying or working in the computing sector (Tickle 2012). The reasons for this are varied: previously, the ICT curriculum was perceived as a negative, geeky subject, an uninteresting subject and a subject with the reputation of being non-academic. To help combat these issues, a new computing curriculum was introduced in 2013, which focused upon computational thinking and programming (DfE 2013). Despite the curriculum change, the proportion of females studying computing is 7% (a decrease since the subject's introduction) (BCS 2014).

This disparity raises an interesting question for debate: why is the number of females opting to take computing still declining? The computing curriculum is relevant and timely: it has been praised by industry leaders such as Google and Facebook (Curtis 2013). This leads on to an important issue for discussion: is it now time to stop blaming the curriculum for the declining numbers and to start looking at us as a society to help reverse the number of female participants?

Even before computers were introduced into schools, the gender gap in education was apparent in secondary schools. Before the Sex Discrimination Act of 1975, it was common for male and female learners to study separate subjects at age 11, for example, cooking for girls and woodwork for boys (Deem 1981). After the Sex Discrimination Act was introduced, there was a move to implement this into the UK to comprehensive schools, where all children regardless of gender, race, ability and social class had access to the same educational opportunities (Deem 1981). During this period, the majority of girls did not have the opportunity to study 'physical sciences' whilst at secondary school. Female students who had a choice often chose to study biology or to opt out of science altogether. (However, it should be noted that the findings discussed were not the case in all schools but those surveyed.) This is demonstrated in a survey conducted in 1973 by the Department of Education and Science, which found that only 17% of female students were offered the chance to take physics in Years 10 and 11 compared with 83% of boys. Of the female students who were offered the chance to take physics, only 17% took this in comparison with 52% of the boys (DoE 1975).

It was clear that even with a choice of subjects, there was a distinction between the types of courses that male and female students preferred to take. Ormerod (1975) conducted a study into course preferences and choices and found that mathematics, physics, chemistry and geography were seen as male subjects, whilst biology, languages and art were seen as female subjects. In addition, Whyte (1986) argued that this distinction in subject choice was due to the way in which physical sciences were taught in mixed-sex schools. This is demonstrated in a study by Pratt et al. (1984) where it was found that those in single-sex schools were less influenced by the image of the various subjects.

During the 1970s and 1980s, there was an increase in funding to get more computers into schools (Fothergill 1981), which resulted in mathematics teachers and computer enthusiasts encouraging the use of computers in schools and experiments with either the Apricot or Commodore. However, at the time these computers were not for general use by children as they did not have graphics or sound cards and were only suitable for word processing and spreadsheets (Forester 1985). Teachers often selected enthusiastic boys to be part of computer clubs and to learn more about the computer (Carter 2006).

In 1992, IT was seen as important enough to be made a core subject in the national curriculum in England, which meant that it was taught along with English, mathematics and science. IT was also applied in other subjects to demonstrate its practical application. As computers became easier to use, there was less need to understand how they worked. This gave the impression that the computer was 'just' a tool necessary to perform certain tasks in Microsoft Office (Opie 2000).

Today in the national curriculum in England, all learners (regardless of gender) are taught similar skills and are examined according to the examining board their school has selected (History Learning Site 2016). However, the ICT curriculum was criticised as being 'boring' as it was not relevant to young people (The Royal Society 2012). The biggest criticism of this GCSE was that it taught learners to be users rather than creators of technology; thus, female students were being put off by ICT (Morris 2013).

After a campaign in 2012, computing was introduced into schools as a curriculum subject. This meant that computational thinking, programming and problem solving were part of the key teaching objectives in the new computing GCSE (Burns 2012).

Participation statistics by gender

There is a stark contrast in the statistics of male and female students opting to do either ICT or computing at GCSE level. It is clear from Table 5.1 that there is a great disparity in the percentage of female students opting to study computing at GCSE and, from the statistics, it is evident that the numbers are getting lower. Since the launch of the computing GCSE in 2004, female participation has decreased from 12% to 7%.

This decline is a cause for social and economic concern, as it would benefit the UK to increase the number of women entering the IT industry. The 2002 Greenfield report drew attention to the reasons why the number of women in science, engineering and technology needs to be increased (Greenfield et al. 2002):

- *Competitiveness* moving the economy forward.
- *Return on investment* cost of training is significantly high and it is vital that good use is made of this investment by retraining women returners.
- *Benefit to science* exploiting diversity enhances the quality of science, engineering and technology. Through highlighting different aspects of science and by bringing a more varied perspective, a more varied perspective of the outcomes results.
- *Mixed markets and skills* organisations are missing markets and maybe missing benefits of different aspects of research and its application. In other words, women are not represented in design and development.

This is reinforced by the more recent report *Women in IT Scorecard*, which highlights the fact that the decline of females in computing will have an impact on the IT industry in the next decade, and that the UK needs to increase the number of women in order to drive the IT industry forward (BCS 2014).

The addition of computing to the national curriculum has been a significant development. We have seen from the statistics that although the curriculum is held in high regard by industrial experts, the number of girls participating is in decline.

There are initiatives which are working to address the gender disparity. These are ever changing and wide ranging, and include e-learning computer clubs, science and engineering days/weeks, women's returner schemes and women's support networks (BCSWomen 2016). Through surveying the different initiatives

Table 5.1 Genders opting to study computing and ICT at GCSE (BCS 2014)

			2004	2005	2006	2007	2008	2009	2010	2011	2012	2013
UK	Computing	Mate	88%	89%	90%	90%	91%	90%	91%	92%	92%	93%
		Female	12%	11%	10%	10%	9%	10%	9%	8%	8%	7%
	ICT	Male	65%	65%	64%	63%	62%	61%	62%	61%	61%	62%
		Female	35%	35%	36%	37%	38%	39%	38%	39%	39%	38%

available, it is clear that there are two types of activity: recruitment of women into computing and retention of women in computing, as well as those that aim to do both. Neither type of activity cannot exist in isolation. These initiatives are often dependent upon external funding bodies or people willing to take the time to manage these networks. A number of networks aim to support schools currently teaching computing. The largest UK network is Computing At Schools, which provides meet-ups and resources to assist in the teaching of computing. A branch of this is 'CAS #Include', which focuses upon issues of diversity (CAS 2016).

The next sections of this chapter look beyond the curriculum to understand societal factors that influence this debate regarding computing and gender disparities.

Other factors impacting gender disparity

Various factors in career decision-making affect both male and female learners. We will be discussing how these factors influence female learners to make certain decisions.

There is a perception that there is a prominent male geek culture present in the IT industry (von Hellens et al. 2000) and this could be a factor in dissuading girls from opting into computing careers and courses (Myers and Beise 2001). In addition, Brownlow et al. (2002) found that both men and women view female scientists negatively; they found that the perception of a female chemistry student was negative, with men saying that "they would not like to go out with her" (p. 141) and women participants indicating that "she would not have a fulfilling career" (p. 141).

A contributing factor to this is the lack of positive female role models, where the need for role models is prominent. Townsend (2002) found that female students on ICT courses may not feel confident if they see a teacher struggling with ICT, as a teacher is seen as an important role model. It is apparent from a number of studies that boys have far more interest and enthusiasm for computers and ICT lessons than girls (Rommes et al. 2007) do. There is a strong correlation between those who are enthusiastic about computers and those who are also interested in computing (Colley and Comber 2003). Studies have also found that computer enjoyment and interest unfortunately decrease as age increases for boys and girls, but that this is more extreme for girls (Camp 1997).

Stereotypes are said to have a significant effect. According to studies conducted by Gatewood, Gowan and Lautenschlager (1993), the media portrays negative images of the IT industry. Their findings emphasise that the more exposure someone has to real information, the more accurate is their image of that particular career. Computing on television does not portray the dynamic pace that the IT workplace boasts (Lister 2005). Instead, it focuses on making fun of the IT geek image. An example of this is a television series called the *IT Crowd*, a programme about a technical support team set in a basement. This denotes a darkened room and the unglamorous side of the IT industry, as described by

Margolis and Fisher (2002), who also found that, in the United States, those who understood the positive aspects of computing were able to look past the stereotypes. The study asked females (studying computing) if they were a 'geek' and found that they denied it, stating that they enjoyed computing but they did not let it take over their lives like 'they' (geeks) did. Females who were informed and understood the virtues of computing paid less attention to its image (Margolis and Fisher 2002). Hodges (1974) highlights that first impressions have an impact on how individuals see the world. This is because they have come from socially undesirable characteristics, which stick in people's minds as being unattractive (Hodges 1974).

The geek culture extends to computer games. Typically, computer games are aimed at boys, as they involve competition, violent graphics and male characters (Klawe and Leveson 2001). Boys begin to play computer games at a young age, sit in front of the computer for a long time and carry on this pattern as they get older; however, girls do not follow this pattern (Cassell 1998). It has been suggested that the early exposure that boys have to the computer is a reason for their higher confidence and for not feeling as anxious as girls (Hartmann and Klimmt 2006). At another level, it is apparent that parents are able to influence the way in which young people feel about certain careers (Ozdemir and Hacifazlioglu 2008). In a study by the Institute of Employment Studies on the influencing factors of science, technology, engineering and mathematics (STEM) career choices (Durbin 2013), it was found that from the age of 8, children pick up ideas about careers and occupations from their parents. This is to the extent of being able to hold stereotypical views about certain careers at this stage: the younger the child, the greater the parental influence (Beyer 2014). Boys are far more likely to be aware of occupational stereotypes than girls are, especially regarding stereotypes of gender in the occupation (Equal Opportunities Commission 2004). The occupations of fathers are seen to be important for women, since those who choose to go into non-traditional careers are heavily influenced by their fathers (Henwood et al. 2008). The strong support of mothers was also seen as important for females wanting to pursue a career in science and technology (Robertson 2001). Although the views and opinions of parents influence factors in decision-making, parents themselves do not feel they are well informed about careers in science, engineering and technology (SET) and do not feel that this is a viable long-term career for their children (Engineering & Technology Board [ETB] 2005).

Teachers are seen as a factor in decision-making, as teachers are able to influence and reinforce gender stereotypes and perceptions of careers through their own attitudes, gender stereotyping roles and choices through their interaction with learners. According to a study by Sanders and Stone (1986), teachers often give learners the impression that males are better at working with computers than females (Galpin 2002). Teachers in primary schools often think boys are more interested in computers and therefore encourage them a lot more (Culley 1988). Careers advisers are a source of information for young people, but it has been documented that they can also be biased (Bimrose 2001). In other words, the advice given is often dependent upon what gender the adviser is alongside what they perceive the learner is capable of doing (ETB 2005).

Peer groups have an impact upon decisions; young people tend to discuss career decisions with each other, and they will be aware of what their friends think and feel about them, especially at a young age, and will be self-conscious about doing something out of the norm. Thomas and Allen (2006) found that friends were the second most important group of people when it came to influencing. Tsagala and Kordaki (2005) discovered that the media and friends are the key drivers influencing girls into choosing particular careers. Since friends often express their views regarding careers, girls are therefore more likely to be negatively influenced by their friends' opinions in computing (Tsagala and Kordaki 2005).

Confidence is said to be a factor in dissuading girls from enjoying using computers (Brosnan 1998, Margolis 2002). However, confidence increases as experience and knowledge increases (Margolis and Fisher 2002). According to Cooper and Weaver (2003), girls prefer not to use the computer in front of others, as they are anxious about making mistakes. Overall, female learners have lower confidence levels, even when they get high grades in their classes, according to Beyer et al. (2003). As a consequence, girls experience a crisis of confidence, which means they are more likely to drop out of their computer courses (Kekelis et al. 2005). Boys are twice as likely as girls to rate their computer skills as above average (Brosnan 1998).

A further study found that female learners suffered more from computer anxiety than boys do, especially at university where males showed a lessening of computer anxiety throughout the years, whereas females became more anxious (Todman 2000). This shows to some extent that prior experience does not influence computer anxiety for females, but demonstrates a key difference in computer-related behaviour (Whitley 1996). However, female learners do perform better in the presence of another female (Corston and Colman 1996). This relates to self-efficacy, which can be broken down into perceived competence, skill and aptitude. Like confidence and anxiety, female learners tend to underestimate their skills in ICT lessons when working on the computer (Hasan 2003).

The difference between using the computer out of school and at home is that it does not follow a curriculum of any kind, nor is it subject to testing for qualifications. It is self-directed, and understanding is gained through communication online, face-to-face or through learning by doing a task. Technological experience out of school allows pupils to explore technology for enjoyment rather than for educational merit. It gives pupils the freedom to do what they want to do. This can be in the form of games, social networking and other IT-related activities that take place outside school hours.

The ways that females and males use technology out of school is different and highlights personal preferences rather than being restricted to curriculum-based learning materials. Singh (2001) found that women were more likely than men to use the computer for social networking and for a specific purpose rather than just for fun, and female learners use computers less, like them less and underestimate their ability compared with boys. It is important that girls have a positive interactive experience with the computer. Where this occurs, girls are more likely to continue taking courses or enjoying ICT career options (McCormick and McCormick 1991, Camp 1997).

Conclusions

The computing curriculum is still in its infancy and, therefore, it is unfair to make any presumptions with regard to its success. However, the issue with gender is clear from the statistics (see Table 5.1). Through understanding the changes of computing education through the years, it is clear that throughout every change a problem with gender has persisted. Is changing the curriculum enough? From the statistics, this would not seem to be the case: barriers exist in society, with role models and at an individual level. It is only by pushing through these barriers that we can increase the number of girls opting to study computing. Figure 5.1 summarises what we have been discussing in this chapter.

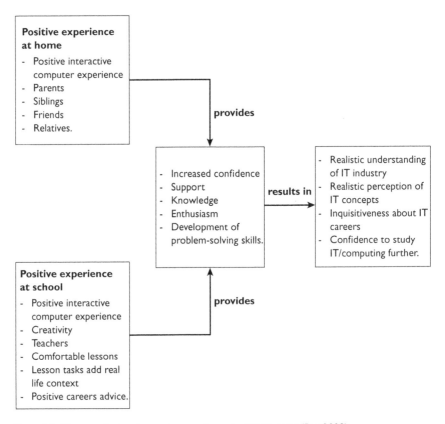

Figure 5.1 Home and school experiences - impact of IT learning (Pau 2009).

At a societal level, we need to realise that girls build their impressions of computing and IT on images and experiences that they receive from outside sources. First impressions are very strong, especially if they are negative. The media, and other external sources of information, need to refrain from using negative stereotypes too heavily, instead using role models to reinforce consistently that the industry is a good one for girls.

At a familial level, parents need to be better informed of careers in the computing industry to dispel the negative stereotypes that may be held and to reinforce it as a viable career option for women. Female learners like computing, but they are still being given the wrong messages about whether they should take these courses; role models, including teachers and career advisers, should be aware of their own biases when influencing young people in their studies or careers.

Finally, at an individual level, young women rely on the enthusiasm of their role models to help ignite interest in different aspects of computing. The use of a computer at home is important, within a safe environment where they can explore the computer, thus reducing issues of anxiety, enhancing their computer experience and building their confidence.

Changing the curriculum is a step forward, but society also needs to provide a positive, safe and engaging environment for all girls and young women to flourish in the world of computing.

References

BCS (2007). *Computing's too important to be left to men*. Available from: http://www.bcs.org/content/ConWebDoc/10791

BCS (2014). *BCSWomen score card report. Scorecard*. Available from: http://bcswomen.bcs.org/the-bcs-women-in-it-scorecard-for-2016-is-out-now/

Bcswomen.bcs.org. (2016). *BCSWomen – The BCS specialist group that provides networking opportunities for all BCS professional women working in IT around the world* [online]. Available from: http://bcswomen.bcs.org/ [Accessed 22 Jun. 2016].

Beyer, S. (2014). *Why are women underrepresented in Computer Science? Gender differences in stereotypes, self-efficacy, values, and interests and predictors of future CS course-taking and grades*. Computer Science Education, 24(2–3), pp.153–192.

Beyer S., *et al.* (2003). Gender differences in computer science students. *Proceedings of the 34th SIGCSE technical symposium on computer science education* pp. 49–53 Reno, Nevada, USA — February 19–23, 2003.

Bimrose, J. (2001). *Girls and women: challenges for careers guidance practice*. British Journal of Guidance & Counselling, 29(1), pp. 79–94.

Brosnan, M. (1998). *The impact of computer anxiety and self-efficacy upon performance*. J Comp Assist Learn, 14(3), pp. 223–234.

Brownlow, S., Smith, T., and Ellis, B. (2002). Journal of Science Education and Technology, 11(2), pp. 135–144.

Burns, J. (2012). *School ICT to be replaced by computer science programme* [online]. Available from: http://www.bbc.co.uk/news/education-16493929

Camp, T. (1997). The incredible shrinking pipeline. *Communications of the ACM*, vol. 40, no. 10, pp. 103–110, Oct. 1997.

Carter, L. (2006). Why students with an apparent aptitude for computer science don't choose to major in computer science. *SIGCSE* 38: 27–31.

CAS (2016). *CAS #include: Computer science for all* [online]. Available from: https://www.computingatschool.org.uk/custom_pages/270-cas-include [Accessed 30 June 2017].

Cassell, J. (1998). *From Barbie to Mortal Kombat*. Boston: MIT Press.

Colley, A., and Comber, C. (2003). Age and gender differences in computer use and attitudes among secondary school students: what has changed? *Educational Research* 45 (2), pp. 155–165.

Computingatschool.org.uk. (2016). *Computing At School* [online]. Available from: https://www.computingatschool.org.uk/ [Accessed 22 Jun. 2016].

Cooper, J., and Weaver, K. (2003). Gender and computers. Mahwah, NJ: Lawrence Erlbaum.

Corston, R., and Colman, A. (1996). *Gender and social facilitation effects on computer competence and attitudes toward computers*. Journal of Educational Computing Research, 14(2), pp. 171–183.

Culley, L. (1988). *Girls, boys and computers*. Educational Studies, 14: 3–8.

Curtis, S. (2013). *Computing curriculum: Digital skills versus computer science*. Telegraph.

Deem, R. (1981). *State policy and ideology of women, 1944–1980. British Journal of Sociology Education* 2(2): 131–143.

DfE (2013). *National curriculum in England: computing programmes of study* [online]. Available from: https://www.gov.uk/government/publications/national-curriculum-in-england-computing-programmes-of-study [Accessed 30 June 2017].

DOE (1975). *Curricular differences for boys and girls education survey*, London: Department of Education, Her Majesty's Stationery Office.

Durbin S. (2013). *It's a boy's thing really isn't it? The factors affecting career choices amongst male and female engineers*. Bristol: Centre for Employment Studies Research (CESR), University of the West of England.

Equal Opportunities Commission (2004). *Occupational segregation, gender gaps and skill gaps* [online]. Available from: http://www.voced.edu.au/content/ngv%3A32480 [Accessed 22 Jun. 2016].

Engineering and Technology Board (ETB) (2005). *Factors influencing Year 9 career choices* [online]. London: ETB. Available from: www.etechb.co.uk/_db/_documents/factors_influencing_year_9_career_choices.pdf

Forester, T. (1985). *The information technology revolution*. Cambridge, Mass.: MIT Press.

Fothergill, R. (1981). *Microelectronics education programme: the strategy*. London: Department of Education and Science.

Galpin, V. (2002). Women in computing around the world. *SIGCSE Bulletin*, 34, pp. 94–100.

Gatewood, R., Gowan, M., and Lautenschlager, G. (1993). *Corporate image, recruitment image and initial job choice decisions*. Academy of Management Journal, 36(2), pp. 414–427.

Greenfield, S., *et al.* (2002). *SET fair: a report on women in science, engineering and technology from the Baroness Greenfield CBE to the Secretary of State for Trade and Industry*. London: HMSO.

Hartmann, T., and Klimmt, C. (2006). *Gender and computer games: exploring females' dislikes*. Journal of Computer-Mediated Communication, 11(4), pp. 910–931.

Hasan, B. (2003). The influence of specific computer experiences on computer self-efficacy beliefs. *Computers in Human Behavior*, 19(4), pp. 443–450.

Henwood, K., Anne Parkhill, K., and Pidgeon, N. (2008). *Science, technology and risk perception*. Equal Opportunities International, 27(8), pp. 662–676.

History Learning Site (2016). *Gender and educational attainment – history learning site* [online]. Available from: http://www.historylearningsite.co.uk/sociology/education-and-sociology/gender-and-educational-attainment/ [Accessed 22 June 2016].

Hodges, H. (1974). *Conflict and consensus: an introduction to sociology*. New York: Harper & Row.

Kekelis, L., Ancheta, R., and Heber, E. (2005). Hurdles in the pipeline: girls and technology careers. *Frontiers: A Journal of Women Studies*, 26(1), pp. 99–109.

Klawe, M., and Leveson, N. (2001). Refreshing the nerds. *Communications of the ACM*, 44(7), 67 ff.

Lister, R. (2005). Feminist citizenship theory: an alternative perspective on understanding women's social and political lives. *In:* J. Franklin (ed.), *Women and social capital*. South Bank University, London: Families and Social Capital ESRC Research Group Working Paper No. 12, 2005.

Margolis, J., and Fisher, A. (2002). *Unlocking the clubhouse*. Cambridge, Mass.: MIT Press.

McCormick, N.B., and McCormick, J.W. (1991). Not for men only: why so few women major in computer science. *College Student Journal*, 85(3), 345–50.

Morris, J. (2013). *Women in computing*, Elsevier.

Myers, M.E., and Beise, C.M. (2001). Nerd work: attractors and barriers perceived by students entering the IT field. *Proceedings of the ACM SIGCPR Conference on Computer Personnel Research*, San Diego, California, USA.

Opie, K. (2000). *A tale of two national curriculums: Issues in implementing the national curriculum for ICT Teacher training*. Journal of Information Technology for ICT Education 9(2): 79–94.

Ormerod, M.B. (1975). *Subject preference and choice in co-educational and single sex secondary schools*. British Journal of Educational Psychology 45: 275–267.

Ozdemir, N., and Hacifazlioglu, O. (2008). Influence of family and environment on students' occupational choices and expectations of their prospective universities. *Social Behaviour and Personality: An International Journal*, 36(4), pp. 433–446.

Pratt, J., Bloomfield, J., and Seale, C. (1984). *Option choice: A question of equal opportunity*. Slough: EOC/NFER-Nelson.

Robertson, G. (2001). *Public understanding of science*, 10(1), pp. 71–82.

Rommes, E., *et al.* (2007). I'm not interested in computers: Gender-based occupational choices of adolescents. *Information, Communication & Society*, 10(3), pp. 299–319.

Pau, R. (2009). *Experiential factors which influence how female students perceive computing and computing careers at different stages in their education*. Thesis (PhD). University of Southampton.

The Royal Society (2012). *Shut down or restart? The way forward for computing in UK schools*. The Royal Society.

Sanders, J., and Stone, A. (1986). *The neuter computer: computers for girls and boys*. New York: Neal-Schuman.

Singh, S. (2001). Gender and the use of the internet at home. *New Media & Society*. 3 (4): 395–415.

Tickle, L. (2012). *ICT teaching upgrade expected ... in 2014*. Digital Literacy Campaign [online]. Available from: http://www.theguardian.com/education/2012/aug/20/ict-teaching-programming-no-guidance [Accessed 20 June 2016].

Thomas, T., and Allen, A. (2006). Gender differences in students' perceptions of information technology as a career. *Journal of Information Technology Education*, 5, 165–178.

Todman, J. (2000). Gender differences in computer anxiety among university entrants since 1992. *Computers and Education* 34, 27–35

Townsend, G. (2002). People who make a difference. *SIGCSE Bull.*, 34(2), p.57.

Tsagala E., and Kordaki M. (2005). Gender differences in computer science: the views of prospective computer engineers. *CBLIS Conference Proceedings 2005 Integrating New Technologies in Science and Education.*

von Hellens L., Pringle R., Nielsen S.H., and Greenhill, A. (2000). People, business and IT skills: the perspective of women in the IT industry. *Conference Proceedings of the 2000 ACM SIGCPR Conference on computer personnel research.* Chicago, Illinois, pp. 152–157.

Whitley, B.E. (1996). Gender differences in computer-related attitudes: it depends on what you ask. *Computers in Human Behavior* 12(2):275–289.

Whyte, J. (1986). *Girls into science and technology: the story of a project.* London, Boston and Henley: Routledge & Kegan.

Chapter 6

Towards tomorrow's successful digital citizens

Providing the critical opportunities to change mindsets

*Christina Preston, Moira Savage,
Malcolm Payton and Anthony Barnett*

Alerting the citizens to the issues

In recent years, there has been shift in the UK curriculum from *Information and Communications Technology* (ICT) to *Computing*. The debate amongst professionals has been whether the 'softer' aspects of ICT might be downgraded by a concentration on computing science and especially coding. In this chapter, we recommend a rounded approach to the subject. We suggest that skilled computer experts will provide a better service to society if they are able to understand and debate the benefits and dangers of computer literacy.

We tackle the topic of digital citizenship by first defining the term based on the literature, which gives the reader an outline of the different perspectives. We then report on a knowledge creation event that was attended by a number of expert educators who debated the value of digital citizenship in the classroom context. We suggest that the methods used for running the event, as well as the collaborative knowledge that was created, would provide a good basis for a teacher who wants to set up such a debate in the classroom. Learners who debate this subject will develop a strong affiliation with the issues.

Defining digital citizenship

What is meant by 'digital citizenship'? Can it be a global concept where being a digital citizen means being a citizen of the digital world, or must it remain more localised? For example, would we expect a citizen of the United Kingdom as a digital citizen to be any different from a citizen of the United States or China as a digital citizen? Political ideology inevitably disrupts digital boundaries (e.g. China's decision to prohibit access to Google), and only 162 of the 192 countries in the world have adopted the Berne Convention on copyright (www.firstwriter. com/copyright/berneconvention.shtml). Also, the digital divide highlights a lack of universal access whereas citizenship implies rights and responsibilities based on a common rule of law within the nation–state. However, Selwyn (2013) draws attention to multiple metaphors, for example cloud and cyberspace, and to the alternative view emphasising connectivity and society as networked with the "increasing tendency of dominant functions and processes within contemporary societies to be organised around networks rather than physical boundaries" (p. 3). Ribble (2014) also starts to question the possibility of a global concept of digital citizenship in such a fragmented digital space. In education, therefore, a debate on digital citizenship needs to raise awareness of the changing nature of society and specific national standards as well as to engage with the issues at a fundamental human level.

Statements relating to digital literacy in the national curriculum for England, Computing Programmes of Study, imply aspects of digital citizenship (DfE 2013). For example, one of the aims of this document is to educate learners so that they become "responsible, competent, confident and creative users of information and communication technologies" (DfE 2013, p. 1). At first glance, a competency model of teaching might be presumed sufficient; however, the terms responsible and confident hint at wider dimensions: identities, values, ethics, attitudes, beliefs and a sense-of-self in relation to others. Quickly it becomes apparent that education about digital citizenship must be a lived educational experience, over time, across the physical and digital landscape within and beyond the school setting: a challenge for teachers.

At Key Stage 3, the curriculum requires that learners are taught to "understand a range of ways to use technology safely, respectfully, responsibly and securely, including protecting their online identity and privacy; recognise inappropriate content, contact and conduct and know how to report concerns" (DfE 2013, p. 2). The phrase "protecting online identity and privacy" within the programmes of study reminds teachers that pedagogical approaches adopted must support learners in appreciating the construct of a digital representation of themselves (DfE 2013, p. 2).

The theme of "protecting online identity and privacy" is explored in detail by boyd (2014) when unravelling various dimensions of the online life of networked teens in her book *It's Complicated*. It is imperative, boyd believes, to facilitate learners to reflect on their digital persona and notions of privacy as citizens operating in digital spaces. Being aware of and understanding complex procedural elements involved in protecting or constructing privacy online can in itself be a challenge for learners. Privacy is defined by external organisations, often commercial, in typical digital contexts. The locus of control, in terms of pre-defined privacy settings users can opt in or out of or customise within parameters, are often set by others. Online counter-cultures can ironically be equally as persuasive in terms of privacy: think no further than the glorification of anonymous hackers in films and television portrayals. Anonymity and real or assumed identities are recurring themes for learners to consider in relation to digital citizenship. The Joint Information Systems Committee (JISC, 2015) is currently revisiting its digital capability model with the education community and now propose 'identity and well-being' as a fundamental component of digital literacy to incorporate these themes.

Notions of digital citizenship are embedded within several popular models of digital literacy. This is sometimes related to discussions of individuals as passive consumers and/or active producers of digital content and services (Resnick 2012), the implication being that digital citizenship goes beyond a set of technical competencies and becomes a mindset or way of being and acting in the digital world. Sharpe and Beetham's (2010) model of defining digital literacy refers to the 'I am' stage of identity development as the top of the pyramid (see Figure 6.1).

The description of digital citizenship as a 'mindset' is also reflected in the purpose of study in the national curriculum for computing, referring to learners "becoming active participants in a digital world" (DfE 2013, p. 1). On a personal level, identification, interpretation and understanding of norms and patterns of interaction in varied digital environments means engagement (consciously or otherwise) with individual and collective representations of values, beliefs and attitudes.

The JISC emphasises "capabilities which fit an individual for living, learning and working in a digital society" (2014, n.p.). The notion of fit is in itself interesting and implies a sense of belonging to a group or communities inhabiting digital landscapes in terms of conformity, rebellion or independence. boyd's (2014) research suggests that teenagers' use of social media reflects rather than transcends basic social divisions. Facebook networks were found to be closely matched to the segregated racial groupings that characterised the Los Angeles schools, and this can be easily transferred to other contexts such as the UK. Are the processes for humans connecting fundamentally different in the physical and digital world? It could be argued they are one and the same, especially where there is a strong affective element, positive or negative, isolating or affirming. What is potentially different are the scale, impact and transparency of digitally mediated social interaction and reaction across platforms. For example, a Twitterstorm would fall into this category. A Twitterstorm typically relates to a "sudden spike in activity on a topic, typically on a breaking or controversial topic, using a particular hashtag with subsequent retweets and tweets" (Techopedia 2015). We can easily cite examples where social media has been used to empower and promote a

Defining digital literacy: a general model

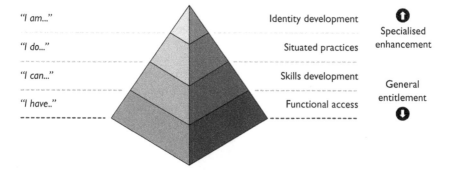

"I am..."   Identity development

                            Specialised
"I do..."   Situated practices   enhancement

"I can..."   Skills development
                            General
"I have.."   Functional access   entitlement

Figure 6.1 Model of digital literacy (Adapted from Sharpe and Beetham, 2010)

cause or voice of members of society who may not traditionally have the political or economic resources to be heard by mainstream society, thereby contributing to positive change. In a classroom context learners can now easily write, publish and promote digital content to that real audience teachers often talk of when setting tasks. However, by contrast, many individuals have been called to account or vilified by social media responses. As teachers, we instinctively think of cyberbullying victims, but equally we need to empower young people to gain a sense of the impact of taking less constructive or unkind actions as perpetrators (CEOP 2015). The educator's challenge is to provide contexts that prompt reflection on how citizenship contains both rights and responsibilities, and, importantly, real-world consequences on inter-personal, social and legal levels resulting from online behaviours. It is important for educators to recognise that a lived experience of the rights and responsibilities of being online is developed over time, evolving, and not without controversy.

Belshaw (2011) echoes this notion of a digital literacy as a condition. Hobbs (2010) similarly emphasises that there are a "constellation of life skills necessary for full participation" including "making responsible choices", "reflecting on personal conduct and communication behaviour by applying social responsibility and ethical principles", "taking social action by working individually and collaboratively to share knowledge and solve problems in the family, workplace and community, and by participating as a member of a community" (Hobbs 2010 pp. vii–viii). Belshaw's comprehensive eight-component model of digital literacy directly highlights that digital literacy is highly "contextual and situational with co-constructed norms of conduct" (2011 p. 207). Belshaw goes on to state that "In each of these contexts are found different codes and ways of operating, things that are accepted or encouraged as well as those that are frowned upon and rejected" (ibid.).

In Savage and Barnett (2015), the authors reflected on what this means for teachers working with learners in these hybrid physical and digital spaces. Primarily, it is fundamental to realise these elements need to be lived, not talked about or speculated about from afar. Belshaw (2011) reminds us of the self-limiting technical proficiency models, and the element that underpins the models is providing space and contexts for learners to consider 'the issues, norms and habits of mind surrounding technologies used for a particular purpose' (2011, p. 207). To operationalise this into a pedagogical approach, Savage and Barnett (2015) prompted teachers to reflect on the range of digital environments provided for learners to explore in the classroom. As risk-aware professional teachers, we need to navigate the tension of providing safe but sanitised opportunities in classrooms, with an awareness of beyond-school digital experiences. Personal agency as digital citizens is actualised "through immersion in a range of digital environments" (Belshaw 2011, p. 207). Belshaw extends the exposure aspect and persuasively argues that 'mind expansion' comes from "exposure to various ways of conceptualising and interacting in digital spaces helps develop the cognitive element . . . it is not the practise of using tools, but rather the habits of mind such use can develop" (2011, p. 208).

The communicative element of Belshaw's model highlights the forms and norms of digitally mediated communication. Again, for teachers the tension resurfaces: to "truly understand networks you need to be part of them" and have a sense of the lived experience rather than the perceived experience (2011, p. 209). However, the presence of teachers and adults may not be welcome in these digital spaces even if they can be identified and located.

Two final elements Belshaw draws attention to have a very direct connection to digital citizenship: critical and civic (2011, pp. 212–213). Returning to the DfE requirement for educating learners to be 'responsible users', the potential for individuals to "participate, engage and act for social justice and have civic responsibility" (DfE 2013, p. 1) is potentially very powerful. Criticality is closely linked in terms of recognising and challenging power relations (Belshaw 2011).

Table 6.1 below, from Savage and Barnett (2015), explores three further considerations of digital citizenship (p. 108). Ribble (2014) defined digital citizenship as "the norms of appropriate, responsible behaviour with regard to technology use and identifies nine key themes that are intuitively directly relevant to understanding digital citizenship" (Ribble 2014, cited in Savage and Barnett 2015, p. 107). Savage and Barnett (2015) also explored the approach by Common Sense Media (CSM, 2014) in relation to digital citizenship, and details of related resources are presented below. "The digital citizenship strand is based on five units and the South West Grid for Learning (SWGfL) has developed the CSM scheme for teaching digital literacy and citizenship in the UK using eight themes" (Savage and Barnett 2015, p. 108).

Inherent in any conceptualisation of digital citizenship are dimensions relating to values and dispositions. By their nature they cannot be taught, but teachers

Table 6.1 Key themes in defining digital citizenship (Savage and Barnett 2015, p. 108)

Ribble (2014) 9 key themes	Common Sense Media (CSM) Planning and resources	SWGfL Linked to CSM
1 Digital Access	1 Digital Life – This relates to the impact of digital media and what it means to be a responsible digital citizen	1 Internet safety
2 Digital Commerce		2 Privacy & Security
3 Digital Communication		3 Relationships & Communication
4 Digital Literacy	2 Privacy and Digital Footprints – This relates to personal information, both of self and others	4 Cyberbullying
5 Digital Etiquette		5 Digital Footprint & Reputation
6 Digital Law	3 Connected Culture – This relates to ethics including cyberbullying	6 Self Image & Identity
7 Digital Rights and Responsibilities	4 Self-expression and Identity – This considers communicating through digital means	7 Information Literacy
8 Digital Health and Wellness	5 Respecting creative work – This relates to intellectual property rights	8 Creative Credit & Copyright
9 Digital Security		

have some responsibility for providing critical and dialogical opportunities for learners to reflect on their values and beliefs in relation to others in both face-to-face and digitally mediated contexts. For example, freedom of (self) expression is often cited as a British value but in contemporary times, and with the Prevent Duty (DfE) agenda, this no longer is as clear cut for teachers. Protecting children and young people from radicalisation, the Prevent Duty (DfE, 2015) outlines expectations for teachers and makes direct reference to social media channels. Ohler (2011) tackles the notion of character education head on, challenging policy makers to "create academic and character education programs tailored for raising an intelligent, caring generation of students who understand the responsibilities and opportunities associated with living a digital lifestyle" (p. 25). Also, it might be worth including the alternative view of digital citizens as netizens (Webster 2004) or digizens (www.digizen.org) as well as contrasting the nine key themes of Ribble (2014) with the themes of CSM's curriculum (though the resources are no longer free).

The term 'lifestyle' again is a term that relates to a Western notion of choice. The democratisation of knowledge is often aligned with the growing ownership/access of technologies and access to digital information. Whilst the digitisation of, for example, archive materials is constructive, access can still be moderated by traditional groups, and how open the access is can be problematic. Raza et al. (2007) critique that

> e-learning materials are still very much European or North American centric. The potential is to give opportunities for revolutionary socio-cultural transformations created by e-learning. In this manner knowledge is created, codified, retrieved, managed and transmitted across the boundaries of different cultures.
>
> (p. 64)

Recent wars in the Middle East, particularly Syria, and the use by ISIL of social networking to entrap teenagers into active service, makes an understanding of digital citizenship even more important in UK schools. Just teaching digital citizenship at a factual, information transmission level is not enough. The central need here is for learners to relate to the issues and be able to articulate them in a way that is meaningful to their lives outside school as well as inside. Teachers have a vital role in promoting this kind of debate. The next section makes some suggestions about how to encourage engagement amongst learners.

Setting up a digital citizenship debate

Providing critical and dialogical opportunities

In this section, we suggest how dimensions relating to values and dispositions that cannot be taught can be stimulated by active debate. Creating the right conditions for providing critical and dialogical opportunities means that learners reflect on their values and beliefs in relation to others in both face-to-face and digitally mediated contexts. One way to emphasise the digital context is to use digital tools to enrich the texture of the debate.

The debate that we are drawing on was designed to give international educators from different professional organisations an opportunity to contribute fully even if they could not attend face-to-face (www.mirandanet.ac.uk/blog/2015/08/digital-citizenship-report/).

The digital knowledge creation context

A website was set up so that all the opinions and contributions could be collected, analysed and published. The day was organised on the principles of a MirandaMod (www.mirandanet.org.uk/mirandamods). This is a knowledge creation event that has been developed by MirandaNet Fellows over several years. The professional organisation of educators works on the principle that knowledge is often built and owned by teams in the world of work. This process has been given new diameters by the social media and is an important focus of digital citizenship. In the view of the Fellows, learners need to be encouraged to make the most of the richness of collaborative social opinion and understand the dangers. This kind of event could be reproduced in classrooms and in approved online communication environments in order to promote more understanding of how collaborative knowledge is formed. Also, more acknowledgement and reward for this process in education is required, as this kind of event could provide learners with techniques to understand how crowdsourcing of knowledge might work.

In this event, all the contributors provided a profile beforehand and wrote a summary of their views about the topic for everyone to read as well as any references and publications they recommend. This pre-session actively meant that the lead speakers and the participants needed only to present the headlines of their arguments for 3–5 minutes, during which presentation software was discouraged in order to engage fully with the audience and encourage participation. First, this leaves time for many more participants to engage. Second, there is time to analyse the similarities and the conflicts. When possible, the sessions are video streamed to those who cannot attend in person. Some expert speakers also engaged through online conferencing packages like Skype.

What makes a MirandaMod different from a conventional debate is that those inside the room and viewing the video stream can contribute to a Twitter or Padlet wall in real time. Others record their responses in online digital concept maps that can be collaboratively developed remotely. This element of digital contribution provides a visual recording of the concepts as they emerge, that provide a collaborative analysis for the debate if the map makers have been primed beforehand.

Organising the debate on 'digital citizenship'

The proposal that was provided beforehand was:

This professional community believes the importance of ethics and values in relation to digital technologies is not emphasised sufficiently in today's digital society.

The following definitions of five key terms that relate to digital citizenship were sent to the debaters beforehand so that they started with a common understanding of the concepts under discussion:

Digital literacy is the ability to find, evaluate, utilise, share and create content using information technologies and the Internet. (www.digitalliteracy.cornell.edu/)

Digital citizenship is the norms of appropriate, responsible behaviour with regard to technology use. (www.digitalcitizenship.net/Nine_Elements.html)

A Digital society is characterised by three cultures:

- Digital tools which allow humans to maintain their social life in the digital society and considered as the ground for other elements of the digital culture;
- Digital values which form a belief system that provides meanings or goals for human behaviours or social activities in the digital society;
- Digital norms which represent normative procedures and rules that are socially acknowledged in carrying out digital activities.

(Kwon and Zmud 1987).

Digital Equity is the social justice goal of ensuring that everyone in society has equal access to technology tools, computers and the Internet. It is when all individuals have the knowledge and skills to access and use technology tools, computers and the Internet.

Digital wisdom is the ability of individuals and/or societies to make informed decisions in relation to the appropriate use and exploitation of information technology in all its forms.

In this case, the event lasted a day, but if enough organisation takes place beforehand, such a debate could be conducted in half a day or even a double lesson. In the event under discussion, the day was divided into a number of sessions, each of which consisted of presentations and position papers followed by discussion. Some key experts were invited to present their headline views on the day about the following four questions:

- What is important today with regard to digital literacy, digital citizenship and digital wisdom?
- What do we mean by a digital society?

- What do you think will be important in the future?
- How do you think we get to that future?

Analysing the data generated by the debate

This event generated significant quantities of data that you can read on the public website. However, the important element of this activity is to assemble a group of learners who can learn to analyse the data and publish a collaborative report.

The excerpts from the report below are a compilation of the thinking and insights of the educators who gathered to contribute There is a certain inconsistency in linguistic style and wording; however, it was decided that, in exploring a new area in this way, it was important to use the language of the contributors rather than creating a more consistent but less accurate record of the discussions. A discussion of this approach will challenge the usual convention of a report, which is to find a middle way and leave out the contradictions. This leads to the question: are contemporary opportunities to share through digital networking demanding new ways of expressing the collaborative results? Does it matter that the report of the debate raises more questions and is not conclusive?

The debate outcomes

A significant outcome of the debate was that a series of key questions should be considered if we aspire to ensure the technology evolution can deliver better outcomes for all. These include:

1   Do we need the term digital citizenship, or is it just citizenship?
2   Do different countries, cultures and institutions play a part in influencing how digital citizenship is evolving, or people's perception, or their role as a digital citizen?
3   Must a computer scientist be literate in social informatics and digital wisdom?
4   Is it possible to infuse 'soft' technological systems into 'hard' educational systems?

Additionally, some of the conclusions (which require further exploration) reached were:

Digital citizenship

Instead of asking, "Does the digital world need to have a concept of wisdom?" we can reverse the question and ask, "Does our understanding of wisdom need to include understanding of the digital world?" The latter question leads to a much more conclusive outcome and call to action.

What is the relationship between computer science, social informatics and digital citizenship?

As well as looking at the overlap between these disciplines, these discussions explored the purposes behind the different fields and the integration of values into their objectives. Whilst this is a complex area that led to much debate, the most important conclusion of this section can be summarised very simply and succinctly: you cannot abstain from the ethical or technical debate.

How can we ensure the professional development of digital citizens?

Schools' teaching of the use of ICT tools, as they have in many cases done over the past 20 years, falls short of preparing children for successful digital citizenship. We need to move from an emphasis on digital literacy towards digital empowerment, where people of all ages, individually and collectively, are able to harness digital tools to enhance their lives and the lives of others.

Responses

As is common in these explorations, the discussion and responses generated a number of key questions that can be used to evaluate the underlying issues and the impact of current approaches or alternative proposals.

Whilst the discussions then continued to reach some important conclusions and to identify areas for further exploration, the questions generated are in many cases the most important insight into issues around digital citizenship.

Diagrams 6.1 and 6.2 highlight these key questions, conclusions and areas for exploration against the three key themes.

Moving forward and developing the debate

Key aspects for further exploration are outlined above. Some of these are open-ended areas for exploration.

In spite of the breadth of the issues explored, however, some key themes did emerge. We expect to see these continuing to shape the debate going forward. These themes can be explored with your learners and are set out in the list of statements for debate and questions below.

The need for citizenship

Whether the digital world needs a concept of citizenship is open to debate. Whether the concept of citizenship needs to include reference to the digital world is not.

Questions raised by the term, Digital Citizenship

- Do we need the term "Digital Citizenship"? What about different countries, cultures and institutions? Do these things play a part in influencing in how Digital Citizenship is evolving or people's perception or their role as a Digital Citizen? What about languages? Does the language spoken influence Citizenship perceptions and possibly even disenfranchise Digital Citizens?

- How important are awareness, and understanding of the systems [e.g. in relation to Privacy and Data collection?]

- Are we digital citizens? – or Digital Participants, Digitals Subjects or Digital Servants?

- Do we need norms and rules? Who forms these?

- Can we separate citizenship from the idea of nation-state?

- Do we need a concept of Digital Citizenship – or is it just Citizenship?

- How do we identify society in a digital world where the nation-state has less relevance? Is there a danger of digital ghettos – or tribalism, where people identify only with their own tribe?

- How different is the digital world. Is, for example, anonymity different, and does this lead to different behaviours?

- Does the digital revolution lead to a change in what we need to achieve in terms of; confidence, self-belief; empowerment; resilience and so on?

Exploring ideas such as Digital Literacy, Digital Citizens and digital empowerment allows us to look at how the Digital revolution is having an impact on our role as Citizens.

Citizenship is normally defined in terms of a nation-state. In the digital world, some thought has to be given to the "state" to which a citizen belongs, and whether this is just one digital world state.

Whether the digital world needs a concept of citizenship is open to debate. Whether the concept of citizenship needs to include reference to the digital world is not.

Diagram 6.1 Digital Citizenship

The need to recognise different cultures and societies

How do we identify 'society' in a digital world where the nation–state has less relevance? Is there a danger of digital ghettos or tribalism, where people identify only with their own tribe and do not contribute to wider society?

What about different countries, cultures and institutions? Do these things play a part in influencing how digital citizenship is evolving or people's perception or their role as a digital citizen? What about languages?

The need to ensure the ethical dimension is included in all disciplines

Computer systems should not be built without involving the social context.

You cannot abstain from the ethical or technical debate.

With computers being an inseparable part of our everyday life, it is necessary that the systems they employ should be constrained by ethical and legal standards. How do we ensure that those consigned with the task of designing and developing these systems are aware of the necessity of these constraints?

Questions this raises:

- *Must a computer scientist be literate in social informatics and digital wisdom?*
- *How do the different terms inter-relate – Digital Literacy, Digital Fluency, Digital Citizenship, Digital Wisdom?*
- *If wisdom is the ability to make a decision for positive outcomes, are these outcomes personal, local to a group or global?*
- *What is acceptable, and who decides?*
- *Is there a risk of a mechanistic rather than a humanistic approach to the teaching and learning of computer science and ICT?*

Conclusions from discussions:

- *There is considerable overlap between Computer Science, Social Informatics and Digital Wisdom. None can exist in isolation, and none can exist apart from the moral dimension;*
- *Teaching internet safety is more like teaching swimming and water safety than teaching smoking-related safety. It is knowledge and skill that saves lives, not avoidance;*
- *Computer systems should not be built without involving the social context;*
- *Digital/blended wisdom comes from a humanistic perspective and that of understanding the broader impact of change, decisions, leadership, drive and motivation in developing education change towards the improvement of lives of others;*
- *We cannot abstain from the ethical or technical debate in schools.*

Areas for further exploration

- *How do we move the teaching of internet safety away from a smoking-related safety approach (i.e. can't be our fault, we don't allow it here – must have learned it at home) to a swimming-based approach (i.e. the more experience and knowledge you have, the safer you will be)?*
- *How do we minimise the risk of a mechanistic approach (e.g. coding, machine level control/instruction, silo-based learning etc.) rather than a humanistic approach (e.g. computational thinking and system thinking, lateral thinking, project-based learning etc.) to the teaching and learning of computer science and ICT?*
- *With computers being an inseparable part of our everyday life, it is necessary that the systems they employ should be constrained by ethical and legal standards. How do we ensure that those consigned with the task of designing and developing these systems are aware of the necessity of these constraints?*

Diagram 6.2 What is the relationship between Computer Science, Social Informatics and Digital Citizenship?

The need to develop new pedagogies

There is an urgent need to reflect and elaborate around digital pedagogies.

Teachers are teaching every day, finding ways of using digital technology, discovering what works and what does not. They are in the crucible of innovation learning from and with their students.

The need to design assessment around learning, not the learning around the assessment

We need to design assessment systems flexible enough not to constrain pedagogy.

How can approaches such as constructive technology assessment, value sensitive design and other iterative, multi-stakeholder approaches be used to support a more interactive approach to assessment?

Conclusions

In this chapter, we have assembled the views of several eminent writers on the topic of digital citizenship, and we have also engaged a community of practitioners in a debate about the topic. The writers provides us with well-considered views and the debate created an opportunity to consider conflicting views and engage with the passion that this topic can engender.

In the literature, digital citizenship as a 'mindset' rather than a set of rules emerges from the various definitions. The teachers' task is to balance the notion of empowerment against the dangers of cyberbullying, giving voice to the oppressed and marginalised whilst still maintaining a message of hope. The complexity of the notion is captured by the JISC report:

> a learner needs functional access to digital tools, skills development, situated practices and the development of their own digital identity. In this context, the teacher must grapple with the knowledge that each culture has a different approach to the development of an individual identity and that in the classroom different cultures are often represented. As a result of this complexity, lessons about digital citizenship should have been backed up with in-depth training to support the teacher in this endeavour. In UK schools, the emphasis on British Values is also a strategy that applies particularly to this area of teaching.

In order to create a digital citizenship mindset, we have shown how teachers might engage their classes in the kind of vibrant debates that underpin democracy. By presenting a 'digital knowledge creation approach' to a debate, we have intended also to challenge some of the conventions of reporting that include a linear approach and a unified approach. Whereas digital media provides ways of collaboration and networking that have not been available to digital citizens in the past, the new media also challenge the ways that we report agreement and disagreement. These issues about collaboration and responsible reporting are issues of digital citizenship that teachers can discuss with their learners. These writing dilemmas pertain particularly to searching for the information on the web and the provenance of the information that is found.

In the end, this chapter makes it clear that the way in which schools deal with digital citizenship will have a profound impact on the health of society and the preservation of democracy. Leaving digital citizenship out of the curriculum does not seem to be an option.

Acknowledgements

Thanks to all those who attended the Think Tank on 24 February 2015 and, in particular, to those who prepared presentations to stimulate thinking. As with any exploration of this nature, it is inevitable that some valuable comments will have been omitted, and the emphasis may not reflect the particular interests of each individual. Apologies in advance for any omissions or inaccuracies. See more about the event here: www.mirandanet.ac.uk/blog/2015/08/digital-citizenship-report/

References

Belshaw, D. (2011). *What is digital literacy?* [online]. Available from: http://neverending thesis.com/index.php/Main_Page [Accessed 15/09/2015].

boyd, d. (2014). *It's complicated: the social lives of networked teens* [online]. London: Yale University Press Common Sense Media. Available from: www.digital-literacy.org.uk [Accessed 31/10/2014].

CEOP Command (formerly the Child Exploitation and Online Protection Centre) (2015) [online]. Available from: https://ceop.police.uk/ [Accessed 04/06/2016].

Common Sense Media (2014). *Earn digital passport online* [online]. Available from: www. commonsensemedia.org/educators/blog/announcing-new-ios-andandroid-versions-for-the-award-winning-digital-passporttm [Accessed 31/10/2014].

Common Sense Media (n.d.). Available from: www.commonsensemedia.org/ [Accessed 04/06/2016].

Department for Education (2013). *The national curriculum in England: framework document* [online]. Available from: https://www.gov.uk/government/uploads/system/uploads/attachment_data/file/239067/SECONDARY_national_curriculum_-_Computing.pdf [Accessed 15/09/2015].

Department for Education (2015). *Protecting children from radicalisation: the prevent duty* [online]. Available from: https://www.gov.uk/government/publications/protecting-children-from-radicalisation-the-prevent-duty [Accessed 15/09/2015].

Digizen.org. (n.d.) Available from: www.digizen.org [Accessed 31 October 2014].

Hobbs, R. (2010). *Digital and media literacy: a plan of action* [online]. Available from: http://www.knightcomm.org/digital-and-media-literacy-a-plan-of-action/ [Accessed 15/09/2015].

JISC (2014). *Developing digital literacies* [online]. Joint Information Systems Committee. Available from: https://www.jisc.ac.uk/guides/developing-digital-literacies [Accessed 15/09/2015].

JISC (2015). *Revisiting digital capability for 2015* [online]. Joint Information Systems Committee. Available from: http://digitalcapability.jiscinvolve.org/wp/2015/06/11/revisiting-digital-capability-for-2015/ [Accessed 15/09/2015].

Kwon, Tae H., and Robert W. Zmud (1987). Unifying the fragmented models of information systems implementation. *In:* R.J. Boland and R. Hirschheim (eds.), *Critical issues in information systems research.* Chichester: John Wiley. pp. 227–251.

Ohler, J. (2011). Digital citizenship means character education for the digital age. *Kappa Delta Pi Record, 48*(1), pp. 25–27.

Raza, A., Kausar, R., and Paul, D. (2007). The social democratization of knowledge: some critical reflections on e-learning. *Multicultural Education & Technology Journal, Vol. 1 Iss: 1, pp.64–74.*

Resnick, M. (2012). Lifelong kindergarten. *Cultures of Creativity*, pp. 50–52.

Ribble (2014). Available from: digitalcitizenship.net/Nine_Elements.html [Accessed 31/10/2014].

Savage, M., and Barnett, A. (2015). *Digital literacy for primary teachers.* Critical Publishing.

Sharpe, R., and Beetham, H. (2010). Understanding students' uses of technology for learning: towards creative appropriation. In R. Sharpe, H. Beetham, and S. de Freitas (eds.), *Rethinking learning for a digital age: how learners shape their experiences.* London and New York: Routledge Falmer, pp 85–99.

Selwyn, N. (2013). *Education in a digital world.* New York: Routledge.

Techopedia (2015). *Definition of a Twitterstorm.* Available from: https://www.techopedia.com/definition/29624/twitterstorm [Accessed 15/09/2015].

Webster, F. (2004). The information society reader. London: Routledge.

Resources

1   A good starting point for teachers engaging in classroom activities is the **Digizen** website at www.digizen.org/. A detailed glossary and a range of classroom activities are included. The resource is also something that can be recommended to parents: for example, there is a useful 'home agreement' document at www.digizen.org/digicentral/family-agreement.aspx. All parties can obtain accurate knowledge to help evaluate popular social networks www.digizen.org/socialnetworking/evaluating-sns.aspx.

> *The Digizen website provides information for educators, parents, carers, and young people. It is used to strengthen their awareness and understanding of what digital citizenship is and encourages users of technology to be and become responsible digital citizens. It shares specific advice and resources on issues such as social networking and cyberbullying and how these relate to and affect their own and other people's online experiences and behaviours.*

2   **Common Sense Education** is an American educators' site offering age-appropriate lesson plans and resources relating to digital citizenship. Appropriately they give teachers and learners open questions to promote reflection and discussion, for example, 'What is the place of digital media in our lives' and 'What are the consequences of over-sharing online' at an introductory level to more philosophical questions about 'collective intelligence' online at www.commonsensemedia.org/educators/lesson/collective-intelligence-9–12

The home page is located at www.commonsensemedia.org/educators/curriculum, and they describe their digital citizenship curriculum by stating, "*Our materials are designed to empower students to think critically, behave safely, and participate responsibly in our digital world*".

3   **Thinkuknow Toolkit for Key Stage 3 and 4** (www.thinkuknow.co.uk/teachers/): Many educators will be aware of CEOP's Thinkknow e-safety resources. These are continuously updated and

> The Thinkuknow Toolkit, is a new downloadable set of lesson plans for education practitioners to use with young people aged 11+. The Toolkit helps you transform the Thinkuknow website from a reference tool into

an interactive resource to get young people thinking and talking about key issues related to sex, relationships and the internet; encouraging learners to return to the website in their own time.

4   **Digitalme** (www.digitalme.co.uk/) is primarily about offering educators and learners a tool, based on Mozilla's Open Badge scheme, a way of recognising and rewarding engagement in digital activities. It is included here as throughout the emphasis has been on facilitating constructive lived experiences in digital spaces.

   "Badge the UK is a new project which will enable learners to demonstrate all their achievements using digital badges". See more at: www.digitalme.co.uk/home#sthash.4JvwSn7V.dpuf.

Recommended reading

1   Shelley, M. (2004). Digital citizenship: Parameters of the digital divide. *Social Science Computer Review*, 22 (2) 256–269.
2   Gorman, G.E. (2015). What's missing in the digital world? Access, digital literacy and digital citizenship. *Online Information Review*, 39 (2).
3   Hill, V. (2015). Digital citizenship through game design in Minecraft. *New Library World*, Vol. 116 Iss: 7/8, pp. 369–382. Here the researchers undertook a study to explore the effectiveness of employing a gamification approach to provide learners with an opportunity to explore digital citizenship. The usefulness of an abstraction approach using Minecraft is an interesting point to reflect upon in light of previous discussions. "The students designed and built a 3D virtual world library game for younger students to help them learn digital citizenship and information literacy" (Hill 2015).
4   Mossberger, K., Tolbert, C., McNeal, R., and Ramona, S. (2008). *Digital citizenship: the internet, society, and participation*. Cambridge, MA: MIT Press. A North American text examining the historical context, economic and civic implications of digital citizenship for a diverse national population. The implications of a digital divide are explored and many considerations are equally applicable to a UK context. This is not written for teachers as a classroom guide but poses questions for educational policy makers and societal observers.
5   Ribble, M. (2012). Digital citizenship for educational change. Kappa Delta Pi Record, 48:4, 148–151. In this article, it is identified that *"a process needs to be in place so that all teachers can learn and understand the skills and concepts involved in digital citizenship"*. Further, *"as the impact of technology continues to grow, both inside schools and out, the skills needed to become effective digital citizens will be ever increasing. Educators can no longer wait for the next digital tool or federal mandate to be released. Digital citizenship education is needed today"*.

Part II

Whole school learning environments

Learning spaces

Exploring physical and virtual pedagogical principles

*Christina Preston, Allison Allen and
Richard Allen*

> If you can design the physical space, the social space, and the information space
> all together to enhance collaborative learning, then that whole milieu turns
> into a learning technology and people just love working there and they start
> learning with and from each other.
>
> (Seely Brown, 2000)

In this debate, we explore the notion that learning spaces should be considered
as a whole and the designs should be overseen by educators whether the space is
physical or virtual, and whether intended for social collaboration or independent
discovery.

We frame the debate with two definitions of learning: agile and traditional:

Agile learning is *adaptive*, where learning milestones are identified but
there is flexibility in the learning to reach them; it is learner-centric, focusing
on individuals and interactions, getting resources that work, responding to
change – an iterative process that often relies on social collaboration.

Traditional learning is *predictive*, based on analysing abilities and planning in detail with risks known. Learners can be directed onto pathways
through the Internet in their research, but often a school will prefer to engi-
neer a 'walled garden' to prevent learners discovering information that is
unexpected or inappropriate. This is teacher-centric, and sometimes teachers describe exactly what is planned for the entire length of a topic but may
have difficulty changing direction if something goes wrong (Williams 2014,
Alchemi 2010).

We use these definitions to provide a simplified view of two key approaches to
pedagogy without implying that either one is 'right' or 'wrong'. Each decision
about pedagogy is as unique as the organisation's learning landscape and as different as the context of the learners and their teachers.

We explain our definitions of learning spaces, virtual and physical, and how
integration between physical and virtual learning environments has enriched

notions of effective learning in the 21st century. We then turn our attention as an example to a new pedagogical strategy with the integration of virtual and physical spaces called flipped learning.

The term flipped learning describes a different way of using physical and virtual spaces from traditional approaches: learners are encouraged to research a topic outside the classroom through safe use of the Internet, preferably with the Internet search scaffolded by their teacher. Armed with new information on the topic, learners return to the classroom to debate with their peers and their teacher. In this way, the view is, their understanding is internalised and reinforced.

The independent learning principles that underpin flipped learning also cause us to focus on the security and safeguarding strategies that teachers and learners must know about if they are to research and collaborate via cloud storage or productivity tools on the Internet. Whereas ensuring a pupil's physical safety in a learning space has always been a priority, there has been far less training for professionals on how to ensure safety when pupils are using the new cloud tools without clear restrictions.

Integrating physical and virtual spaces

According to the Organisation for Economic Co-operation and Development (OECD) (Kuuskorpi et al. 2011), it is widely acknowledged that teachers' roles have changed dramatically since the last century, and we have witnessed rapid social and cultural changes with advances in communication and information technologies. These factors have contributed to shape the teaching and operating cultures of schools and created shifts in our expectations of the physical learning environment. These changes have given rise to an urgent need for a new generation of facilities to cater for 21st century teaching and learning needs.

The concept of learning space is expanded by the ubiquity of technology in the modern world; for example, by 2030 we will arrive at zettascale computing which is 1,000 times more powerful and faster than the human brain – just at a time when children who are entering school now will be leaving university (Brown Martin 2014). This convergence of powerful technology matched with innovative approaches to pedagogy suggests that we are on the cusp of a change in how we choose to learn.

In his book, *Stratosphere* (2013), Fullan describes in detail the fortuitous convergence he senses between the three forces of technology, pedagogy and knowledge about how to change systems. Fullan (2014) argues these three elements now have the power to transform education:

> There is a grand convergence spontaneously erupting. I think it is the natural dynamic of push and pull. The push, to put it directly, is a combination of the boredom and alienation of students and teachers. Students won't wait, teachers can't wait.

We contend that close attention to a fourth element is also important: the quality of the learning spaces, virtually as well as physically, where this convergence takes place. We are analysing the integration of pupils' learning outside the school with their learning in school, and bridging the gap with digital tools.

Our contention is that one of the greatest factors in the success of online tools and agile learning is that some of the principles we would automatically apply to physical classroom space can also be applied to new ways of learning online.

The OECD (von Ahlefeld 2009, p. 1) defines "an educational space" as

> a physical space that supports multiple and diverse teaching and learning programmes and pedagogies, including current technologies; one that demonstrates optimal, cost-effective building performance and operation over time; one that respects and is in harmony with the environment; and one that encourages social participation, providing a healthy, comfortable, safe, secure and stimulating setting for its occupants.

In its narrowest sense, a physical learning environment is seen as a conventional classroom and in its widest sense, as a combination of formal and informal spaces where learning takes place both inside and outside of schools (Manninen et al. 2007). Put briefly, according to the Joint Information Systems Committee (JISC 2006), the design of our learning spaces should become a physical representation of the institution's vision and strategy for learning – responsive, inclusive and supportive of attainment by all.

As far back as the Romans, Marcus Vitruvius Pollio (15BC) in his treatise on architecture, *De Architectura*, asserted that there were three principles of good architecture:

- Firmatis (durability) – It should stand up robustly and remain in good condition;
- Utilitas (utility) – It should be useful and function well for the people using it;
- Venustas (beauty) – It should delight people and raise their spirits; impact – a 'wow' factor.

Few learning space designers would argue with these Roman principles. If we are to use technology effectively in learning, we also need to consider what that might be and how it might fit into our physical spaces. Vitruvian principles can also be the basis for good virtual space design and can be used to help analyse why we prefer certain websites to others. In addition, using the principles of 'sense-sensitive design', cash-strapped schools can also cheaply and effectively enhance the learning environment. The concept of sense-sensitive design was developed by the IBI Group (2013) in response to 12 years of extensive research that has shown that a range of built environmental characteristics can have powerful healing and therapeutic benefits. Explained by Mazuch (2013), the design ideas are based on the way the body perceives and responds to sensory stimuli.

According to Mazuch, using the basics of light levels, colour, vista, sound, touch, temperature and atmosphere, we can impact learning through physiological, psychological, emotional and physical means. For example, dimming light leads to quieter movement in school whilst good levels of natural lighting in classrooms can increase productivity by 18–20%; whereas poor ventilation leading to CO_2 build-up negatively impacts learning and attentiveness. There are cost-effective ways to address ideas of improving classroom ambience through sense-sensitive design: low natural light can be enhanced through the use of natural light bulbs; colour (through paint or projection) can affect mood; scent can affect attitude – for example citrus oil enlivens the environment and increases productivity; sound – learners can benefit from the Mozart effect, birdsong or gentle wind through trees, which is supported by research from the University of South Wales (2013).

Research by Barrett et al. (2015) suggests that informed use of colour can improve learning; their three-year investigation concludes that good primary classroom design can boost progress in reading, writing and mathematics by up to 16% a year. The study suggested that the results of an average child in the most effectively designed classroom, compared with a child in the least effectively designed, could be boosted by 1.3 sub levels in a year. Similar research is anticipated in secondary schools, taking into account the complexities of subject spaces as well as the contexts of older pupils.

Teachers quoted in *The Price of Beauty and Usefulness in Learning Research* (Preston 2015) argued that classroom furniture should be visually inviting, restful and durable. Furniture inspired imaginative play when the design was not too prescriptive. A head who had been closely involved in the classroom design process was convinced that there is significant impact on learning based on how a room is designed.

> Understanding what makes an effective design is important. The best are likely to assist all within the institution to work more productively and to produce learners who are confident, adaptable, independent and inspired to learn. In short, the design of our learning spaces should become a physical representation of the institution's vision and strategy for learning – responsive, inclusive, and supportive of attainment by all.
>
> (JISC 2006, p. 4)

If we are seeking to empower our learners through technology, we need well-designed virtual spaces. In this context, Vitruvian principles apply equally well to technology if they are adapted:

- Firmatis (durability) – It won't break, is sustainable and it can scale;
- Utilitas (utility) – It should do what the teacher and learner need and function well;
- Venustas (beauty) – Learners should enjoy the experience and want to revisit it.

However, this debate cannot be led by the design of the virtual environment, important though this is. More important is that if they are well designed, learning environments can build on our desire as social animals to learn together. Most individuals are motivated to pursue knowledge for personal or professional reasons as a means of improving social inclusion, citizenship, personal development and a sense of self. We tend to develop informal personal learning networks (PLNs) that are made up of the people with whom a learner interacts and from whom they gain knowledge, as well as the technologies that support such communication and knowledge exchange.

This concept of a PLN is related to the theory of connectivism developed by Siemens (2005) and Downes (2005) where learners create connections and develop a network that contributes to their professional development and knowledge – they do not have to know or meet these people personally.

Many of the early online learning environments were designed as 'simply storage places', whereas the newer environments have been influenced by social media and have tried to harness the effect of online exchanges for specific classes and for massive open online courses (MOOCs). These represent a global experiment in engaging large numbers of students in courses designed by universities and companies that are often free. There is, however, a significant dropout rate before the courses are completed, but there are nevertheless fears that these free global courses available to anyone with Wi-Fi will damage the capacity of local and national universities to compete. Despite the desirability of MOOCs engaging with courses from the best universities in the world, the viability of their business model is still not proven (Laurillard 2014).

The Open University produces annual reports titled *Innovating Pedagogy* (Sharples 2012, 2013, 2014) that explore emergent pedagogies. In 2014, Sharples identified an innovative pedagogy developing in informal virtual spaces and microblogging, which they called rhizomatic learning, as it invokes the biological metaphor of a rhizome. The authors use the plant to explain the way in which knowledge is constructed by self-aware communities adapting to environmental conditions like the stem of a rhizomatic plant that sends out roots and shoots. Each of these can grow into a new plant. Rhizomes resist organisational structure and have no distinct beginning or end. The complementary learning experiences may build on social, conversational processes, as well as a personal knowledge-creation process, through the creation of large, unbounded PLNs that may incorporate formal and informal social media. This chaotic rhizomic approach to learning is clearly a challenge to schools where learning is far more regulated (ibid.).

The MirandaNet Fellowship, established in 1992, is an online community of practice and network of educators who have been working in this area of virtual chaos in order to see how learning can be managed. They have found the metaphor of a rhizome helpful in understanding a phenomenon they have observed in their online knowledge-creation activities in their network. This community of professional educators has been experimenting with collaborative communication tools to see whether learning experiences can be extended. These thought leaders contend that the most important creation of wisdom comes from the meeting of minds in what is known as liminal space, where digital environments provide an innovative way of exploring learning:

> The informal dynamic knowledge creation in collaborative contexts occurs as participants move from textual debate in a conventional mailing list to video conferencing, micro blogging contributions and collaborative concept maps. This collaborative technology can be seen as creating a liminal space – a passage, in which a person moves from one state of being to another. Participants in this liminal space are transformed by acquiring new knowledge, a new status and a new identity in the community. This change is of critical importance if learning is to be successful. Whilst remote and informal learning is largely is *[sic]* what has been understood about mobile learning, the concept can now be extended to include these informal spaces in which learning takes place – the liminal spaces that those who push the boundaries of digital possibilities now inhabit intellectually.
>
> (Cuthell et al. 2011, p. 2)

So how can these newly defined processes of learning be assessed? The authors of the *Innovative Pedagogy* reports advocate 'dynamic assessment', which works well in a flipped classroom and virtual rhizomatic learning spaces because it focuses on the *progress* of the learner. The assessor interacts with learners during the testing phase of the process, identifying ways to overcome each person's current learning difficulties. In the dynamic assessment process, assessment and intervention are inseparable.

Of course, these new pedagogies and assessment processes present schools with some significant rethinking and readjustment. Using technology to its advantage, this growing range of pedagogies can be explored and discussed on the website where all three publications can be found (Sharples 2012).

Arguably, the virtual space in a school is often more controlled and restricted because teachers are in *loco parentis*. Learners in most schools have access to virtual learning environments (VLEs) and learning platforms that include both personal spaces and various social media features. Social media are defined as computer-mediated tools that allow individuals to create, share or exchange information, ideas, and pictures/videos in virtual networks: in short, to create and modify user generated content.

However, the pace of change within schools is traditionally slow, and Davidson and Goldberg (2009, p. 3) argue that "institutions of learning have changed far more slowly than the modes of inventive, collaborative, participatory learning offered by the internet and an array of contemporary mobile technologies".

Clearly, the technology is there to support learning – but is our education system capable of using it to meet the needs of learners? McFarlane (2015) does not think that the system works yet. She argues that currently, schools are not preparing learners to function at their full capacity in a digital world.

Sugata Mitra (2007) had come to the same conclusion. He first came to notice this during his groundbreaking work on children's self-organised learning, through his Hole in the Wall project, where Indian children found a computer he had mounted in a hole in a wall outside his office in the slums of Delhi. He watched these children as they worked out how to use the device in groups – and then taught other children. If these talents emerge naturally, school or no school, he asks, what else can children teach themselves?

> It's quite fashionable to say that the education system is broken – it's not broken, it's wonderfully constructed. It's just that we don't need it any more. It's outdated.
>
> (Mitra 2013)

Mitra argues that a self-organised learning environment (SOLE) is character-ised by discovery, sharing and spontaneity. Mitra argues that anyone can create a SOLE – sparking curiosity in children by asking them to explore a Big Question using the Internet and then facilitating their ability to work together: learning.

Flipped classrooms

A survey commissioned in 2014 by Virgin Media Business found that there is a "growing divide" between technology that is available in UK classrooms and teachers' ability to use it; only 15% of teachers are "totally computer savvy" and 70% of teachers said they do not tailor learning to digital skills relevant to the workplace. However, the ubiquitous ownership of mobile devices is making the lack of integration into classroom spaces more difficult to accept. Should educa-tors go on avoiding the global influence of mobile devices outside school and continue with a model where they behave as if they are still the gatekeepers of knowledge? The London Mobile Learning Group (Pachler et al. 2010) argues that in their opinion, schools and other educational institutions are facing a crisis of legitimacy.

An understanding of the principles of flipped learning as a pedagogy can help schools to embrace the new convergences and validate their role as the bridge between learning spaces at home and at school. However, too many institutions, regions and even governments spend significant sums on devices for all before they have considered how to ensure that they will improve learning. In the schools that are applying flipped learning, pupils watch videos on digital devices at home – sometimes they undertake a quiz to check their understanding. When they arrive in class they may, for example, start with an interactive discussion stimulated by the video content that allows deeper thinking around the topic. Pupils might then work on problems in groups or have more individual support. Importantly, this pedagogical method frees up time for a variety of learning activities – the teacher and pupil roles may change according to need, adding a layer of excitement to knowledge transfer and collaboration. 'Flipping' the role and the responsibility of learning to pupils means that the teacher becomes more of a facilitator whilst pupils collaborate, coach and instruct each other; technology allows small groups or individuals to present strategies and solutions to help each other.

In a small-scale study (Allen 2013), teachers found that flipped classrooms often evolve rather than being the result of a step change, producing a strong, reflective model. The teachers reported that leadership support was essential and that staff needed time to become confident with the technology. Using the technology in this way changes the way pupils and teachers interact; pupils gain confidence, becoming more engaged and less fearful of making mistakes. They use forums and develop PLNs, supporting each other and relying less on needing answers solely from a teacher. Pupils request and practise independent learning, and deliver short lessons to their class – there is real and sometimes extraordinary impact on the quality and quantity of work produced. Unexpectedly, the school found a positive impact on parental communication and parental engagement using a parent virtual classroom and parent forum – links are posted so parents can understand and relate to what their child is learning in the classroom; with access to a virtual classroom, they can see what their child is doing and support them. The flipped classroom is changing the pedagogy from the traditional model of starter, introduction, main and plenary; now lessons are based on "What do they need to learn?", "What skills are missing?", "Where are the gaps?" and "How are we going to fill them?"

Indeed, the greatest challenge to leaders in education is embracing pedagogical innovation of any kind. In this context, flipped learning as a pedagogy has gained a strong following since the use of mobile devices has become more pervasive.

Mazur (2013) has been experimenting with flipped learning since the early 1990s when he referred to the technique as "peer instruction" or "inverted" approach. The components in his implementation, that make for a thoughtful, rigorous experience, are those advocated by November and Mull (2012), which are:

- Learners prepare for class by watching videos, listening to podcasts, reading articles, or considering questions that access their prior knowledge.
- After accessing this content, learners are asked to reflect upon what they have learned and organise questions and areas of confusion.
- Learners then log in to a Facebook-like social tool, where they post their questions.
- The instructor sorts through these questions prior to class, organises them, and develops class material and scenarios that address the various areas of confusion. The instructor does not prepare to teach material that the class already understands.
- In class, the instructor uses a Socratic method of teaching, where questions and problems are posed and learners work together to answer the questions or solve the problems. The role of the instructor is to listen to conversations and engage with individuals and groups as needed.

The schools that are successful in achieving the Naace Third Millennium Learning Award (Naace, 2016) are enlightened in the adoption of flipped learning. These schools demonstrate that they are providing an education fit for the 21st century. They celebrate creating an environment and curriculum that stimulate deeper and better learning, making full use of the opportunities presented by technology. These schools feature the development of higher thinking skills, problem-solving and creativity that form the basis of the award:

1) Teacher dependent learning changing to self-directed, lifelong and personal-ised learning.
2) 20th century, pre-computer and pre-network learning skills changing to third millennium learning skills.
3) Schools following externally imposed approaches to teaching and learning changing to schools deciding themselves what are the most appropriate approaches for their pupils and community.
4) Notions of fixed intelligence and limits in ability to learn changing to reflec-tion on learning to develop the capacity to learn more and an understanding of brain plasticity.
5) Learning as something that happens in individual schools, classrooms and pupils changing to learning that uses connections with other people to a far greater extent.
6) Learning in extrinsically imposed ways changing to learning that happens through intrinsic learning behaviours and attitudes.
7) School learning largely isolated from home learning changing to two-way parental engagement with young peoples' learning.
8) Accredited learning happening mainly in schools changing to extended learning.
9) The amount of creativity in teaching and learning becoming considerably greater.
10) Teachers and pupils becoming increasingly aware of, and using, the kinds of pedagogy and learning that are more effective, such as learner enquiry-based learning.
11) Celebrating failure as the route to success, combined with providing better feedback to learners on good learning and their achievements.

We describe two examples where school leaders have successfully implemented flipped learning. In the first example, pupils at School A have a much clearer understanding of what flipped learning includes and how it can help their learn-ing. In the school's video submission for their Third Millennium Learning Award (2016), the learners list 10 features that they like about flipped learning, including:

- developing co-operative values, sharing and collaborating online;
- a creative approach to learning, being able to use online creative tools at home;
- changing the fabric of the building to enable learning to happen more easily outside classes;

- collaborative groups online, with pupils joining groups they want to, to extend their learning;
- an 'educational Facebook' style application using mobile access;
- vertical apps for creating groups, with pupils from different year groups working together;
- having ownership of their work and being able to make it visible to wider audiences;
- enabling greater enjoyment of work by presenting in varied styles;
- multiple access to things they work on together, online, working co-operatively;
- regularly accessing video and written materials prior to lessons.

The second example, School B (Naace 2016) demonstrates a wide range of activities and attributes that are exemplary of a Third Millennium Learning school, where pupils and staff recognise the changes from the traditional predictive teaching style and the "sage on the stage" as described by Stinson and Milter (2006) towards heutagogy or self-directed learning, with the teaching style becoming more of the agile 'guide by the side' approach.

School B uses technology to support learning:

- for pupils to be in control of their own learning;
- for creative cross-curricular work;
- to collaborate;
- to reach out to the wider community;
- to complement skills that the workplace needs.

In classrooms where deeper learning is the focus, you find students who are motivated and challenged, showing evidence of deeper learning and able to transfer learning skills to new contexts; how can 'deeper learning' be defined and measured? Considering 'flipped learning' causes us to ask whether or not it exemplifies 'agile learning' and if it supports enquiry-based learning. Many of us believe that new forms of learning like the agile mode that are self-organised and encourage self-starting resilience can be better than the traditional predictive models.

One of the most important new concepts in teaching is creating opportunities to make thinking visible when teachers see learning through the eyes of their students. Hattie (2012) claims that learning becomes visible when teachers are also learners (i.e. evaluators of their own teaching), helping students to become their own teachers (through metacognitive strategies, feedback and reciprocal teaching). When teachers can really see the thinking of their students, they can provide these students with the support and encouragement they need to be successful. Web-based video is the technology that is taking this pedagogical strategy to new levels in terms of teachers and pupils being able to reflect on their teaching and learning performance (Preston 2016). The flipped learning method offers teachers a means and a method of making learning visible. However, caution in using online learning spaces is needed, and we examine the need for this in the next section on safety.

Although flipped learning is not defined by technology, it is largely dependent on it, and the technology may include newly developed technologies or older technologies repurposed for the task. One of the main concerns of using the flipped classroom approach is that in some cases, learners may not have completed the prior activity before attending the lesson. In particular, the flipped technique can emphasise the problem that some learners have no access to technology at home and are thus disadvantaged. Some schools open computer rooms out of lesson time or suggest a visit to the local library; however, this deprives the learner of the benefits of time to reflect and review the activity, leading to an impoverished experience. It is worth considering how to bridge this digital divide for even the small minority so that no learner is disadvantaged.

Security and e-safeguarding in virtual spaces

Understanding about e-safety, privacy and data security has a significant effect on the use of online tools and social media, and how the benefits and challenges are managed and communicated (McGee and Begg 2008).

Madge et al. (2009) and Siemens and Weller (2011) note resistance from learners when what they regard as fun, social spaces like Facebook are 'invaded' by authority figures like teachers.

Many schools use successful learning platforms; although school-owned learning platforms remove many concerns over e-safety, privacy and data security, their functionality is sometimes not well understood and consequently poorly used. Some schools have therefore moved to use social media such as Facebook or Twitter, or alternatively to popular, more secure tools built for education use and providing teachers, learners and parents with a private learning network that they could use to connect and collaborate with each other, such as Edmodo. Cloud productivity and storage tools are beginning to be used in schools, but some are causing serious safeguarding concerns and risk to learners. The real key to the successful application of technology in learning dialogues is fitness for purpose.

We are all familiar with the reasons why children should be safeguarded from danger in public spaces. Rules like not talking to strangers and staying near the parent or guardian are absorbed early on, and teaching of e-safety is part of an Ofsted inspection. But classroom use of virtual learning spaces and social media is relatively new in education: the dangers are not as clear-cut, nor the rules of engagement as fully established.

McFarlane (2015) explains, reassuringly, that research studies indicate that most young users of social media have little or no interest in communicating with people they do not know online. But she also remarks:

While somewhat reassuring this still leaves a percentage who are vulnerable to strangers and much adverse exposure comes via people who are not strangers at all. Additionally, cyber fraud is a major and growing crime, difficult to police and often international in nature. It is never too early to learn to be cautious online.

(p. 44)

The new pedagogies mentioned above – such as visible thinking, PLNs and flipped learning – all require teachers to not only consider e-safety issues in the classroom, but to address issues of safeguarding. All school staff have a responsibility to provide a safe environment in which children can learn; the term 'e-safeguarding' addresses all safeguarding issues which relate to the use of digital tools and includes e-security and e-safety. Further, senior managers also need to think about the whole school culture as virtual spaces, as storage and tools become part of the learning landscape.

Increasingly popular, cloud computing tools increase the benefits of mobile devices and virtual spaces, in addition to potential cost savings, making it an attractive option for schools considering, for example, flipped classrooms. Working 'in the cloud' means that files are stored (and often created) in the cloud, rather than on the computer where the file was originally created. According to Maresova and Kacetl (2015), cloud computing is a kind of computing which is highly scalable and uses virtualised resources that can be shared by the user, making it very attractive for flipped learning and online space. There are an increasing number of services offering cloud storage and productivity tools where schools can upload documents, photos, videos and other files to a website to share with others. These files can then be accessed from any location or any type of device. Benefits are usually attractive including affordability and reliability, and Maresova and Kacetl (2015) describe enrichment of technology-enabled education and reduction of budgetary impact, but schools may come across risks to their data of which they were previously unaware. For example, there may be content or artefacts online that are created by pupils and carry identification tags. Rich data about pupils and teachers within records containing sensitive information about identifiable adults and children may be stored in the cloud rather than in addition to storage on school servers.

Indeed, in terms of a school's lack of knowledge, many teachers and educators are unclear on what computing in the 'cloud' really means. A survey of school comprehension of cloud security by the Information Commissioner's Office (Gould and Polemon 2013) shows that although UK schools are rapidly adopting cloud computing, including productivity tools and/or storage space, some school staff are deeply concerned by the threat to student privacy posed by data mining of student email and online documents for profit by cloud providers. The report revealed that more than half of responding teachers either did not understand the contractual agreements of the cloud suppliers they used or did not know the detail of what they had signed.

Data protection, in particular, has always been a school safeguarding responsibility, and technology presents new challenges to security; however, reducing the risk can be similar to using school-hosted services. Many cloud contractual documents have clauses that schools have agreed, giving permission to the supplier to "communicate, publish, publicly perform, publicly display and distribute such content" (Google 2014, n.p.); bearing in mind content may identify pupils and teachers, it is an alarming statement. In contravention of UK data protection legislation, some suppliers also store data outside of the United States and Europe – in turn, it may be deleted unexpectedly.

Whilst understanding the benefits to learning of cloud computing and the technologies supporting flipped classrooms, teachers are rightly beginning to question the security of pupil and staff data on some cloud storage and productivity tools. Although such tools are enabling and empowering, some protect data robustly whilst others do not. It is no longer possible to decide by virtue of whether the tool is 'free' or has a cost.

If we handle and store information about identifiable, living individuals – for example, about school pupils – we are legally obliged to protect that information. The Data Protection Act states that we must only collect information that we need for a specific (specified) purpose and keep it secure. Many schools follow good practice, but not all. In most schools, the head teacher or senior manager is the senior information risk officer (SIRO) and data protection officer – sometimes the two are combined. But in some schools, teachers are not aware of who has that role.

It is easy to identify the benefits of using cloud computing in school, especially when the product has no budgetary cost. It is also very easy to tick the box to agree with the terms and conditions of use. In terms of law, the responsibility for due diligence regarding data security in the cloud and in transmission rests squarely with schools. Pinto and Younie (2014) outlined the need for parental responsibility with e-safety, especially as learning in virtual spaces frequently takes place on home equipment. When flipped classroom principles are implemented, it is clear that the learning community expands and so do the responsibilities for ensuring safety in learning spaces.

Technology-enhanced learning such as flipped learning and the use of online spaces can encourage family learning and reinforce a love of lifelong learning. Learners deserve that teachers know where data about themselves and their learners is stored and what might be done with it – particularly if the school is considering adopting cloud computing tools. It is worth reviewing trusted alternative cloud services suppliers such as those in partnership with the NEN (National Education Network), SuperJanet and Regional Broadband Consortia (RBC) cloud services. In the end, however, we as educators need to think wisely about how safety and security affect the quality of learning. Not just knowledge but wisdom is needed on the topic of e-safety.

Conclusion

We have discussed incremental changes that learning in virtual spaces is making to the pedagogy of the classroom. We have also investigated what teachers need to consider to ensure that their learners have an exciting, productive and safe learning experience in both virtual and physical spaces. But how much will access to virtual space impact the ways that schools are managed? How will it affect their physical space? Schools who want to undertake new pedagogies empowered by technology-enhanced models like visible thinking, SOLE, PLNs and flipped classrooms will want virtual spaces to underpin these collaborative approaches to learning. But developing respectful learning relationships between the partners requires far more effort and commitment than mastering the technologies that accompany transformation.

Of course, once these partnerships are forged between learners, teachers, parents, carers, grandparents and mentors in virtual spaces, will school as a physical space, however much impact, be required at all?

References

Alchemi, D.J. (2010) *Dick Moore on agile learning, agile software development and the mobile internet* [online]. Available from: http://alchemi.co.uk/archives/ele/dick_moore_on_a.html [Accessed 8 December 2016].

Allen, R. (2013, February) *The flipped classroom – Gonville Academy* [online]. Edfutures. Available from: http://edfutures.net/The_Flipped_Classroom_-_Gonville_Academy (A Primary academy study that has relevance to the secondary phase) [Accessed September 2014].

Barrett, P.F., Davies, Y., and Zhang, L. (2015) The impact of classroom design on pupils' learning: Final results of a holistic, multi-level analysis. *Building and Environment Journal* [online]. Elsevier. Available from: http://www.sciencedirect.com/science/article/pii/S0360132315000700

Brown Martin, G. (2014) *Learning reimagined*, London: Bloomsbury Academic.

Cuthell J., Preston, C,. and Cych, L. (2011) *Learning in liminal spaces* [online]. Available from: http://www.virtuallearning.org.uk/wp-content/uploads/2011/03/Liminal-Spaces-Bremen.pdf [Accessed 14/3/17].

Davidson, C.N., and Goldberg, D.T. (2009) *The future of learning institutions in a digital age*. The MIT Press.

Downes, S. (2010) New technology supporting informal learning. *Journal of Emerging Technologies in Web Intelligence*, 2(1), 27–33.

Fullan, M. (2013) *Stratosphere*. Canada and UK: Pearson.

Fullan, M. (2014) *There is something different about 2014* [online]. Available from: http://michaelfullan.ca/there-is-something-different-about-2014 [Accessed 7 March 2017].

Google (2014) *Google terms of service* [online]. Available from: https://www.google.com/policies/terms/ [Accessed 7 July 2017].

Gould, R., and Polemon, B. (2013) *SafeGov.org and Ponemon Institute UK schools study summary* [online]. Available from: https://brianpennington.co.uk/203/05/30/schools-are-concerned-about-cloud-security/ [Accessed 06 March 2017].

Hattie, J. (2012) *Visible learning for teachers*. New York & London: Routledge.

IBI Group (2013) *IBI nightingale think* [online]. Available from: http://www.ibigroup.com/wp-content/uploads/2013/03/IBI-Group-Brochure-Sense-Sensitive-Design.pdf [Accessed 20 November 2014].

JISC (2006) *Designing spaces for effective learning.* Bristol: Joint Information Systems Committee.

Kuuskorpi M., Kaarina, N., and Cabellos González, N. (2011) *The future of the physical learning environment: school facilities that support the user.* CELE Exchange 2011/11 OECD 2011.

Laurillard, D. (2014) *Hits and myths: Moocs, may be a wonderful idea but they are not viable.* Times Higher, 6 January 2014.

Madge, C., Meek, J., Wellens, J. and Hooley, T. (2009) Facebook, social integration and informal learning at university: 'It is more for socialising and talking to friends about work than for actually doing work'. *Learning, Media and Technology* 34: 4–55 [online]. Available from: http://dx.doi.org/0.080/7439880902923606 [Accessed 30 November 2016].

Manninen, A. *et al.* (2007), *Oppimista tukevat ympäristöt. Johdatus oppimisympäristöajatteluun.* Opetushallitus, Helsinki.

Maresova, J.. and Kacetl, J. (2015) *Effective use of cloud computing in educational institutions* [online]. Social and Behavioral Sciences. Elsevier Ltd/Procedia, Available from: http://www.sciencedirect.com/science/article/pii/S1877042815030566 [Accessed March 2016].

Mazuch, R. (2013) *Sense sensitive design and the learning environment* [online]. Learning Spaces Conference, Cardiff. Available from: http://www.slideserve.com/weldon/sense-sensitive-design-and-the-learning-environment [Accessed November 2016].

Mazur, E. (2013) *The flipped classroom will redefine the role of educators* [online]. Harvard School of Engineering and Applied Sciences, March Interview. Available from: http://www.seas.harvard.edu/news/203/03/flipped-classroom-will-redefine-role-educators [Accessed 0 March 2015].

McFarlane, A. (2015) *Authentic learning for the digital generation.* London: Routledge.

McGee J.B., and Begg M. (2008) *What medical educators need to know about "Web 2.0"* University of Pittsburgh School of Medicine, USA.

MirandaNet Fellowship (n.d.) Available from: mirandanet.ac.uk [Accessed July 2017].

Mitra S. (2007) *Kids can teach themselves.* TED Talks [online]. Available from: http://www.ted.com/talks/sugata_mitra_shows_how_kids_teach_themselves?language=en Sugata Mitra professional profile http://www.ncl.ac.uk/ecls/staff/profile/sugata.mitra [Accessed November 2016].

Mitra S. (2013) *Build a school in the cloud.* TED Talks 2013 [online]. Available from: http://www.ted.com/talks/sugata_mitra_build_a_school_in_the_cloud/transcript [Accessed November 2016].

Naace (2016) *Third Millennium Learning Award* [online]. Press release: February. Available from: http://www.naace.co.uk/thirdmillenniumlearningaward/2015/ [Accessed 7 March 2017].

NEN (n.d.) The Education Network [online]. Available from: http://www.nen.gov.uk/ [Access July 2017].

November, A., and Mull, B. (2012) *Flipped learning: a response to five common criticisms* [online]. November Learning, March 2012. Available from: http://novemberlearning.com/educational-resources-for-educators/teaching-and-learning-articles/flipped-learning-a-response-to-five-common-criticisms-article/ [Accessed 7 March 2017].

Pachler N., Bachmair, B., and Cook, J. (2010) *Mobile learning: structures, agency, practices.* Springer.

Pinto, T., and Younie, S. (2014) Developing e-safety in school. *In:* S. Younie, M. Leask and K. Burden (eds.), *Teaching and learning with ICT in the primary school.* London: Routledge.

Pollio, M.V. (15BC) *The elements of architecture* [online]. Translation H. Wotton (1624). Available from: http://news.lib.uchicago.edu/blog/2011/05/04/firmness-commodity-and-delight-architecture-in-special-collections-special-collections-research-center-exhibition-gallery-may-9-2011%E2%80%94july-29-2011/

Preston C. (2015) *The price of beauty and usefulness in learning: A study of value for money in a nursery setting MirandaNet publications* [online]. Available from: http://mirandanet.ac.uk/about-associates/associates-research/community-playthings-research/

Preston C. (2016) *Innovation in professional development: collaborative classroom coaching with web-video and web-audio* [online]. Available from: http://mirandanet.ac.uk/about-associates/associates-research/iris-connect-research-into-web-based-video-in-professional-development/ or http://www.irisconnect.co.uk/

Seeley Brown, J., and Duguid, P. (2000) From interview by Creelman with John Seely Brown and Paul Duguid, based on their book *The social life of information* (2000) [online]. Available from: https://www.hr.com/en/communities/human_resources_management/chief-scientist-seely-brown_eacu2tmg.html [Accessed March 2017].

Siemens, G. (2005) Connectivism: a learning theory for the digital age. *International Journal of Instructional Technology and Distance Learning*, 2(1), 3–10.

Siemens, G., and Weller, M. (2011) Higher education and the promises and perils of social network. *Revista de Universidad y Sociedad del Conocimiento (RUSC)* 8: 64–70

Sharples, M. (2012, 2013, 2014) (series ed.) *Innovating pedagogy* [online]. Milton Keynes: Open University. Available from http://www.open.ac.uk/blogs/innovating/ [Accessed March 2017].

Stinson, J.E., and Milter, R.E. (2006) Problem-based learning in business education: Curriculum design and implementation issues. *New Directions for Teaching and Learning,* Vol. 996, Iss. 68, pp. 33–42

University of South Wales (2013) Learning Spaces Pedagogic Research Group. Learning spaces and the student experience: do spaces matter? [online] Sense Sensitive Design and The Learning Environment, University of South Wales. Available from: http://http://pedagogic.research.southwales.ac.uk/ [Accessed March 2017].

Virgin Media (2014) *Three-quarters of teachers use technology in most lessons but only 5% are 'totally computer savvy' risking digital divide, survey finds* [online]. Available from: http://www.virginmediabusiness.co.uk/Search/?q=70%25+of+teachers/ [Accessed 7 March 2017].

Von Ahlefeld, H. (2009) *Evaluating quality in educational spaces: OECD/CELE pilot project* [online]. Available from: www.oecd.org/edu/innovation-education/37783219.doc [Accessed 7 March 2017].

Williams, L. (2014) *Introducing computing: a guide for teachers.* London: Routledge.

Chapter 8

Using Web 2.0 technologies to enhance learning and teaching

Leon Cych, Lawrence Williams and Sarah Younie

This chapter debates the efficacy of Web 2.0 technologies for learning and teaching. Further, it examines the pedagogical affordances of a range of applications that use these technologies, considering their value for classroom practice and professional development. 'Web 2.0' is a term that is understood to refer to interactive, user-generated content, which is easily usable, with high levels of interoperability. It allows online content to be utilised by a number of different systems and devices. Another key feature is the linking between online objects and users of those objects. Whereas Web 1.0 was taken to refer to read-only content, Web 2.0 is characterised by links between objects and the ability of users to interact with, and collaborate over, those objects. Examples of the use of Web 2.0 technologies include social networking sites, video sharing sites and web-based applications (apps), the merits of which will be debated in this chapter.

Interestingly, the inventor of the World Wide Web, Tim Berners-Lee, dismissed the term Web 2.0 as a 'piece of jargon' precisely because he had intended the Web to be, from the very outset, 'a collaborative medium, a place where we [could] all meet and read and write' (Richardson, 2009, p.1). Berners-Lee argued that the Web 2.0 technology itself may not be fundamentally different from Web 1.0, but the implications for the development of social constructivist ways of learning and teaching are significant and will be explored in these debates, along with practical examples. There has been an expansion in Web 2.0 technologies, and, as teachers, we need to examine the new possibilities for creative and collaborative working that these offer to learners.

This chapter thus explores the debates concerning the pedagogical implications of using Web 2.0 tools in the classroom and the way teachers can appropriate these technologies for their own professional development, too. Given that the early Internet developed simply as an online encyclopaedia, now we need to explore the intended purpose of the Web by Berners-Lee – collaboration. There is potential for a paradigm shift in learning and teaching, brought about by the collaborative and creative use of Web 2.0 technologies. Whether these technologies have led, or can lead, to such a shift is at the crux of the debate. Further, this chapter considers, as part of this debate: the rationale behind the use of Web 2.0 technologies; the potential for mobile learning, assisted by Web 2.0 technologies and tablet devices; examples of a range of Web 2.0 tools that could be used to enhance learning and teaching; examples of effective practice for using popular Web 2.0 technologies and uses for teachers' professional development.

Web 2.0 technologies can provide a social constructivist online learning environment, and we argue that, within this, learners are more able to develop creative and collaborative skills, rather than focusing merely on content (Bryant, 2006). Web 2.0 has now become an essential learning and teaching toolbox, particularly with the arrival of devices such as tablets with wireless connectivity to the Internet. These powerful mobile devices provide a ubiquitous connection to Web 2.0 software and with it the opportunity to view, create, edit and upload user-generated Web 2.0 content.

The rate of growth of Web 2.0 applications is increasing. However, from a teacher's point of view, they can usefully be subdivided into a number of curriculum areas, such as collaborative writing (e.g. Google Drive and PrimaryPad), animation software (GoAnimate), creating storyboards and comic characters (ToonDoo and Pixton), collaborating on whole-class projects (VoiceThread), developing 3D modelling (SketchUp) and so on. They could equally, however, be categorised in terms of broader skill development such as creativity, collaboration, motivation, reflection, visualisation, interaction or the co-construction of knowledge. It is a bewildering array, but we hope that the projects described in this chapter will provide some detailed practical guidance in traversing the debates around tools and uses, and perhaps some inspiration on how to start integrating these tools into classroom practice.

The good news, of course, is that it is likely to be the case that our learners already use interactive social networking applications such as Facebook, Instagram, Snapchat and Twitter, and so they may well start ahead of us. Our task, as teachers, is to guide them safely forward in their learning. Below are some of the tools described briefly, with practical examples of how they have been used effectively in the classroom to support the development of digital literacy, collaborative work, creativity, higher order thinking skills and the co-construction of knowledge, which provides a stimulus for your reflection on how you could appropriate such tools for pedagogic practice.

Digital literacy skills: developing collaboration and creativity in the classroom

A key debate concerning digital citizenship focuses on the moral imperative to equip learners with 21st century skills of digital literacy. To support digital literacy development, an accessible tool for learners to start collaborative writing is 'PrimaryPad' (see www.primarypad.com). This is a web-based application that allows several learners to write together synchronously – that is, on the same web page, all at the same time in 'real time'. Each learner who is contributing to the writing is assigned different coloured text at login, and then they can write freely on the web page anywhere they want. Writing from anyone who is logged on appears concurrently so that the writing is a collaborative endeavour.

Initially, learners may find this both exciting and confusing, and may experiment to try and over-write each other's work, but a system of protocol and behaviour guidelines for focused writing sessions, together with immediate peer pressure and transparency of 'who is writing what', usually means any over-writing is short lived. Unlike a wiki, where written contributions compete for space and time (contributors usually have to lock and unlock the page and cannot write simultaneously), one of the immediate effects of seeing three or more people writing on the same topic is that it increases the pace of writing; learners can measure themselves against each other and modify anything that might be seen as duplication. The second significant difference is that learners can see writing modelled and are scaffolded immediately in relation to writing tasks. Learners then do not tend to copy each other but choose variants or different aspects for their writing, which is especially true if learners are engaged in collaborative activities.

The advantage of real time, synchronous transparency like this is that all the participants, teachers and learners can make immediate decisions about their activities and learning, and the lesson can be highly dynamic. Because the writing is publicly available in the classroom for everyone to see, either on an electronic whiteboard or on mobile or desktop devices, everyone is yoked together in what is, essentially, a small ad hoc network.

With collaborative writing, for example, creating an information leaflet, answers can be sought from different sites on the Internet and brought back to the pad. In this way, learners develop search and source skills, which also gives the lie to the fact that learners will just cut and paste. Working collaboratively (in groups) and competitively (between groups), learners are motivated to find the right information and to reflect on it before representing it within a written context. These are higher order thinking skills, and this online tool facilitates this development aptly, thereby enhancing the development of digital literacy. You may want to debate the advantages of learning to write collaboratively and how this may enhance employability skills for learners.

Notably, this online application is constantly being updated to include more features, and one of the most useful (in many ways the strength of Web 2.0 tools) is the ability to record the whole teaching session and to play it back in full or with highlights. Each learner or group can be given a colour at the beginning of the session, and it is easy to replay the 'writing' and to discuss the thinking behind what occurred. In this respect, the application is both a summative and a formative tool for assessment. Teachers are able to unpack where specific writing happened, and to tutor someone in how or what they did, or use it to assess what input and further work is needed with a specific learner or group. It is also a worthy tool for peer assessment. Screen recording is instantaneous and easy and would be suitable to embed in a virtual learning environment (VLE) or other portfolio system of work; this then allows for review and reflection. Arguably, this Web 2.0 tool engenders a more collaborative, dynamic and fluid approach to writing and brings a set of affordances that are markedly different to individual pen and paper writing.

Digital literacy can also be supported by learners creating avatars, which engage learners in novel ways with writing. Voki (see www.voki.com) is a web application that allows learners to create a cartoon avatar, which can be used to read out text entered into the application. Or, a recording can be made of the learner's own voice and synchronised to the avatar's mouth, or a pre-recorded audio made to do the same. With disengaged learners or reluctant writers (Gardner 2011, 2014), this Web 2.0 tool can help overcome a learner's reticence to write. This is because the use of avatars is very helpful for anonymising learners' work or allowing more reluctant learners in real-life class situations to express an opinion through a persona. The pre-supplied voices reading the text have different accents, which can be modulated using different effects. As a result, Voki has been used in literacy lessons as a means of creating 'character' for story openers. The different Voki graphical options, when creating a character with the Web 2.0 app, allows the learner to use a variety of elements – clothes, jewellery, skin colour, hairstyle, stylised drawing – to construct a cartoon avatar very quickly.

Learners can take a screen grab of the avatar and paste it into a word processor. They can use this picture as a stimulus for a written description of the character for a story starter. To get the creative process flowing, learners are asked to form pairs – each person would then create a Voki character online, take a screenshot, write a description in a Word document, but then hide the picture of their character. Their partner does the same, and then they swap descriptions. Each learner then has to go online and reconstruct the character (avatar) using the description they have been given in the Voki web app; then they compare and discuss the pictures.

In subsequent lessons, learners put the descriptions they have written of the avatars into the avatar's speech, using the programme by either typing the descriptions into the box for speech or recording their voices. These can then be used as story starters, which can be uploaded onto the school VLE, and form the basis of much longer stories. This can form an innovative pedagogical approach to literacy and engage hard-to-reach learners through technology.

Voki also has wider curriculum applications; for example, it can be used for the recording of voice for modern foreign languages, poetry or other oral literacy work. A cartoon avatar is a very practical motivational tool. It allows quick recording of what the learners have written. Also, Voki is a very useful tool for both summative and formative assessment in that the teacher has a concrete record of the learner's achievements that can be 'embedded' in a learning platform, web page or blog.

In addition, Voki can be used as an effective way of conducting peer review and assessment. It helps develop critical assessment in peers and enables them to be more specific. The use of this tool helps learners to make choices or at least gives the perception of choice. A variety of options can be created for the learning materials, and so a richer set of stimuli is available. Effective class organisation usually involves working in pairs or threes – it is supportive and encourages co-learning.

With media-rich applications such as Voki, there is often learner discovery of new features as time goes on – the teacher does not need to be the expert. The more one explores the tools, the more ideas develop as practice supports deeper understanding. These tools are often 'emergent' and lend themselves to creative exploration for their use in learning. In this sense, such Web 2.0 tools facilitate a learner-centred approach to writing through exploration and discovery.

Encouraging learners to annotate multimedia objects is another strategy that supports digital literacy skills, and another Web 2.0 tool that facilitates this is VoiceThread (see www.ed.voicethread.com). VoiceThread is a very simple idea. It is an online web application (and educational community portal) that allows users to annotate pictures or videos uploaded to a webpage. Users can write text, record audio or upload video comments about the central photo or piece of media. This is an extremely powerful tool for language and reflection and can be organised around specific topics.

For example, a teacher could upload a video on the Dissolution of the Monasteries, or a 3D model of one of the monasteries, plus a commentary on the Reformation, and learners can add information around these media. In this way, you can build a small information source around the digital assets for other learners, or year groups, to use at a later date. You may want to consider examples that relate more specifically to the computing curriculum, which these tools could be applied to as well.

VoiceThread can be used to enable peer assessment of work too. It is an asynchronous writing/media tool and another multimodal way of presenting and reflecting on information. Even young learners can give feedback on scanned writing, because VoiceThread has an annotation feature. Learners can outline words and comment verbally on the writing scanned in. This could also be used to highlight pieces of video, or a specific photograph or part of a graphic. In this way, VoiceThread has been used quite extensively as a type of video elicitation tool. From these examples, you may want to debate the merits of engaging multimedia forms of literacy for learners and consider any drawbacks to developing this approach.

Digital literacy: ordering and sorting information using Web 2.0 applications in the classroom

Developing multimedia skills so learners are digitally literate can be facilitated through the use of Lino (see www.en.linoit.com). Lino can best be described as an electronic 'sticky note' website. It allows learners to create an immediate 'sticky' that can be moved around a noticeboard. This note could be a video, text, calendar, photo or graphic. The noticeboard can be accessed by multiple learners in real time (synchronously). Lino can be used to put up and share resources around a topic: it is a kind of electronic collaborative scrapbook. It is also extremely useful for eliciting and garnering information about learners' knowledge at any one time. It can be used before introducing a topic or skill set and again after a lesson, or series of lessons, has taken place, and therefore can be used to show learning progression.

Another tool that facilitates visual literacy skills is SpicyNodes (see www. spicynodes.org). SpicyNodes is a Web 2.0 application that allows users to make visual concept maps and to structure information around a topic using spider diagrams and mind maps. For example, it has been successfully used with learners in a history project to find and collate information about the Spanish Armada. Some learners were quite critical of the application at first, because they could not see the benefit of 'outlining' a topic in text when they could do this quite easily with pencil and paper, which would have been faster, too. It was only when the class began to embed video and pictures into the application that the benefits became more apparent.

Despite criticisms, the strength of online mind mapping is that it is easy to assemble and reassemble information quickly and in a logical outline. SpicyNodes and equivalents like Bubbl.us (www.bubbl.us) and MindMeister (www.mindmeister. com) are effective tools for reconfiguring and reflecting on information gathering. Unlike tools like Lino, online mind maps allow for the structuring of information into sets and subsets, thus making it easier to get an overview of the subject or to record a brainstorming session quickly so that it can be re-edited and re-ordered later. Essentially, SpicyNodes is an outlining and planning tool for the classroom, which helps to familiarise learners with online tools for ordering information.

Another tool is Glogster (see www.edu.glogster.com). This is an accessible way to make multimedia posters of information. Pictures, videos, text, hypertext and almost any web element can be embedded in a web page to make a bricolage of different media types around a subject. Bright and colourful posters for classroom display can be made fairly quickly. However, when viewed online they take on a different dimension because video, audio, animation and graphics can be added, as well as hyperlinks to other different resources.

The Glogster application can be used to get learners to make an interactive poster of any subject, for example, when teaching Shakespeare and the different characters in a play such as *Twelfth Night*. The multimodal aspect of the medium enables learners to link to pictures, films and text about the characters from the play. These posters can be printed out but also put up on individual blogs on the school's VLE.

Toneva's (2011) research with learners using Glogster found learners included text, images and sound. All learners, even those who were not extremely confident in using technology, were engaged and eager to work on their multimedia poster. Evidence of learners' work in progress was published at the Glogster blog, together with learners' reflective comments (see www.glogsterproject2.blogspot. com/2011/06/learners-share-their-views-about.html).

Blogging has the potential for enhancing teaching and learning – blogs are not only great tools for personal reflection and sharing opinions, but they can also be used effectively in the delivery of formal curricula and can boost learners' communication skills.

In Toneva's (2011) case study school, she reported seeing good initial practice emerging where teachers were guiding learners on how they could effectively utilise blogging for their learning. Key features of this case study were that the information in a blog is accessible 24/7 and could be used for revision and reflection, and as evidence for learning and assessment; learners can use blogs to develop their e-portfolios, and reading the blogs will allow the teacher to get feedback on what the learners have understood or misunderstood. This will allow the teacher to structure the lessons to assist with more personalised learning. Learners can also learn from their peers and take control over their own learning. Those with special needs, including those who have English as a second language, can blog at their own pace. Such blogging could be used as a catalyst for sharing opinions between learners and could encourage learners to explore their comments in face-to-face discussions.

Initially, teachers created blogs for publishing learners' work and providing comments for feedback. The published examples were used for reflection and provided evidence of learning and an effective way of keeping records to demonstrate progress. When sharing their views about using Glogster, learners reported 'I like it because you can make it private or you can publish it for everyone to see it and this is much easier than making a poster by hand with paper' (Student M). 'I think it's good because we can share what we understood and how we understood it; we can say what happened . . . and share it with different people everywhere' (Student F) (Toneva, 2011).

However, with any debate it can be argued that Web 2.0 technologies can also be developed in very different ways, especially when combined with other mobile technologies. In the next section, we examine using tablets and Web 2.0 technologies to facilitate mobile learning, and briefly outline what is understood by the term mobile learning and how such devices can be deployed to support a learner-centred pedagogy.

Mobile devices to support learner-centred pedagogy

Traxler (2007) argues that whereas some advocates conceptualise mobile learning in terms of devices, he prefers to define mobile learning 'in terms of the mobility of learners and the mobility of learning, and in terms of the learners' experience of learning with mobile devices' (Traxler, 2007, p. 1), and he stresses the importance of understanding mobile learning to be 'essentially personal, contextual, and situated' (ibid.). Similarly, Sharples and Pea (2014, p. 2) highlight learner mobility rather than the technology, citing how 'learning interweaves with other everyday activities, complementing yet at times also conflicting with formal education'.

Sharples et al. (2009) argue that with mobile devices we have the opportunity to design learning differently, particularly as these devices have become more pervasive and gained significant traction since the proliferation of low-cost tablets and smart phones since 2008 (Sharples and Pea, 2014). Figures which demonstrate such penetration show that in Europe more than 90% of children aged 9 to 16 years go online weekly, with 60% going online almost every day (Livingstone et al., 2011). Figures are similar for Australia and USA. For the UK, significant numbers of adults and teenagers own a smartphone, with adolescents reporting that they watch less TV and read fewer books, and mobile use is significant in social settings including mealtimes, but also the bathroom and in restricted areas (Ofcom, 2011).

Arguably, mobility is about increasing a learner's capability to physically move their own learning environment as they move (Barbosa and Geyer, 2005). Benefits include anywhere and anytime access and facilitated interaction between learners (Sarrab et al., 2012). Our understanding of mobile learning is based on social constructivist approaches to learning, where constructivism creates a learning environment that emphasises collaboration and the dialogic exchange of ideas. Constructivism gives learners ownership of their learning, since they are engaged through questions, explorations, inquiry and possibly also designing assessments. A learner-centred approach may be the main focus in a school's technology strategy for using mobile devices and Web 2.0 technologies, where the slogan 'It's not about the technology, it is about the learning' is most appropriate.

It is suggested (Bryant, 2006) that mobile technologies can support social constructivist theories of learning by expanding discussion beyond the classroom and providing new ways for learners to collaborate and communicate. Leask and Younie (2001) developed the concept of communal constructivism to mean that learners can learn 'for and with each other', where the affordances of the technologies allow learners to create, share and build new knowledge online together. Our challenge is to identify practical approaches that support the process of gaining new knowledge, skills and experience within mobile learning environments, assisted by the technology.

Case studies utilising mobile technologies

In Toneva's (2011) research with schools, she worked with one school that provided tablets for all learners and staff. Learners valued having their own device, which they did not have to share. The tablets were used for creating engaging learner-centred environments and for enhancing learners' creative activities, specifically, taking and editing photos, producing sound and video clips, animations, creating online multimedia posters to present project ideas and homework, writing digital multimedia stories and creating websites. Learners reported that they were able to produce independent work that they felt was a reflection of their ideas and imagination. Toneva (2011) found that the flexibility and connectivity were great catalysts to the success of the collaborative activities. The learners were more enthusiastic about teamwork than in previous learning environments, as they found out-of-class sharing of information and communication was greatly assisted by Web 2.0 technologies. The initial learners' feedback collected via web surveys has been very encouraging. You may wish to debate the extent to which you could consider Web 2.0 technologies to engender a learner-centred pedagogic approach.

Research would seem to suggest that mobile devices and Web 2.0 technologies have the capacity to support a range of individual and collaborative learning tasks, and participation appears to be promoted through tools that are intrinsically social and open. Thus, the use of such technologies can be argued to be aligned with the principles of education theories such as connectionism (Medler, 1998), social constructivism (Vygotsky, 1978) and communal constructivism (Leask and Younie, 2001).

Using Web 2.0 technologies to enhance teachers' professional development

We argue that the examples of Web 2.0 tools described in this chapter allow for the development of digital literacy in imaginative ways, to order and sort information, and to encourage collaboration and creativity. While for learners digital literacy skills can be developed using these Web 2.0 technologies, teachers, too, can benefit from these tools, which can be effectively deployed for teachers' professional development. The competences which underpin digital literacy are also arguably a set of professional skills required for 21st century teachers, too. Thus, the rise in the use of Web 2.0 technologies, such as social media, can be seen in the context of online connections between individual groups of teachers (as professionals learning together) and teachers' relationships to formal and ad hoc organisations.

With the use of interactive, collaborative online tools, there has been a rise of 'niche' communities of practice. The proliferation of mobile devices, particularly smart phones with smart networks and apps, is leading to a cultural shift in teachers' professional development insofar as they can, and do, interact and collaborate (see online teacher communities at www.l4l.co.uk/?p=3395). With this changing landscape of mobile devices have come 1:1 schemes in schools (Norrish et al., 2014), and although the mass tablet rollout in California has been problematic (see www.larryferlazzo.edublogs.org/2013/09/30/a-very-beginning-list-of-articles-on-the-ipad-debacle-in-los-angeles-schools/), conversely, in parts of the UK, with a different strategic plan, it has been a great success (see www.independent.co.uk/news/education/education-news/the-school-where-every-teacher-has-an-ipad-and-every-student-has-an-ipod-7578167.html).

The key to the effective utilisation of such technologies lies in their strategic deployment by school leaders and education ministries, in tandem with teacher organisations and communities. However, unless teachers can see a purpose and a better way to blend traditional teaching (and professional development) with Web 2.0 technologies and face-to-face activity, they may be resistant to change (Younie, 2007), particularly if it is imposed 'top down'. If, however, teachers join up willingly to form professional groups from grass roots to address and inform each other, this will have more chance of empowering the profession, which is arguably starting to happen.

Many teachers are now coming together to form ad hoc groups to share ideas and resources (see www.workingoutwhatworks.com/). There are now over 1000 UK teacher blogs covering all areas of the curriculum, and a growing interest in research in education. For example, there have been pop-up conferences organised by teachers talking on Twitter. There is also a new *Journal of Applied Research Education* run by teacher peers being proposed. See Gilchrist (2015), as well as the College of Teaching (www.collegeofteaching.org), which is also developing a journal for teachers. Subject associations are co-opting Web 2.0 technologies to pull together their members' subject specialist areas in a variety of different ways (see, for example, www.pinterest.com/TheASE/). Twitter chats by curriculum leaders and Key Stage coordinators are coalescing around local geographical hubs, as well; for example, see the regional mathematics hubs (http://www.mathshubs.org.uk/). In addition, there are also TeachMeets (see www.teachmeet.pbworks.com/w/page/19975349/FrontPage) and Lesson Study Groups (see www.elac.ex.ac.uk/lessonstudymld/page.php?id=170) that have emerged to discuss and reflect on practice and drive professional development activity and change. It may be that this Web 2.0 approach will become the norm in a few more years for teachers' professional development, thereby providing a low-cost sustainable model for self-improvement.

Another example of using digital tools to update teacher's professional knowledge using a low-cost sustainable model can be seen in the MESH Guides project (Mapping Education Specialist knowHow), which utilises Web 2.0 technologies. This is a knowledge mobilisation initiative that provides summaries of research for teachers (see www.meshguides.org). The aim is to establish easy online access to evidence-based research that can inform teachers' professional practice and enable teachers to support their professional judgements with research evidence. In the same way that the medical profession justifies its practice on research evidence, so too can education move to a position where this is possible (Jones et al., 2015).

Overall, schools and teachers in the UK are tending to follow the late-adoption model of technological innovation, as outlined by Rogers (1983) in his model of innovation and diffusion (originally postulated in 1962), which he developed from extensive longitudinal research across a range of different areas and disciplines, and found the model to be consistent across varying contexts. Rogers found that with any innovation, there were always the innovators who were the first to experiment with new techniques and technologies; this was followed by the early adopters, and then there were the early majority, followed by the late majority and the laggards. This process of diffusion follows an 'S' curve of adoption rates with successive groups adopting the technology, starting with the first 2.5% innovating, then 13.5% being the early adopters, then 34% the early majority, followed by 34% late majority, with the laggards last at 16%. Interestingly, Younie's (2007) longitudinal research with teachers' adoption of technology in schools in the UK also found supporting evidence for this pattern of innovation and diffusion outlined by Rogers (1983).

Innovations with technology, like the emergence of Web 2.0 tools with applications like Google Drive and YouTube, are being used by teachers, but a fair amount of scepticism is still expressed and many teachers, though less conservative than in previous years, still prefer their tried and trusted approaches. A case study example that outlines this approach can be seen in the blog of a teacher who is a late adopter of technology who outlines their journey of transformation and adoption, which reflects a wider pattern of take-up amongst teachers (see www.heatherfblog.wordpress.com/2014/12/11/technology-has-transformed-my-teaching/).

Many Web 2.0 pedagogic applications are still emergent, however, and their use in the classroom and for professional development has not been adequately researched, although, this is slowly being documented. The research surrounding this area, as it exists at present, can still be seen to be fairly patchy (Haßler et al., 2015), but what is clearly evident is that many schools and teachers are beginning to use Web 2.0 online apps and mobile devices at both an individual and strategic level. However, the pace of technological change in this area is arguably faster than researchers' ability to publish in traditional print form; therefore, we will signpost to more immediate online uploading of continuing professional development (CPD) activities to support teachers' professional practice.

Using Twitter for professional development

The number of apps online, and the skills of being able to navigate, make sense of and select what might prove useful in the classroom, is a challenge for teachers. The answer is to harness the teaching community to decide which are most effective for professional practice and to share via social media. What appears to be happening is threefold:

1) Dedicated individual teachers, 'smart nodes' in the social network, have begun to build blogs and resources around practice and social media activity.
2) Education organisations are beginning to pull together attention and debate quite forensically through Twitter, where a number of dedicated 'Twitter chats' have begun to emerge for various teacher interest groups.
3) These individuals and groups are coming together and connecting, forming a smart, cohesive though not homogenous network, in novel and exciting ways to share their learning via Twitter.

For example, UKEdChat, which is a weekly Twitter session for teachers, has now developed an allied resource magazine (see www.ukedchat.com). Run by the dedicated Martin Burrett (@ICTmagic; see www.twitter.com/ictmagic), the ICTmagic wiki is a compendious listing of the main apps sorted by curriculum (see www.ictmagic.wikispaces.com). Similarly, SLTchat (see www/twitter.com/ SLTchat) is a Twitter chat for senior leaders run by @TeacherToolkit (see www. teachertoolkit.co.uk) to discuss leadership issues and share blog posts.

Teacher membership of Twitter as a communication medium to facilitate professional sharing of ideas is continuing to grow, and teachers are coming to understand that it is a place where professionals can garner information faster than previous traditional print media. The debate about teachers' CPD and how Web 2.0 technologies can be harnessed to meet teachers' needs and facilitate updating of information is explored next through Pinterest, which is being used by some subject associations.

Teachers' use of Pinterest

The ASE (Association for Science Education) and CAS (Computing At School) are organisations that have both developed a strategic use of social media for teachers. ASE has a Pinterest board sorted by curricular areas (see www.pinterest. com/TheASE/), and they also have dedicated local TeachMeets for members to meet up and an ASEChat – a regular online Twitter chat. These social media networks are all co-ordinated through these subject association websites.

In addition to subject associations and teacher organisations using social media, leading practitioners are garnering these novel ways of online networking to communicate en masse to other teachers. For example, individual teachers like Rachel Jones (see www.twitter.com/rlj1981) have curated and pulled together publications like the book *Don't Change the Lightbulbs* (Jones, 2014), which are way-markers to the use of effective Web 2.0 resources in the classroom. Rachel Jones' Pinterest board has a wealth of links to educational pages and apps (see www.pinterest.com/rlj1981). Likewise, Mark Anderson has a host of neatly arranged pins on the Pinterest site that are extremely practical for use as ideas in the classroom (see www.pinterest.com/ictevangelist). Both Anderson and Jones also have blogs that you may consider worth further reading, too.

Teacher websites like Pedagoo and *The Echo Chamber* have also emerged and act as online portals to much greater professional collaboration, activity and debate among teachers. Pedagoo is built around the simple desire to share classroom practice, in the form of a collaborative blog, and it is a popular grass roots network organisation that has now had several successful conferences and workshop days (see www.pedagoo.org; also see www.educationechochamber. wordpress.com).

Although not secondary-focused, dedicated websites, such as QuadBlogging and the Hundred Word Challenge, are drawing schools into global writing initiatives run by dedicated teachers (see www.quadblogging.net and www.100wc. net/about-100-word-challenge). These examples demonstrate how teachers are engaging in Web 2.0 technologies both for classroom practice and to enhance their own CPD.

Another grass roots teacher network is the Digital Leader Network, which encourages teachers to train up pupils to help maintain the digital infrastructure and equipment in schools. Again, this is an organisation which has developed from the bottom up to serve a direct need in the classroom and schools (see www.digitalleadernetwork.co.uk). With respect to developing digital leaders in schools, it is important that teachers are sufficiently competent in a range of digital skills so they can teach a diversity of learners, which is why emerging teacher communities like the Digital Leader Network are so important. Digital leaders may also be involved in top-down, bottom-up projects, which are explored in the following section.

Digital literacy: a framework for teachers' professional development

An example of a top-down, bottom-up project is DigiLit Leicester. This is an example of a local authority-wide initiative to build digital literacy in schools through a collaboration between Leicester City Council's Building Schools for the Future Programme, De Montfort University and 23 of the city's secondary schools (Hall et al., 2014).

The DigiLit project created a framework for assessing teachers' digital literacy skills. This is a helpful evaluation tool that enables teachers to self-assess their knowledge and understanding and identify which competences they may need to develop further. For this reason, we include it here. The framework consists of a number of strands, each of which is considered in turn:

> **Finding, Evaluating and Organising**. Teachers know that the Internet has a significant range of information, resources and research that can be used to support and develop learning and teaching. This *Finding, Evaluating and Organising* strand of the framework includes the skills required to success-fully search for information and resources online, the knowhow needed to identify reliable sources of information and to be able to apply a range of approaches for organising online content.

> **Creating and Sharing**. As an educator, you will need to be able to manage a wide range of digital information and resources, including those that you create yourself. The *Creating and Sharing* strand covers using online tools to create original materials, and building on or repurposing existing resources for the classroom. You should know how to identify resources that you have permission to use and remix, and also how to openly share your own materials. You should be able to support learners in creating their own resources and portfolios of work. As an educator, you need to be aware of the legal requirements relat-ing to the use of online and digital resources, for example, copyright law, and the range of open licences available, for example, Creative Commons licensing.

> **Assessment and Feedback**. Web-based and mobile technologies provide a range of opportunities for teachers and learners to assess attainment and track progress, to identify where learners are having difficulties and to pro-vide feedback, including peer assessment. The *Assessment and Feedback* strand also includes how teachers make use of technologies to support learners in monitoring and managing their own learning and to ensure teaching approaches are effective, and adjusting these to suit learners' pace and needs.

Communication, Collaboration and Participation. Digital tools and environments offer teachers and learners a range of collaborative opportunities, supporting the co-design and co-production of resources, providing new approaches to participation and supporting learner voice. Teachers and learners can use technologies to connect and learn both with and from other learners and experts from around the world. The *Communication, Collaboration and Participation* strand involves the use of communication technologies, for example, types of social media including wikis, blogs and social networking sites, to support learning activities and enhance school communications, planning and management.

E-Safety and Online Identity. The use of technology is increasingly integrated into everyday life, and the value of using both private and public digital environments to support learning, teaching and communication is well recognised. Schools and teachers support learners in understanding the negative effects of inappropriate online behaviour and in ensuring learners understand what responsibilities they have as members and representatives of a school community. The *E-Safety and Online Identity* strand underpins teachers' and learners' use of digital environments for formal and informal learning, including understanding how to keep both yourself and your learners safe online, and how appropriate and positive online behaviours can be modelled in classroom practice.

Technology-supported Professional Development. For teachers, the challenge with CPD is keeping up-to-date with subject knowledge and with emerging pedagogic approaches. Web- and mobile-based technologies have changed the landscape in terms of how we can connect to other teachers both locally and globally. Personal learning networks (otherwise known as PLNs) developed and managed by educators allow teachers to discover, discuss and share relevant ideas, resources and pedagogic approaches. The *Technology-supported Professional Development* strand focuses on how educators can and are making use of technology to take their practice forward.

A number of classroom research projects have arisen out of this digital literacy initiative, and one such example is that on 'assessment' by Simon Renshaw, whose blog on the use of 'Hinge Questions' and the use of the 'Quick Key App' shows what is possible under such a digital competency framework (see www.srenshaw. wordpress.com/2014/03/08/evaluating-the-use-of-hinge-questions-and-the-quick-key-app/.

Northampton University's Inspire project is another example of a top-down, bottom-up initiative, which reflects a number of years of teachers' work using apps, social media and devices to create a set of exemplar activities for use in the classroom (see mypad.northampton.ac.uk/inspire/). Similarly, the Art and Computing STEAM-based website aims to join together aspects of the computing and art curriculum – it has a range of very rich exemplars and video of work developed by classroom teachers (see mypad.northampton.ac.uk/inspire/stem-to-steam-project/).

Uses of social media to support teachers

Teachers are currently exploring the use of social media to help with assessment and feedback. See, for example, Mr. Benny (www.mrbenney.wordpress.com/2014/04/14/quickkey-multiple-choice-and-hinge-questions/), which has some very worthwhile examples that we recommend for further reading.

The key issue to debate here regarding Web 2.0 technologies for teachers' CPD concerns the question of whether teacher networks are sufficiently mature and well organised to be self-reliant, or are they at present only appealing to the teacher 'innovators' in Rogers' (1983) pattern of diffusion and therefore only engaged in by a minority of the teaching profession? To what extent does this emergent Web 2.0 model of using social media to support teachers CPD permeate the profession, which in turn is a question of Web 2.0 technology penetration amongst the profession. This issue warrants further research to garner a better understanding of the factors that facilitate and hinder teachers' uses of Web 2.0 technologies to support their classroom practice and their professional development.

Conclusions

This chapter highlights the complexity of the contemporary digital landscape for teachers and outlines the interplay of activity concerning Web 2.0 technologies, which cover apps, use of mobile devices, social media and emerging online teacher networks. The possibilities that Web 2.0 technologies generate for professional development for teachers include the sharing of curriculum resources and ideas for application, the development of learner-centred pedagogies, providing new audiences for learners to address and co-constructing knowledge. Certainly, the growing teacher networks coalescing around these technologies are quite a marked and distinct development in recent years. These will allow teachers to explore how these technologies can facilitate higher order thinking skills, collaborative learning and social constructivist ways of learning and teaching in the ways originally envisaged by Tim Berners-Lee.

Acknowledgements

Thank you to Kayta Toneva for providing the case studies, which included Maryam Thawfeega, Rose Threlfall, Sarwat Siddiqui and the tutors who participated. Also, thank you to Lucy Atkins for permission to cite the Digilit project.

References

Barbosa, D.N.F., and Geyer, C.F.R. (2005) Pervasive personal pedagogical agent: A mobile agent shall always be with a learner. In *Proc. IADIS International Conference Mobile Learning, Malta*, pp. 281–285.

Bryant, T. (2006) Social software in academia. *EDUCAUSE Quarterly*, 2, p. 61.

Gardner, P. (2011) *The reluctant writer in the primary classroom: An investigation of mind mapping and other pre-writing strategies to overcome reluctance* [online]. Bedford: Harper Trust. Available from: http://www.harpurtrust.org.uk/wp-content/uploads/2015/11/The-Reluctant-Writer-in-the-Primary-Classroom.pdf [Accessed 8 March 2017].

Gardner, P. (2014) *Reluctant writers*. MESHGuides [online]. Available from: http://www.meshguides.org.uk) (Accessed 1 Feb 2017).

Gilchrist, G. (2015) Kickstarter Project. *Journal of Applied Education Research* [online]. Available from: https://www.kickstarter.com/projects/glengilchrist/journal-of-applied-education-research. [Accessed 7 July 2016].

Haßler, B., Major, L., and Hennessy, S. (2015) Tablet use in schools: a critical review of the evidence for learning outcomes. *Journal of Computer-Assisted Learning*, 32 (2), 139–156.

Hall, R., Atkins, L., and Fraser, J. (2014) Defining a self-evaluation digital literacy framework for secondary educators: the DigiLit Leicester project, *Research in Learning Technology*, 22, 1–17.

Jones, R. (2014) *Don't change the lightbulbs*. Carmarthen: Crown House.

Jones, S., Procter, R., and Younie, S. (2015) Participatory knowledge mobilization: an emerging model for translational research in education. *Journal of Education for Teaching*, Special Issue, Volume 41, No.5, 555–574.

Leask, M., and Younie, S. (2001) Communal constructivist theory: pedagogy of information and communications technology & internationalisation of the curriculum. *Journal of Information Technology for Teacher Education*, 10 (1 & 2), 117–134.

Livingstone, S., Haddon, L., Görzig, A., and Ólafsson, K. (2011, September). *EU kids online II: final report* [online] [Monograph]. Available from: http://www.eukidsonline.net/ [Accessed 26 November 2016].

Medler, D.A. (1998) A brief history of connectionism. *Neural Computing Surveys*. 1: 61–101

Norrish, D., et al. (2014) *Educate 1-to-1: The secret to successful planning, implementing and sustaining change through mobile learning in schools*. CreateSpace Independent Publishing Platform.

Ofcom (2011) *A nation addicted to smartphones* [online]. Available from: http://media.ofcom.org.uk/news/2011/a-nation-addicted-to-smartphones

Richardson, W. (2009). *Blogs, wikis, podcasts, and other powerful web tools for classrooms (2nd ed.)*. California: Corwin Press.

Rogers, E.M. (1983) *Diffusion of innovation. 3rd edition*. New York: The Free Press.

Sarrab, M., Elgamel, L., and Aldabbas, H. (2012) Mobile learning (m-learning) and education environments. *International Journal of Distributed and Parallel Systems*, 3 (4), 31–38.

Sharples, M., Arnedillo-Sánchez, I., Milrad, M., and Vavoula, G. (2009) Mobile learning: small devices, big issues. *In: Technology-enhanced learning*, Balacheff et al. (eds.), Netherlands: Springer, pp. 233–249.

Sharples, M., and Pea, R. (2014) Mobile learning. *In:* K. Sawyer (ed.), *The Cambridge handbook of the learning sciences: second edition.* New York, NY: Cambridge University Press, pp. 501–521.

Toneva, K. (2011) Using netbooks and Web 2.0 technologies to facilitate mobile learning. *10th World Conference on Mobile and Contextual Learning, MLearn*, Beijing, China, 18–21 October 2011.

Traxler, J. (2007) Defining, discussing and evaluating mobile learning: the moving finger writes [online]. *The International Review of Research of Open and Distance Learning,* Vol 8, No 2. Available from: http://www.irrodl.org/index.php/irrodl/article/view/346 [Accessed 1 February 2017].

Vygotsky, L. (1978) *Mind in society* London: Harvard University Press.

Younie, S. (2007) *Integrating ICT into teachers professional practice: the cultural dyanmics of change.* Thesis (PhD). De Montfort University, Leicester, UK.

Chapter 9

Understanding online ethics and digital identities

Pete Bradshaw and Sarah Younie

This chapter discusses two components of ethics in the context of computing and ICT in schools. First, it looks at ethical issues that directly affect the use of technologies in school with learners. Second, it considers wider ethical issues which learners may learn about and discuss but which do not directly impinge on them.

Learners today live, and have lived through, times of continual technological change. To a greater extent than similar changes in the past, these present ethical challenges to those charged with supporting, nurturing and teaching them. There are two reasons for this increase in challenges. New devices and software appear more frequently than has previously been the case, and many of the developments move young people into spaces and activities which previous generations did not experience first-hand as young people. Thus, the world in which the technology is applied is 'unknown' and changing fast. Such a fluid landscape means that the resolution of ethical issues becomes a continuous challenge as new behaviours outpace ethical procedures and controls.

Use of social networks/e-safety

The first, and perhaps the most obvious, arena for ethical consideration with young people is e-safety. The rise in the use of social networks has brought this to the fore, as it is increasingly easy to be in contact with people you do not know or who are not who they purport to be. While schools may offer a more formal structure for Internet use, and hence less opportunity for such encounters, the ethical issues are the same as in more informal settings. Moreover, teachers of computing and ICT should be discussing the issues faced by young people in all contexts. Ethics and e-safety are not just things to have policies about: they are objects of learning in their own right.

The problem of knowing whom one is talking to, or in contact with, online is a particular case of the problem of veracity. In other words, how do people decide whether what they read online is true or reliable? Metzger et al. (2010) report that the development of the Internet as a place of social interaction has changed the way in which people assign credibility to what they read. In today's online, connected world, the wisdom of the crowd creates authority on the web.

If something is not credible then the crowd will expose it – Wikipedia can be edited to correct vandalism or misrepresentations, sites can be rated, social media can be responded to. The problem here, though, is that when someone wishes to present something, or more crucially themselves, online they can play on the indicators of reliability. By developing profiles which adhere to the rules of integrity, they can present an image which is believable. Whereas this is also a problem offline (witness the number of scams reported on consumer programmes) it can be more damaging online because of anonymity – you do not meet people online for some time, if at all – and speed and availability of communication.

The UK Child Exploitation and Online Protection (CEOP, 2014) identified five areas in which the ethics of safe online behaviour (e-safety) should be considered. These are addressed from the point of view of young people themselves:

- Guidance on posting things online
- Communicating with strangers
- Pressures to behave in certain ways as a result of online communication
- Seeing things online that might be disturbing
- Issues of reporting.

Each of these issues calls on the professional values and skills of the ICT teacher. Discussions with learners could focus on what type of information is shared online and with whom. While it is perfectly usual to be asked for telephone numbers when ordering goods, for example, the same data would not normally be posted in a publicly accessible space. This then leads into a discussion of permissions and an understanding of how groups of contacts can be segregated into groups, each of which one interacts with in a different way. So it may well be, for example, that the same mobile phone number entered into an online purchase form might also be put onto a social network but only shared with those close friends who would have it through non-online contacts. It is important to realise that there are no hard and fast rules here. Simply saying 'Do not put your personal details online' might lead to a lack of understanding of the underlying issues. Indeed, having your close family and friends being able to access a phone number or other details online could be beneficial in an emergency.

The issues of communicating with strangers and feeling pressured to behave in certain ways, or do certain things, are related. Here the ICT teacher needs to draw on the experience of young people offline as well as online. They need to be helped to discuss how one decides who to talk to, what to look out for and how to remain in control. From an ethical perspective, the boundaries here are fairly easily defined in terms of only communicating with people that you know, but as with all situations of potential abuse, the danger may come from precisely those people. Teachers of ICT may wish to work with colleagues responsible for personal and social education to develop a whole school approach. While many of the issues are magnified or mediated by technology, they are wider than the subject itself.

There is scope, however, to look at the role technology plays in these issues. So, for example, a consideration of the differences between online and real-world experiences can be a fruitful point of reference. What might a learner consider to be 'safe' in face-to-face situations? How do they judge? Can the same judgements be made online? Issues such as veracity and reliability come into these questions, as discussed above. There are also issues of non-verbal communication, which is missing online. Young people may need to explicitly think about how we judge what is safe by looking at the emotions or disposition of people they are talking to. That this is much harder to do online should be brought out.

The development of technologies also provides opportunities for contextualisation. It may be that learners find some environments so familiar that they cannot see where dangers might lie. It is by thinking about new technologies, familiar to only a few, that a more conscious recognition of the issues is possible perhaps. So one can trace the development of online interactions from text messaging, through forums to social networks, voice-over-Internet protocol (VOIP) systems (with and without video) such as Skype, webcams more generally, online gaming and text/photo/video messaging apps. This list will presumably continue to grow as will the subtleties in their use – would we have predicted the growth of games within social networks, for example? Taking each of these and focusing on those which are less familiar allows for those which are more familiar to be looked at in a new light. For example, thinking about how one behaves in an online gaming environment might inform how one behaves on a social network or in a forum. The same issues as listed in the CEOP concerns above apply, but they are contextualised and given new emphasis by changes in technology. The overarching goal must be to equip young people with understandings of the general issues so that they may apply them to novel situations in the future.

The changes are not merely restricted to software platforms. More universal access to webcams (built in to computers or enabled on mobile phones) means a far higher proportion of learners will be able to access and use them. Teachers need to regularly explore what technology is available and how it might be used. Such exploration is probably best done with learners. As with all of these issues, the CEOP materials provide a good starting point for such discussions. These resources include guidance on the use of applications, advice on online privacy and communications, and reporting and safeguarding procedures in cases where issues arise or are suspected (see www.ceop.police.uk and www.thinkuknow.co.uk).

Some of the common features of social networks and related software will now be considered from the point of view of where ethical considerations may be located. While acknowledging that any such list is only partial and subject to change as technology develops, it provides a starting point for planning work with learners.

Profiles. Learners need to understand implications of putting things in their profile as well as the effect that setting permissions has on these. Discussions could centre around the type of information that one might put in a profile and who one might make it available to, with the possible consequences of so doing.

Friendships. While the terminology differs, the underlying principle of social networking software is to link people to each other. A critical concern here is the relationship between the online friendship and the real-world contact. As well as thinking about who might be considered as a 'friend' online, learners need to be helped to understand that there are not uniform 'rules' and that relationships change. Adding someone to your friendship list is much easier than considering the impact of revealing things to them in the future.

Groups. Some software will allow users to organise their friends or contacts into groups, with different permissions assigned to each. Here is fertile ground for discussions of purpose, audience and what is appropriate to share in these differing contexts.

Applications. Increasingly, social network platforms have a range of other software tools that act with and on individual accounts. Often there is an explicit indication that the tool is going to access one's private information but, equally, this may be done in the background. Learners should take a critical view of how such software is interacting with their profiles.

Multimedia. Social networking spaces will allow the posting of photos, videos and audio. Learners need to think about the differences between sharing images and sharing text. Often the permissions might be set separately. Nearly always, the impression one gains of someone from an image or video is different from that created by text alone. Cyber bullying, for example, takes on a new dimension where video is concerned. Learners should discuss what is appropriate and what is inappropriate with respect to sharing multimedia. Issues of copyright also come in here with potential for infringement and piracy.

Ethical responsibility and digital citizenship

The emergence of smartphones and mobile tablet devices has heralded a dramatic change in how the Internet has become more personalised, with content specifically aimed at producing outcomes based on information provided by an individual.

A key task for us as teachers is to look at empowering learners to become responsible in their own online lives. This involves the need to raise awareness about online identity, understanding the concept of digital footprints and highlighting what it means to be a responsible digital citizen.

The development of e-safety in schools following the Byron review

In tracing the developments of online safety for learners, a seminal publication was the first Byron report *Safer Children in a Digital World* in 2008, which was commissioned by the Department of Education amid fears that children could access harmful and inappropriate material via the Internet and online gaming. The report highlighted that direct contact could be made with children and young people through the Internet, who may lack the skills of critical evaluation when communicating with others online and not fully understanding the risks associated with sharing personal information.

As a consequence of the first Byron report (2008), Ofsted was tasked to evaluate the extent to which schools educate learners to adopt safe and responsible online practices (Ofsted, 2010). Research shows that children and young people reveal their identity to others at a far higher rate than their parents realise (Livingstone and Bober, 2005; Valcke et al., 2006). For example, the CEOP Centre (CEOP, 2014), which was set up to centrally coordinate cases of Internet-related abuse in the UK, reported that 49% of young people surveyed had given out personal information, such as their full name, age, email address, phone number or name of their school, to someone that they met on the Internet, but, by contrast, only 5% of parents think their child has given out such information (Livingstone and Bober 2005, p. 22). Similarly, the Childalert (2011) survey of young people found that the average 6–14 year old communicates with more than 1,100 people online in a year.

To address these concerns raised in the Byron report (2008), a national strategy group called the UK Council for Child Internet Safety (UKCCIS, 2009) was set up. This was a decisive moment in the UK, which set 'a global precedent' (Bryon, 2010, p. 5) by creating a multi-stakeholder Council and established the UK as a world leader in children's digital safety. Most importantly, in order to heighten an understanding of how to keep safe online, UKCCIS stipulated following the 'Click Clever, Click Safe Code', with three simple things to remember to help keep learners safe online – *Zip It, Block It, Flag It.*

The three Cs conceptual framework for understanding e-safety

Arguably, one of the most useful outcomes of the Bryon review (2008) was the creation of the three 'C's of 'contact, content and conduct', which provided a conceptual framework for understanding the complexity of e-safety. This was presented in a grid format and contained four overarching aspects of e-safety that covered commercial, aggressive, sexual and values, which were cross-referenced with the concepts of content, contact and conduct (see Table 9.1).

Much online behaviour is intertwined with commercial activity. It is important for learners to consider the negative impact of advertising, email spam, sponsorship and the way in which websites and social networking sites are used to gather personal information. Learners need to develop strategies and confidence to deal with increasing online commercialised activity, which can be both persistent and persuasive. Similarly, learners must also receive clear guidance and instruction with regard to their own online conduct and be aware

Table 9.1 A framework for e-safety (Byron, 2008, p. 16)

	Commercial	Aggressive	Sexual	Values
Content (child as recipient)	Adverts Spam Sponsorship Personal info	Violent/ hateful content	Pornographic or unwelcome sexual content	Bias Racist Misleading info or advice
Contact (child as participant)	Tracking Harvesting Personal info	Being bullied, harassed or stalked	Meeting strangers Being groomed	Self-harm Unwelcome persuasions
Conduct (child as actor)	Illegal downloading Hacking Gambling Financial scams Terrorism	Bullying or harassing another	Creating and uploading inappropriate material	Providing misleading info/ advice Misuse of online info e.g plagiarism

of the illegality regarding hacking, gambling underage and certain types of downloading activities.

The aggressive online activities identified by Byron (2008) include material that concerns violent and hateful content, the contact aspect of being bullied, harassed or stalked and the conduct aspect of being the bully. When considering these aspects in class, teachers can also make clear connections with the personal and social education curriculum in relation to these issues. The Byron review also made particular reference to the sexual nature of Internet activity and identified the importance of considering the impact of pornographic material, meeting strangers and grooming, and the learner's conduct of making and uploading inappropriate material. With young people, this might be sexting, but with younger learners, this may involve sharing images through social networking sites with exploitative adults. The review also discusses values and states that here, actions are often determined by the individual's moral position. Activities include bias, racism, misleading advice/information, self-harm, misuse of information and plagiarism.

In the later Bryon review of 2010, Byron rightly highlights the importance of situating the issue of online safety within a broader context of building resilience (for example, through learners developing skills of critical evaluation, risk management and self-monitoring), with a view to providing a 'clear understanding of the importance of risk experiences and their management for child learning and development' (Bryon 2010, p. 2). The challenge is to empower learners to manage risks and for individuals

> to be empowered to keep themselves safe – this isn't just about a top-down approach. Children will be children – pushing boundaries and taking risks. At a public swimming pool we have gates, put up signs, have lifeguards and shallow ends, but we also teach children how to swim.
>
> (Bryon 2008, p. 2)

As professionals, we teachers need to be fully conversant with the threats and challenges to staying safe online and support learners' understanding and adoption of safe and responsible practices. In short, this highlights the need for developing learners 'digital wisdom', which embraces responsible and informed use of digital technologies alongside an awareness of risks. These aspects of digital citizenship can also be linked to Belshaw's (2011) eight-component model of digital literacy, which highlights how digital literacy is highly 'contextual and situational with co-constructed norms of conduct' (Belshaw, 2011, p. 207).

Creating safety policies for learners

Teachers address e-safety through developing school policies, and we argue that it is important that these policies are 'living documents' and that they are incorporated into the daily workings of a school and teacher's professional practice. However, such policies are most likely to fail when they are not bespoke, but rather are 'badged' policies from elsewhere. It is important that those writing the policy also address the emotional aspects of using digital technologies and should include those teachers responsible for safeguarding and also PSHE (personal, social and health education) and that the policy reflects behaviour trends in using online technologies. It is also worth including learners in the development of an e-safety policy, as the principles behind protecting learners while using technology in school are equally applicable to their use outside of school. This also supports an understanding of the importance of 'pupil voice' and empowering the learners to appreciate the issues being tackled in writing an AUP (acceptable use policy).

The fact that learners need to be supported in terms of addressing risks and managing inappropriate content has been identified by the EU Kids Online project (see Hasebrink et al., 2011), and the research by Livingstone et al. (2013, 'In their own words: what bothers kids online?') showed that young people were distressed by pornographic images (22%) and violent content (18%). Our role as teachers is to help learners navigate online content, such that they are empowered to know what to do should they come across inappropriate or upsetting content, namely to enact the 'Click Clever, Click Safe Code' – to *Zip It, Block It, Flag It*.

In addition to focusing on technology and behaviour when drafting a policy, it is also equally important to incorporate areas on information and data security. It is necessary to also include how data is managed to ensure that schools are creating an awareness of the importance of passwords and accessing sensitive data sets. Also, as schools integrate more mobile technologies, so this becomes even more significant, as the Information Commissioner's Office (ICO) report on schools (2012) showed it is essential to address issues around data security: 'We advise that procedures should be in place, and be followed, when any personal information that could be considered in any way private or confidential is taken from the school premises in electronic or paper format' (Information Commissioner's Office, 2012, p. 7).

As teachers further adopt online methods of accessing learner data via school management systems, it is important to ensure that procedures and good practices are an inherent part of a teacher's roles and responsibilities. It is also essential that as learners move to a more 'digital life', where passwords and biometrics will play an increasing part in their lives, that they are educated on the importance of electronic security and they become more aware of how to create robust passwords (Pinto and Younie, 2015).

Digital citizenship: managing risk

Ofsted (2010) produced a thematic study on e-safety entitled *The Safe Use of New Technologies*, which highlighted the need for schools to install more managed networks and not lock down all Internet access:

> Pupils in the schools that had 'managed' systems had better knowledge and understanding of how to stay safe than those in schools with 'locked down' systems. Pupils were more vulnerable overall when schools used locked down systems because they were not given enough opportunities to learn how to assess and manage risk for themselves.
>
> (Ofsted, 2010, p. 5)

As schools increasingly move to adopting mobile technologies for learners, care needs to be taken about managing these systems so that learners do not bypass existing structures to access inappropriate online material. To this end, schools and teachers may want to look at mobile device management (MDM) in order that they can maintain suitable control of such sets of devices in school. As stated previously, we suggest that such policies are 'living documents' so that teachers can continue to adapt and modify their policies to reflect changes and advancements with mobile technologies. Both learners and teachers who wish to bring in their own personal device (also known as bring your own device – BYOD) understand and agree to specific stipulations about using such devices in school (Pinto and Younie, 2015).

In recent years, there has been an increase in the number of resources available to teachers through organisations such as CEOP (see www.ceop.police.uk) and Childnet (see www.childnet.com). Access to these resources is free and includes online games, video clips and lesson plans aimed at specific age groups. Arguably, 'digital citizenship' is an effective way of familiarising learners with the key issues relating to e-safety and encouraging appropriate online behaviours, and there is a growing bank of resources to use and adapt. For example, in addition to the above, see Microsoft, Thinkuknow, KidSmart, Digizen and Childnet International: the latter provides materials on their website (www.childnet-int.org). We suggest that you evaluate the suitability of any such resources and look to address issues that are relevant to the specific age groups you teach. We also recommend that you consider training on the delivery of the resources, as the key message should be about empowerment and trust, rather than making learners fearful. The importance of teachers receiving training was highlighted in the review of ICT by Ofsted (2012), which found:

> Despite mostly good provision for e-safety, training for staff was identified as a relative weakness in the schools visited. Training did not always involve all the staff and was not provided systematically. Even the schools that organised training for all staff did not always monitor its impact thoroughly.
>
> (Ofsted, 2012, p. 43)

The prevent debate

Understanding how the Internet can be deployed for propaganda purposes is also crucial for learners in contemporary society, particularly in light of radicalisation and extremism. Consequently, learners need to have a critical awareness of how online activities can be both highly persuasive and also potentially influential and illegal. Through exploring such issues, teachers are able to sensitively highlight areas that relate to the government's 'Prevent' (2011) strategy and counter-terrorism.

The Prevent strategy is the government's counter-terrorism strategy that aims to stop young people becoming terrorists or supporting terrorism. This strategy document provided a set of guiding principles and framework for Prevent; however, it was revised in 2015 following the Counter-Terrorism and Security Act 2015. The Prevent strategy means that all teachers now have a duty to prevent learners from being drawn into terrorism, and in turn, each school's safeguarding policy must include Prevent duty guidance in order to guard against all forms of extremism and radicalisation (see www.gov.uk/government/publications/prevent-duty-guidance).

Schools should be safe spaces in which children and young people can understand and discuss sensitive topics, including terrorism and the extremist ideas that are part of terrorist ideology, and learn how to challenge these ideas. The Prevent duty is not intended to limit discussion of these issues. Schools should, however, be mindful of their existing duties to forbid political indoctrination and secure a balanced presentation of political issues. These duties are imposed on maintained schools by sections 406 and 407 of the Education Act 1996 (HM Government Prevent Duty Guidance, 2015, p. 11).

However, there is another side to this complex issue, as some teachers have claimed that it causes 'suspicion in the classroom and confusion in the staffroom', as reported at the National Union of Teachers (NUT) annual conference in 2016. A motion was backed at this NUT event to reject the government's Prevent strategy, as teachers questioned its effectiveness and raised concerns regarding the poor support offered to schools to implement the strategy.

Since 2015, the strategy has required teachers to refer any child or young person to the police if they suspect them of any involvement in terrorist activity or radical behaviour; however, teaching leaders state that approximately 90% of referrals end without action being taken. To this end, the NUT noted that schools and teachers do have a role in safeguarding and protecting pupils from extremism, but in practice, Prevent was arguably ineffective. Teachers also reported that the training was inadequate and involved crude stereotyping. This highlights the need for appropriate, professional development that enables teachers to sensitively develop tomorrow's digital citizens.

The role of the Internet in these issues would provide a good topic for a debate where learners get to examine the action in the government's Prevent strategy and critically examine the use of the Internet with respect to propaganda and extremism.

Tackling online extremism and propaganda

Teachers may want to consider how to start conversations around extremism and extreme online content as part of exploring critical thinking online. This is important, as learners need to engage in understanding how online content can be inaccurate and yet persuasive at the same time. To this end, Childnet has created a resource called 'Trust Me', which is designed to support teachers in examining online extremism and has been developed in partnership with the London Grid for Learning (LGfL) Safeguarding Board. This resource contains lesson plans that aim to empower teachers and learners to think critically around the areas of online content, contact and propaganda material. Given that propaganda is aimed to persuade readers to change their views, it is crucial that learners are equipped with independent critical thinking skills that enable them to analyse online content and deconstruct the motives and agendas behind what they see online, including who they speak to online. This is all part of developing learners' critical social media literacy, which is part of developing their digital wisdom and broader digital citizenship; see www.childnet.com/resources/trust-me.

The 'Trust Me' resource from Childnet also contains teacher guidance, which includes background documents and provides an overview of the relevant laws online and case study examples to support teachers in answering any questions that may arise during teaching and discussing these issues. The free online resources aim to provoke discussion and debate among learners, so as to challenge them to think critically about the content of websites and social media. The resources can be used in lessons that address digital literacy issues, either as part of the computing curriculum or PSHE, as the content critically examines the idea of trust and provides learners with online examples to debate and challenge. Crucially, the debate should provoke learners' reflection on understanding potential agendas and motives behind what others post as online through social media and the Internet.

Cloud computing and data ownership

The history of computers in schools has moved from a remote connection to local university mainframes, through standalone PCs and then local networks to

Internet connectivity. Today's classroom takes such access to the wider digital world for granted, and further changes are being seen in the use of mobile (and personal) devices and cloud computing. The latter refers to the storage and editing of data files hosted on remote servers rather than on local machines. It also means execution of applications remotely. Thus, today's learners do not need to have programmes stored on their own computer or the school network. Myriad applications are available via the web. These changes bring with them a number of ethical issues.

Perhaps causing most difficulty is the principle of ownership of data. If a learner, or group of learners, is working on a document, presentation or other digital resource that is held remotely, who owns it? There are two dimensions to this problem.

First, there is the ownership among the group. Assessment often requires identification of unique contribution to work. Historically, on computers, this was fairly straightforward. A file would be saved in a user area and the 'properties' of the file would indicate its provenance. This, of course, was far from foolproof. A file could be created by someone and passed on. In the most benign case, this could be a template that was used by all learners with assessable customisation and personalisation indicating ownership. A teacher might make a skeleton spreadsheet or library of programming commands available to learners who then build on it for their own purposes. The original data file may still be tagged with the teacher's name, however. In a collaborative, cloud-based world, this is much more complicated. If learning outcomes are altered to encourage collaboration, how might this be assessed? This is, of course, not a problem of technology per se, but if one single artefact is created then supplementary means of assessing contribution are needed.

Second, there is the ownership of the data in terms of copyright and intellectual property rights (IPR). This is covered below in terms of personal use of material, but in the case of cloud computing there are bigger, more corporate ethical concerns. If a school decides to store its learner data 'in the cloud', who owns it? Is it the learner, the school or the provider of the cloud service? The small print of many such services would indicate the latter. The problem is complicated by the fact that often it is not clear where the data is being held. Modern Internet services often swop data between local and remote machines. This may be particularly true in schools with remote and distributed learning platforms and on mobile devices that sync with remote providers. If you are not sure where the data is being held, the questions of ownership, copyright and IPR are quite intractable.

Copyright and intellectual property rights

One of the most common areas for ethical consideration is that of use of the material of others. As with some of the other issues discussed so far in this chapter, it is not merely restricted to technological contexts but is magnified by them.

Learners have ready access to a vast range of images, videos, audio and texts that are produced by others. Often the ownership is unclear or obscured by the means in which the resource is found. Searching for an image using a search engine may turn up a perfectly usable result that does not require the original source to be looked up at all, let alone checked for permission to use.

Teachers need to help learners navigate these difficulties by making the rights of copyright and IPR holders explicit. They should discuss alternative sources of material, for example, Creative Commons, and model this behaviour themselves. Thus, when material is presented, it should not include material for which clearance has not been granted and, in any case, the provenance of the resource should be explicit.

A related concern is that of software licensing. Traditionally, this is the domain of the network manager in a school; nevertheless teachers need to ensure that they are not using pirated copies of applications or utilities and that neither do their learners.

Professional values

The professional values of a teacher are encapsulated in various documents such as the national standards in England (DfE, 2013) or professional standards in Scotland (GTCS, 2016). Similar statements of standards and values can be found in education systems worldwide. Central to these is the placing of learners' learning and well-being through the creation and maintenance of safe and conducive environments. In the online world, this takes on a further dimension as the environment is not bounded physically or temporally. Learners interact with each other, learning resources and, perhaps, teachers outside of school buildings or hours. Thus, the technology changes the nature of this professional contract with learners.

A particular ethical issue concerns the 'friending' of teachers and learners. A professional distance should be maintained here, which would render such online relationship inappropriate in most circumstances. It might be, however, that a teacher creates separate identities so that they can set up an online classroom in a social networking space. This has to be carefully managed to avoid 'bleeding' of information between the multiple identities. Learners might, more generally, consider what they construe as their own online identity and whether this varies from one space to another – it probably does. The discussion might be widened further to look at identities of 'celebrities' online.

A further dimension to professional ethics in relation to the use of technology in schools concerns the position of the network, or IT, support staff. In schools, this may be a team of people; in smaller schools, it may be a single person. It may be that support is bought in from a managed services company or local authority. It may also be that teaching staff are involved in these activities.

Whereas a teacher is primarily concerned with learners' learning and, in this context, their safety, support staff are concerned with the infrastructure and, in a parallel manner, its security. It may be that the professional codes and approaches of one group are counter to the other. For example, a teacher may wish learners to develop their creativity through access to online resources, whereas the network manager feels that such resources should not be available. A simple example might be access to websites that allow for online editing and saving to the cloud. This may not be possible on a school network if it relies on particular ports being accessed. Similarly, a teacher may want a class to engage in discussions remotely with another class. It might be that access to the sites, or software, for such collaboration may be blocked. Maybe it is not possible to use instant messaging or IP-based video communication.

Another set of issues concern, learners transferring files from home systems to school ones. Teachers might want learners to build on things they are doing outside of school using their own hardware and software. It may simply be that there are incompatibility issues, but it might also be that network security is such that USB memory sticks cannot be used to transfer data for fear of viruses. At the more extreme end, it may be that schools wish to develop curricula that allow learners to manage networks themselves or to be engaged in programming. Such activities require a level of access to systems that is not normally given to learners (or indeed teachers). Here is seen most starkly the conflict between the values and objectives of the two sets of professionals.

A final ethical tension concerns the provision, and control, of access to material on the Internet by learners. Schools have a duty of care, and this includes taking reasonable steps to prevent learners coming into contact with inappropriate or offensive material. Similarly, this is a key dimension of the teachers' and other staff's responsibilities. Before the widespread use of technology, schools were able to do this fairly straightforwardly. The resources provided were controlled by the school and the teachers or other staff. Even with the widespread deployment of ICT, this did not change much. Learners were not allowed to bring in material to load onto computers, and they generally had little need to. Since the wholesale connection of schools, classrooms and individuals' portable devices to the Internet, the situation has changed. Significantly, schools have to take active steps to consider and implement systems for monitoring and controlling access.

Two key components of this strategy are the filtering of sites and the use of AUPs. These are complementary tools in that where sites are not filtered, the way in which they are used can be covered by the AUP. The ethical balance is where to draw the line. Should the filter be rigidly drawn so that, for example, searching for images or accessing instant messaging is not possible from the school network? Or should it be more open with learners learning about the best way of using such tools and the dangers inherent in them. Each school must come up with its own answer to this dilemma and, crucially, be prepared to explain it to all its stakeholders – including learners and parents.

The AUP and access policies must also be understood by teachers. In addition to understanding the principles and requirements, the implications of such measures need also to be considered. If a teacher suspects a learner of violating the AUP then steps need to be taken to ensure that a false judgement has not been made.

What happens if a learner has an inappropriate website loaded into their browser? Can we be sure that there was a deliberate act – or did the learner happen upon it? What if a learner claims their work has been deleted or corrupted? Technology makes many of these types of judgement more difficult and nuanced. Teachers need to exercise professional care and caution in applying the policies. Support staff need to ensure that there are adequate auditing and security tools.

A consequence of an AUP and any use of technology is the "requirement to inform" if things are detected that are in breach of the policy, indications of some malfunction or suspected malpractice. As part of their professional duty, teachers and other staff need to have, and follow, clear guidelines as to who should be told and what should happen next in these circumstances. These requirements are best built into the AUP but should also follow school norms for reporting of similar instances that are not to do with technology. The critical thing is that they are reported and logged. Putting this into an AUP means that learners, too, are obliged to report. The tension here is with the privacy of an individual. If a teacher suspects a learner of doing something that is against school policy, do they have the right to search the learner's online space? No categorical answer can be given but, again, learners need to have opportunities to gain an understanding of the policies in place, and teachers and schools need to ensure that responses to suspected malpractice in technological contexts are proportionate to those in place for non-technological contexts. Thus, in answer to the question about searching a learner's online space, one of the first questions to be asked is 'What would we do if this was a physical space we wished to search?' and hence, 'Is such a response appropriate?' Here, again, the ethical response comes into tension with privacy.

In some circumstances, it may be more appropriate to challenge the learner, to continue to reinforce policy or to monitor for a period to develop the appropriate response. Another important response, again part of the teacher's professional approach, is to model behaviour.

Ethical behaviour and modelling practice

The teacher, in his or her own use of technology, can exemplify what is expected. This can range from simple things like demonstrating good housekeeping in naming and storing files through to the more sophisticated and subtle such as always tagging free-to-use images with their copyright licensing exemption. Similarly, teachers should not be using pirated software or material for which they do not have permission.

Such modelling of practice has been touched on above when considering social networks. If it is deemed unacceptable for teachers and learners to meet in online spaces, then the teacher needs to reinforce this by rejecting any requests and following up with an explanation as to why. On the other hand, if a social networking or collaborative space is set up specifically for a class or project, then the terms of engagement need to be clearly spelt out. In both cases, the teacher's actions are a model for learners. Teachers will feel, perhaps, more able to reject requests (although they may not have or need the opportunity to explain why). They may feel more able to set up their own spaces and establish ground rules. Such rules may, of course, be subject to negotiation. By making this step overt, though in a space set up by themselves, teachers can reinforce this and model how online negotiation might take place. Another consequence of this behaviour is the development of trust between teacher and learners. If things are made overt, explained and negotiated, then trust is more likely to follow.

Individual teachers' behaviours are to be understood here in the context of the wider school strategic attitude to the use of technology. As well as modelling practice for learners, teachers are exemplifying that institutional position. Thus, if it is deemed unacceptable for learners to use instant messaging or social networking, then teachers should not use them either (except in staff-only areas). As it is illegal to use images and audio for certain purposes without permission, teachers should not do this and should, instead, use copyright-free or Creative Commons-licensed material (www. creativecommons.org/). Most significantly, perhaps, this focus on licensing applies to software applications. The school would not expect to use pirated copies of programmes, and it has a duty to ensure that its learners learn about this. One way of doing that is to make overt issues of copyright and piracy. If a piece of software is only licensed for as single user, then teachers should be clear that that is how it is to be used and not allow it to be used by two or more concurrently. This may cause frustrations (for learner and teacher alike) – these perhaps provide a very good opportunity for discussion.

The legalities of copying and distributing software applications and artefacts can also be applied to a discussion of plagiarism and IPRs. While, as teachers, we encourage learners to collaborate, we need to ensure that they understand how to give credit for the work of others – either peers or the authors of materials they have accessed online. This is very easy to model – sources can be given for any third party resources used. If done well, it may become something that is so commonplace it is not noticed by learners – again, overt discussion should be had to draw out an understanding of why it is being done and what the significance of it is.

A further aspect of ethical behaviour that relates to the use of resources concerns the misuses of data. There is an overlap here with the legality of use, but there are concerns which, while they may be legal, are inappropriate. Teachers again should avoid such behaviours, yet make them overt for teaching and for discussion points.

One example of this type of misuse is in the area of sharing of files. In passing, it may be noted that the term 'file sharing' has, perhaps, become imbued with overtones of illegality due to high-profile court cases and disputes over the rights and responsibilities of Internet service providers and individual users. Here, the more prosaic meaning of sharing files in the general sense is intended, for example, as attachments to e-mails or messages, as links to documents online or as embedded objects in documents, spreadsheets or presentations. In passing data to other users in these ways, there is a duty to ensure that the data will not adversely impact their systems. Typical ways this might happen is for files to be very large or to require specialist plug-ins or codecs to be viewable. In this context, teachers can, by example, show how files are compressed, how to resize images (in the sense of their data size) and how to convert to common file formats.

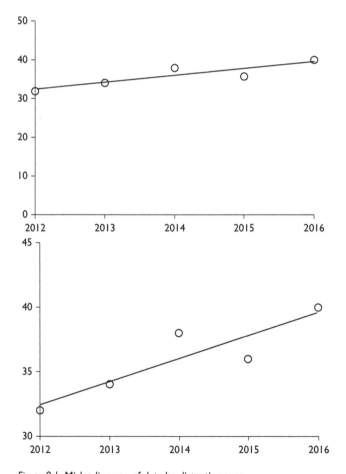

Share of vote

Year	% share
2012	32
2013	34
2014	38
2015	36
2016	40

Figure 9.1 Misleading use of data by distorting axes.

Another more general type of misuse of data is simply when the amount of data available means that it is possible to select a distorted sample to back up a point being made. Learners need to learn to be discerning users of data in this way, just as they need to learn to make value judgements as to veracity and reliability. Teachers should avoid such data misuse by explaining and exemplifying how data can be used reliably. A simple example might be to avoid charts where the axes are scaled for effect without making this clear. This is shown in Figure 9.1 where the first chart gives a true representation (of a share of the vote) whereas the second distorts this.

A related activity, with much scope for learning points although perhaps less clearly misuse, is displaying data in inappropriate forms. This is shown in Figure 9.2 where the data from Figure 9.1 is shown in ways that do not convey its true meaning or obscure it through the wrong choice of format.

A third and perhaps more invidious misuse of data is when data is inaccurate, unreliable or just plain wrong. This is clearly very closely related to the veracity discussion earlier in this chapter encapsulated by the provocation 'Can you trust Wikipedia?' But it goes further. Data can be presented very authoritatively, whereas it may be based on flimsy evidence or insufficient sampling. Equally, it may be out of date or incorrect. Figures 9.3 and 9.4 show some examples of this.

In the first example (Figure 9.3), data has been presented from an out-of-date source. The underlying data comes from a survey in 2005 with extrapolation to 2012. The actual percentage of households with access to the Internet in 2011 was 77%, thus the linear growth shown on the chart was not continued past 2005. In the second example (Figure 9.4), no population size was given. The figures were drawn from a survey in which only 8% of those sent a form returned it.

Share of vote

Year	% share
2012	32
2013	34
2014	38
2015	36
2016	40

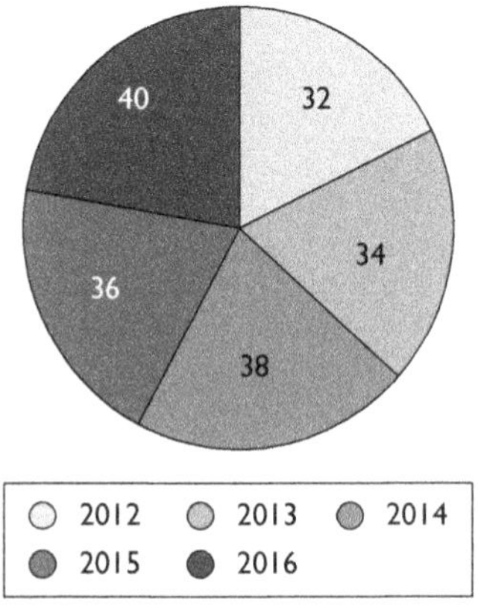

○ 2012   ◉ 2013   ● 2014
● 2015   ● 2016

Figure 9.2 Data misuse through inappropriate representation.

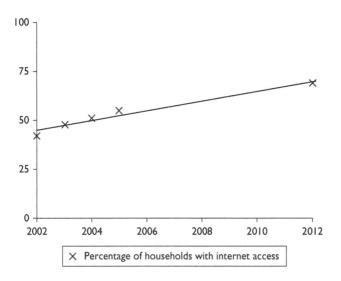

Access

Year	%
2002	42
2003	48
2004	51
2005	55

X Percentage of households with internet access

Figure 9.3 Misleading data (a): Data set based on years 2002–2005 only, with extrapolation to 2012.

It is dangerous to draw conclusions from such a small sample. This highlights the importance of clarity and validity in interrogating data.

As schools become more dependent on IT systems to store and represent data, and as learners become more adroit at its manipulation, these dangers of misuse should be part of the learning of ICT.

Throughout this section, there has been interplay between personal (and professional) behaviours and policies. Not everything can be codified into policy, and any single policy will not cover all eventualities. Some responsibilities will be formalised, and some roles will have specific accountabilities to ensure that these are implemented. As part of professional practice, the overriding approach must be that the ethical use of technology, as with many other aspects of their work, is something that has to be lived and embodied in each individual teacher.

Student evaluation ratings

Rating	n	%
Very good	4	31%
Good	6	46%
Poor	2	15%
Very poor	1	8%
Total	**13**	**100%**

Figure 9.4 Misleading data (b): Data set based on very small sample.

Wider ethical issues

This chapter has so far considered ethical issues in the use of technology that directly affect teachers of computing and ICT and their learners. By this is meant those things which impinge on the teaching and learning process, on the relationship between teachers and learners and their own use of the technology – whether for formal or informal learning purposes.

There is, however, a wider set of ethical issues that the teacher of computing and ICT may wish to consider by way of teaching points. This shorter section considers some of these and attempts to broaden the view of ethics beyond the direct experience of schools and learners. This is then followed by a section on privacy in which further ethical considerations are covered.

Research, psychology and trust

Computers and technology have long been used as instruments in research involving human subjects. Initially this was in the form of data collection or the provision of stimuli. Latterly, the social networking world and alternative realities (e.g. Second Life) have been used as the locale for the interaction with respondents. A further element of this use is in the domain or research into the technology itself – for example, in the use of eye tracking to test websites and applications for usability.

In all these examples, there are elements that need consideration from an ethical standpoint. The consent of those being used as respondents will always need to be freely obtained, but that research being carried out may not always be overt in the technological realm. If a social network, forum or other online space is harvested for opinions, quotes and trends, for example, do all the participants know that when they are contributing? Does the fact that such spaces are sites for research affect the ways in which people act in them? These are key questions for the online researcher in the same way as they are for an ethnographer in the 'real' world.

Participants in an online world need to understand the way in which their contributions will be used. This is, moreover, an extension of the need for the negotiation of ways of behaving in online social communities whether or not they are used for research. Being online hides many of the conventions of interaction that face-to-face meetings have – body language, gestures, the visibility of lurkers. In setting up, managing, facilitating or mediating an online space, this lack needs to be compensated by clear guidelines for use and, through these, a development of trust between members. This development of trust is something which is open to negotiation and will evolve over time, but in a research context, the ways of behaving need to be clearly articulated by the researcher.

A further dimension of trust in the use of technology for research comes from the inherent trust that people may put into things presented online. As discussed elsewhere, the veracity of websites is something that people can easily be convinced of. There is an authority, perhaps analogous to that in other media, that is not always questioned. This is especially true in the case of newly emerging forms of communication and the presentation of information. Evidence of this comes in the ways in which fake websites are easily established and used to trick consumers (see for example BBC, 2009), in the work of Alan November (2012) and in the debates surrounding Wikipedia's value (2016) (the use of Wikipedia as a source for the reliability of Wikipedia is, of course, rather ironic; nevertheless, the page referred to contains numerous links out to other articles that refer to this debate!). Understanding how to 'read' material presented online so that its veracity, accuracy and validity are considered and checked are key aspects of developing a critical digital literacy and for becoming a 'digital citizen' in the 21st century.

Virtual reality and artificial intelligence

As computer systems develop, so there is a blurring of what is real and what is technological creation. Perhaps the most vivid examples of this are in the use of computer-generated imagery (CGI) in the film industry and in the ever increasing reality in games. As an indication of the latter, a search on YouTube for your favourite football team may reveal a number of videos taken from an online game rather than from real life (Danielsaurus, 2012).

There are clearly ethical issues to do with the presentation of artificiality as fact, but there are also other emergent issues. As the power of these technologies increases, they are increasingly replacing the jobs of people. Teachers and learners may wish to consider how this fits with the need for employment and how one imbues machines with moral purpose and values.

As artificially intelligent devices become more prevalent, so the ethical issues in their use increase (for further discussion of these and other ethical issues in computing see the ETICA wiki at www.ccsr.cse.dmu.ac.uk/ETICA-Wiki/index.php/Main_Page). In addition to merely replacing humans in terms of workers, there are problems associated with decision making. Where does the responsibility lie for actions taken by such devices, for example, those that respond to health conditions by administering drugs? If such devices are given autonomous operation and then enhanced by some form of intelligent decision making, what happens if something goes wrong? In this type of usage, the roles of the designer and programmer would presumably need to be scrutinised, along with the role of the professional responsible for diagnosis and deployment of the device. Then there is the patient's own consent and the extent that this can be meaningfully 'informed' given the innovative nature of the technology. It is difficult to agree to something if you cannot understand what the potential consequences are.

The ever greater realism in games and other online environments leads to a whole range of ethical considerations. Some of these will have been experienced by learners themselves, such as online identity, and are covered in the next chapter. Less obvious ones, perhaps, concern the way in which values are distorted online. Pain and harm are not real in games, and there are concerns that those who play games extensively may become addicted and immune to any violence. This leads to questions of what the moral stance of designers of such systems might and should be and how society in general deals with immersion in virtual environments.

Privacy

A final consideration of ethical issues concerns privacy in a digital world. This privacy extends to the identity of individuals as well as to their data. It overlaps with much that has gone before, but some particular aspects have not yet been discussed. Some of these issues will be very much in the day-to-day realm of school learners, whereas others may be more remote.

When using any online services, learners will be familiar with the notion of security to protect their privacy. Thus, concepts such as usernames, passwords, memorable information, personalised questions and so on provide a landscape that learners can readily engage with. Discussion can focus on what makes for strong security in these respects – mixing types of character in passwords, changing passwords regularly, not sharing personal information. There is also scope here to look at the differences between this information – only usernames are unique: passwords can be the same as other users, for example. A further consideration is the purpose to which they are put – usernames for unique identification, passwords for access control.

Learners might also consider the different permissions settings in web spaces that they are familiar with – for example, social networks. Here the concept of access is central. Who can access what and, perhaps less obviously, which applications can access what. Thus, if one logs into one web application and allows another to link to it, how are the permissions cascaded?

An overarching topic here is the notion of identity fraud or theft. Learners could consider what information about themselves they share and what they consider private. They could be invited to find out as much as they can about people from Internet searching – for example, what happens if you enter your postcode, name and mobile number into a search engine?

A different sort of privacy stems from this very personal view of data, access and permissions. This is the privacy that is compromised by storage and transfer of data and of surveillance. Discussion of this might be linked to how police, security or the media find out information about people (fairly or otherwise). Thus, the trail left by mobile phone usage, ATM machines and use of bank cards could be considered. What data is transferred in each of these transactions? How might it be put together to build up a profile of someone's private movements? How might this be supplemented by the imagery from CCTV systems?

A significant technological development in this arena is that of geo-tagging or position-sensitive devices. While mobile phones have always logged approximate location through the masts being accessed by calls and messages, this is now much more widespread. Thus, many devices will be locatable via satellite and cellular systems. Whenever a status is updated online or a user logs into a home page on a computer, their location is often tagged to their account. This may be overt – for example, in opting to display locations with photos uploaded. It may, on the other hand, be covert – when you use some search engines they will look at the location of your device as reported by the service provider and then customise your results to that location. While very helpful if you are looking for a local fast-food outlet or petrol station, there are privacy concerns here.

This chapter has looked at a very wide range of ethical and privacy issues. For the teacher of computing and ICT, this is a rich area and one to which learners will bring their own personal experience. Often the issues are well known, such as e-safety. In other cases, however, learners may not have considered them or even noted that there is an issue. As with much teaching of computing and ICT, the media is a very rich resource for discussion of these topics.

References

BBC (2009) *Fake websites shut down by police* [online]. Available from: http://news.bbc.co.uk/1/hi/8392600.stm [Accessed 10 August 2016]. London: BBC.

Belshaw, D. (2011) *What is 'digital literacy'? A Pragmatic investigation.* Ed.D thesis, Durham University, Durham. Available from: http://neverendingthesis.com/index.php/Main_Page [Accessed 15 May 2016].

Byron, T. (2008) *Safer children in a digital world: the report of the Byron review.* Nottingham: DCSF publications.

Byron, T. (2010) *Do we have safer children in a digital world? Review of progress since the 2008 Byron review*. Nottingham: DCSF publications.

CEOP (2014) *Think U Know* [online]. Available from: https://www.thinkuknow.co.uk/11_13/need-advice/ [Accessed 10 August 2016]. London: Child Exploitation and Online Protection Agency.

Childalert (2011) *How to keep children safe online* [online]. Available from: http://www.childalert.co.uk/article.php?articles_id=206. [Accessed 11 February 2014].

Danielsaurus (2012) *Watford FIFA 12 manager mode: EPIC FA cup semis vs. Liverpool – S1 Ep16* [online]. Available from: https://www.youtube.com/watch?v=7Q9MPYIYbA4 [Accessed 10 August 2016].

DfE (2013) *Teachers' standards* [online]. Available from: https://www.gov.uk/government/collections/teachers-standards [Accessed 10 August 2016]. London: Department for Education.

GTCS (2016) *The standards* [online]. Available from: http://www.gtcs.org.uk/professional-standards/professional-standards.aspx [Accessed 10 August 2016]. Glasgow: General Teaching Council for Scotland.

Hasebrink, U., et al. (2011) *Patterns of risk and safety online. In-depth analyses from the EU Kids Online survey of 9–16 year olds and their parents in 25 countries*. LSE, London: EU Kids Online.

HM Government (2015) *Revised Prevent Duty Guidance: for England and Wales*, London: Crown Copyright. Available from: https://www.gov.uk/government/publications/prevent-duty-guidance [Accessed 27 May 2016].

Information Commissioner's Office (2012) *Report on the data protection guidance we gave schools in 2012* [online]. Available from: http://ico.org.uk/~/media/documents/library/Data_Protection/Research_and_reports/report_dp_guidance_for_schools.pdf [Accessed 12 February 2014].

Livingstone, S., and Bober, M. (2005) *UK Children Go Online project* [online]. Available from: http://www.lse.ac.uk/collections/children-go-online [Accessed 8 February 2014].

Livingstone, S., Kirwil, L., Ponte, C., and Staksrud, E. (2013) *EU Kids Online: In their own words: What bothers children online?* [online]. LSE, London: EU Kids Online. Available from: http://www.lse.ac.uk/media@lse/research/EUKidsOnline/EU%20Kids%20III/Reports/Intheirownwords020213.pdf [Accessed 9 February 2014].

Metzger, M., Flanagin, A., and Medders, R. (2010) Social and heuristic approaches to credibility evaluation. *Online Journal of Communication* 60 (3), pp. 413–439, September 2010.

November, A. (2012) *3 websites to Evaluate* [online]. Available from: http://november learning.com/educational-resources-for-educators/information-literacy-resources/3-web-sites-to-validate/ [Accessed 10 August 2016].

Ofsted (2010) *The safe use of new technologies*. Manchester: Ofsted

Ofsted (2012) *ICT in schools 2008–11*. Manchester: Ofsted

Pinto, T., and Younie, S. (2015) Developing e-safety in the primary school. *In:* S. Younie, M. Leask, and K. Burden (eds.), *Learning to teach using ICT in the primary school*, London: Routledge.

UK Council for Child Internet Safety (2009) *Click clever click safe: the first UK child internet safety strategy*. London: UKCCIS.

Valcke, M., Schellens, T., Van Keer, H., and Gerarts, M. (2006) Primary school children's safe and unsafe use of the Internet at home and at school: an exploratory study. *Computers in Human Behavior*, 23(6), 2838–2850.

Wikipedia (2016) *Criticism of Wikipedia* [online]. Available from: https://en.wikipedia.org/wiki/Criticism_of_Wikipedia [Accessed 10 August 2016].

Chapter 10

Computational thinking and creativity in the secondary curriculum

Moira Savage and Andrew Csizmadia

Introduction

The new Computing Programme of Study (PoS) (DfE 2013), implemented in English state schools from September 2014, began with the bold statement that 'a high quality computing education equips pupils to use *computational thinking* and *creativity* to understand and change the world' (italics authors' own). The implications of the disapplication of the prior Information and Communication Technology PoS (Gove 2012) and the introduction of the Computing PoS for secondary schools include: the development of a new GCSE Computer Science qualification by all the awarding bodies, the inclusion of GCSE Computer Science with the English Baccalaureate (EBacc), a greater number of students taking GCSE Computer Science and computational thinking being the keystone of the revised GCSE Computer Science qualifications first taught from September 2016. These developments received a mixed response and discussions reflected diverse opinions about what the new curriculum should look like. One recurring theme articulated was, 'Where have all the creative aspects of the ICT curriculum gone with the shift in emphasis to computer science? Isn't programming the opposite of creativity?' For many teachers, computing is associated solely with either computer programming or coding, which is 'viewed as a narrow, technical activity, appropriate for only a small segment of the population' (Resnick 2012a p. 42). The changes in the curriculum prompted many in the profession to undergo a fundamental reappraisal of what they understood by computational thinking, creativity and the relationship between the two. This is evidenced in the analysis of the responses by 339 teachers to the annual Computing At School's survey, which was conducted in February 2014 (Sentence & Csizmadia 2016), in which teachers cited computational thinking as a strategy for teaching computing.

The chapter begins by exploring definitions of *creativity* and *computational thinking*, with particular reference to the extent to which they are oppositional or whether a synergy exists. The appropriateness of the emphasis on computer science will be questioned by looking at whether the *product* and/or the *process* is the reward when not all students will want to be programmers. What, if any, are the benefits of computational thinking and programming for all learners? This leads us to the question as to whether there are identifiable attitudes, aptitudes or dispositions that lead to success as a creative learner and/or computational thinker. Finally, what pedagogical approaches should teachers adopt to enable creative computing in their classrooms?

Defining creativity and computational thinking

What is creativity?

Wilson reminds us that creativity is a quality we almost universally feel should be valued even when sometimes we are not precisely sure what we mean by it or how we can foster it in others (2009). As teachers, do we first need to challenge the notion that creativity is the preserve of artistic disciplines such as literature, drama, music, dance, art and so on? Can other disciplines be creative? The National Advisory Committee on Creative and Cultural Education (NACCCE) in 1999 listed five characteristics of creativity: 'using imagination, a fashioning process, pursuing purpose, being original and judging value' (p. 31).

The Qualifications and Curriculum Authority (QCA) 'emphasised creativity in terms of purposeful shaping of imagination, producing original and valuable outcomes' (Craft and Hall 2009 p. 9). Specifically, QCA 'suggested that creativity involves pupils in thinking or behaviour that includes

- questioning and challenging
- making connections, seeing relationships
- envisaging what might be
- exploring ideas, keeping options open
- reflecting critically on ideas, actions, outcomes.

(QCA, 2005)

These ideas were further built upon following the 2006 Roberts Review expanding the definition of creativity: 'creativity involves thinking or behaving imaginatively – this imaginative activity is purposeful: that is, it is directed to achieving an objective; this process must generate something original; and the outcome must be of value in relation to the objective' (DCMS/DfES 2006 p. 13).

What is computational thinking?

The term computational thinking was posited, advocated and popularised by Wing in her seminal work (2006 p. 33–36):

Computational thinking involves solving problems, designing systems, and understanding human behaviour, by drawing on the concepts fundamental to computer science ... It represents a universally applicable attitude and skill set that everyone, not just computer scientists would be eager to learn and use.

Wing's call was to make thinking like a computer scientist a fundamental skill for everyone across the whole curriculum. As a result, an opportunity was presented to promote the concepts and processes of computer science to a wider audience; however, Wing did not articulate a precise definition of the term computational thinking. Since then, there have been attempts by both individuals and groups to derive a definition for computational thinking.

The International Society for Technology in Education (ISTE) with the Computer Science Teachers Association (CSTA) in 2011 produced an operational definition of computational thinking. This states that computational thinking is a problem-solving process that includes the following characteristics as being inherent in that process:

- Formulating problems in a way that enables us to use a computer and other tools to help solve them
- Logically organizing and analysing data
- Representing data through abstractions such as models and simulations
- Automating solutions through algorithmic thinking (a series of ordered steps)
- Identifying, analysing, and implementing possible solutions with the goal of achieving the most efficient and effective combination of steps and resources
- Generalising and transferring this problem solving process to a wide variety of problems.

(ISTE and CSTA 2011)

Brennan and Resnick (2012) proposed a framework for assessing computational thinking, indicating that it should include the following:

- *Computational concepts* – the concepts that designers engage with as they program, such as iteration, parallelism, etc.
- *Computational practices* – the practices that designers develop as they engage with concepts such as debugging projects or remixing others' work
- *Computational perspectives* – the perspectives that designers form about the world about them and themselves.

The Computing curriculum in the UK

In England, the Department of Education initially funded the *Barefoot Computing* project, a national initiative to support primary teachers' understanding of the Computing curriculum with an emphasis on promoting computational thinking. The project articulated a vision of computational thinking concepts to be developed by learners and approaches to embedding these concepts.

Secondary computing teachers will need to be aware of the concepts promoted, approaches advocated and the computational thinking vocabulary articulated, as this may shape their engagement with learners during the transition from the primary to secondary phase of education and their engagement in outreach work in primary school.

In 2016, *Tenderfoot,* a complementary project to Barefoot Computing was launched whose target audience is Secondary Computing teachers. This project refines and adopts the vision of computational thinking concepts as advocated by Barefoot Computing for a secondary school setting.

Concurrently with the developments and rollout of both Barefoot Computing and Tenderfoot, a Computational Thinking Working Group was commissioned by Computing At School (CAS), the grassroots subject association for computer science teachers in the United Kingdom, to investigate how computational thinking concepts and practices could be clearly and concisely articulated, promoted and developed within the classroom. This working group initially amended CAS's Progress Pathway Assessment Framework (Curzon et al. 2014) to include sign-posting opportunities when computational thinking concepts could be promoted in activities and developed by learners. Subsequently, this working group built upon their previous work and published *Computational Thinking: A Guide for Teachers* (Csizmadia et al. 2015).

These previous initiatives to promote computational thinking could be considered as complementary and supplementary to one another in shaping aptitude, attitude and ability in learners following the Computing curriculum at Key Stage 3 as well as supporting Secondary Computing teachers. At Key Stage 4, the development of GCSE Computing/Computer Science qualifications, by the different awarding bodies, clearly indicates the rapid adoption, promotion and prominence of computational thinking. For example, in OCR's GCSE Computing specification (OCR 2012), there is a reference to critical thinking but no mention of computational thinking at all. Within the Edexcel GCSE Computer Science specification (Pearson 2015), there are 13 references to computational thinking (CAS 2015). The revised GCSE Computer Science specifications from the awarding bodies, first taught from September 2016, now have explicit reference to computational thinking. For example, one of the examination papers that students will sit as part of OCR's GCSE Computer Science is entitled: Computational Thinking, Algorithms and Programming (OCR 2015).

The new A level Computer Science qualification (OCR 2015) to be first assessed in 2017 places computational thinking not only in a pivotal role as an area of study in its own right but also in a supportive role as computational thinking principles and practices are applied to solve a wide range of problems. In addition, the A level Computer Science qualification is regarded as a vehicle for learners to develop their computational thinking skills.

The challenge is, if computational thinking is the gift of computer science to other subjects as articulated by Wing (2006), how can computational thinking be embedded within and articulated by other subjects in the curriculum?

A third definition: tinkering

Within the current popularity of the *Maker Movement* (Cohen et al. 2016; Peppler et al. 2016), we often hear references to *tinkering*; this approach has a great deal of relevance in relation to definitions of creativity and computational thinking, and moving towards an operational approach for the classroom. Resnick and Rosenbaum (2013 p. 2) argue that 'The tinkering approach is characterised by a playful, experimental, iterative style of engagement, in which makers are continually reassessing their goals, exploring new paths, and imagining new possibilities'.

Tinkering resonates with the view of the creative process articulated by, for example, Robinson (2006) where there are 'three distinct but related concepts':

- See-Imagination, seeing something in the mind's eye
- Think-Creativity, using imagination to solve problems
- Produce-Innovation, applying creative ideas and implementing solutions.

(Robinson 2006, cited in Wisconsin Task Force on
Arts and Creativity in Education 2010 p. 1)

Does computational thinking oppose or complement creativity?

This section explores the relationship between creativity and computational thinking and whether they are divergent or convergent. Traditionally they may have been viewed as conflicting in nature, but the advent of modern technologies challenges us to reconsider whether there is a greater level of synergy than is apparent at first.

Thus, has the shift in emphasis to computer science in the Computing curriculum meant that the creative elements have disappeared? The College Board (2014) may respond no; in 2014, they argued that fundamentally, 'computing is a creative activity':

> Creativity and computing are prominent forces in innovation; the innovations enabled by computing have had and will continue to have far-reaching impact. At the same time, computing facilitates exploration and the creation of computational artefacts and new knowledge that help people solve personal, societal and global problems.

(p. 6)

The Computing PoS (DfE 2013) requires that students 'design, use and evaluate computational abstractions that model the state and behaviour of real world problems and physical systems'. This seems to echo in particular the characteristics that NACCCE used to describe creativity (Robinson 2001), specifically, the 'fashioning process – the active and deliberate focus of attention and skills in order to shape, refine and manage an idea' (cited by Loveless in Wilson 2009 p. 23). References to creativity in national policy documents do not appear in themselves to be incompatible with notions of creativity as implied by the Computing curriculum.

The Maker Movement

In many ways, the current Maker Movement echoes traditional arts and crafts approaches, in a technology-rich age with 3D printing and more permeable subject boundaries than often operate in secondary schools. In particular, the Maker Movement brings together Science, Design and Technology and Computing, and this has implications for how the curriculum is presented to learners. Martin (2015, p. 31), referring to the long-established Montessori (1912) tradition, states:

> The Maker Movement is a new phenomenon, but it is built from familiar pieces, and its relevance to education has deep roots. It has long been argued that children and youth can learn by playing and building with interesting tools and materials.

Resnick and Rosenbaum (2013) consider that the 'emerging Maker Movement is catalysed by both technological and cultural trends. New technologies are making it easier and cheaper for people to create and share things, in both the physical world and the digital world' (p. 2). Their definition of tinkering itself 'prioritises creativity and agility' (Resnick and Rosenbaum 2013 p. 2–4). At first glance, computation is about logic and precision, but 'what if you want to create things that move, sense, react, interact, and communicate' (Resnick and Rosenbaum p. 5)? They cite an example where 'a child might start with the goal of building a security system for her bedroom, and then experiment with many different materials, strategies, and designs before coming up with a final version' (p. 3).

Recommended Maker Movement organisations to explore

The Fab Lab movement: This began in the United States and Gershenfeld's TED talk (see below) gives a comprehensive overview of its philosophy and history of Fab Labs. Notably, Fab Central can be accessed at www.fab.cba. mit.edu. Fab Labs UK list local branches at www.fablabsuk.co.uk.

Make: This movement began in 2006 and Dougherty's 2011 TED talk (see below) gives a comprehensive overview of its philosophy and history and the sub-components internationally (Maker Faire, Maker Con, Maker Shed, Maker Camp and Maker Space etc.). Maker's tagline is 'We are all makers' and they state their aim as to 'inspire Makers of all ages and types with DIY projects, How-tos, tech news, electronics, crafts and ideas'. More information can be accessed at www.makezine.com. Maker Faires are events run by Make: International, including the UK, and can be located at www. makerfaire.com/global/school/. Within this movement, it is possible to host/attend School Maker Faires, and resources are available at the School Maker Faire resource page. The organisation describes a Maker Faire as 'a celebration of invention, creativity, and resourcefulness. It's a place to show what we've made and to share what we've learned with others – a great match for any educational community'.

TED talks: To understand the philosophy and background of the Maker Movement, the TED talks of Gershenfeld (2006), Dougherty (2011) and Silver (2013) are a useful watch.

What attitudes, aptitudes and dispositions do learners need to be creative and/or computational thinkers?

Can we identify characteristics common to creative learners?

Munro (no date) highlighted the complexity of the question of ascribing behavioural characteristics in relation to creativity due to personal, situational and other factors. However, some commonly cited criterion for creativity include:

> fluency (producing numerous ideas in words, images or actions); flexibility (variety and relevance); originality (uncommon or unique ideas); elaboration (ability to develop or embellish ideas); abstractness (sensing the essence of a problem); and resistance to premature closure (keeping an open mind, keep working on unresolved issues using information from a variety of perspectives).
>
> (p. 3)

In 2010, the Wisconsin Task Force on Arts and Creativity in Education identified the following contributing attitudes for learners engaged in creative work: 'curiosity, willingness to take risks, flexible and adaptable, comfortable with ambiguity and there being more than one right answer, and being open and responsive to diverse perspectives' (p. 3).

Can we identify characteristics common to computational thinkers?

ISTE and CSTA list a number of attitudes needed when engaged in computational thinking:

- Confidence in dealing with complexity
- Persistence in working with difficult problems
- Tolerance for ambiguity
- The ability to deal with open ended problems
- The ability to communicate and work with others to achieve a common goal or solution.

(ISTE and CSTA 2011)

Table 10.1 Desirable attitudes for creative and computational thinking

Wisconsin Task Force on Arts and Creativity in Education (2010) identified the following contributing attitudes for learners engaged in **creative** *work:*	*ISTE and CSTA (2011) listed a number of attitudes needed when engaged in* **computational thinking**:
• *Comfortable with ambiguity and there being more than one right answer*	• *Tolerance for ambiguity*
• *Curiosity*	• *Ability to deal with open-ended problems*
• *Willingness to take risks*	• *Confidence in dealing with complexity*
• *Being open and responsive to diverse perspectives*	• *Ability to communicate and work with others to achieve a common goal or solution*
• *Flexible and adaptable.*	• *Persistence in working with difficult problems.*

Table 10.1 aligns these descriptors for desirable attitudes alongside each other, revealing that these learner attitude descriptors are closely aligned; for example, acknowledging and being comfortable with sometimes working with ambiguity as part of the process.

Attempts to provide a detailed description of what 'thinking like a computer scientist' involves have proven quite problematic (Dede et al. 2013). The Advanced Placement Computer Science Principles Curriculum Framework detail six computational thinking practices including: 'connecting computing and impact on people; developing (creative) computational artefacts in many forms and selecting the appropriate techniques; ability to applying abstracting at multiple levels; analysing problems and artefacts, communicating and collaborating' (The College Board, 2014 p. 6–8).

Returning to the key question as to whether the inherent processes are divergent or convergent, is there more of a synergistic relationship than initially assumed? Dede et al. (2013) extend this discussion through their consideration of the extent to which 'the ability to think computationally is essential to conceptual understanding in every discipline'. 'Knowledge of computer science and mathematics' are undoubtedly key components, but this alone would not necessarily produce successful outcomes. In addition to that knowledge, what is key is 'imaginative capacities like innovative thinking and curiosity' which brings us back to aptitudes commonly associated with creativity (Dede et al. 2013).

What we can conclude with some confidence is that both are intellectually demanding and require high levels of metacognition. Both require confidence and perseverance when outcomes are unknown; therefore, emotional resilience as a learner is essential. Both require awareness of the 'self', 'others' and alternative perspectives. Finally, an intimate and detailed knowledge of context is crucial as successful outcomes are based upon usability and satisfaction of an external audience. How do these processes manifest in classroom settings? As Resnick and Rosenbaum (2013 p. 2) remind us:

Tinkering is undervalued (and even discouraged) in many educational settings today, but it is well aligned with the goals and spirit of the progressive–constructionist tradition—and, in our view, it is exactly what is needed to help young people prepare for life in today's society.

Should everyone learn to program?

Returning to the current Computing curriculum in the UK and the emphasis on computer science, some commentators might suggest the programmes of study are ambitious in scope and challenging to fit in the time and space constraints of the school day. Should everyone learn to program? For everyone to learn programming, there needs to a strong case that precious time is being used effectively. To help resolve that question one distinction to explore is whether it is the *product* or the *process* that is the most important element. Wing states that 'computational thinking is a skill for everyone, not just for computer scientists. To reading, writing and arithmetic, we should add computational thinking to every child's analytical ability' (2006, p. 33). Similarly, Resnick argues that all students can benefit from learning to code: firstly, it helps them understand their media-rich world, and secondly it offers an outlet for creative expression (2013). Coding is viewed as an extension of writing, as 'the ability to code allows you to write new types of things – interactive stories, games, animations and simulations' (Resnick 2013). Further, there are transferable skills beyond 'computational ideas . . . they are also learning strategies for solving problems, designing projects and communicating ideas' (Resnick, 2013).

> Engaging in the creation of computational artefacts prepares young people for more than careers as computer scientists or as programmers. It supports young people's development as *computational thinkers* – individuals who can draw on computational concepts, practices, and perspectives in all aspects of their lives, across disciplines and contexts.
>
> (ScratchEd, 2011)

A 'computational artefact (something created by a human using a computer) can take many forms, including but not limited to, a program, an image, audio, video, a presentation, or a web page file' (The College Board, 2014, p. 6). Further, we are all aware of the extent to which innovations in 'creating digital effects, images, audio, video, animations has transformed industries' and indeed the capabilities anticipated of recruits in a wide range of professions (The College Board, 2014, p. 8).

Resnick reflects on how one contributor to the Scratch community learned, in addition to coding, 'how to divide complex problems into simpler parts, how to iteratively refine designs, how to identify and fix bugs, how to share and collaborate with others, how to persevere in the face of challenge' (Resnick, 2013). This suggests perhaps that computational thinking not only supports the development of 'product' or 'outcome' capability but also facilitates emergent, and transferable, process aptitudes, for example, resilience and goal orientation.

What pedagogical approaches support creative computing?

Social-constructivism, connectivism and constructionism

As a teacher, how are you to organise the physical space, resources and learners to engage in creative computing projects? Is the traditional computer suite adequately equipped and suited to this style of learning and teaching? Should traditional computer suites morph into cross-disciplinary Maker Spaces in our schools if we are to excite and enthuse our pupils about STEM subjects? Should teachers be organising school-based Maker Faires? To answer these questions, we can return to what we know about learning and pedagogical approaches.

The Maker Movement would typically align as social-constructivism, where collaboration, communication and sharing knowledge are often fundamental to founding principles. Scully and Hind (2015) declare:

> Community interaction and knowledge sharing are often mediated through networked technologies, with websites and social media tools forming the basis of knowledge repositories and a central channel for information sharing and exchange of ideas, and focused through social meetings in shared spaces such as hackspaces.
>
> (p. 57)

Also, they proclaim:

> Maker culture is seen as having the potential to contribute to a more participatory approach and create new pathways into topics that will make them more alive and relevant to learners.
>
> (p. 57)

In 2005, Siemens proposed rethinking established learning theories in relation to the digital age and introduced the notion of *connectivism.*, the central tenet being:

> … learning (defined as actionable knowledge) can reside outside of ourselves (within an organisation or a database), is focused on connecting specialised information sets, and the connections that enable us to learn more are more important than our current state of knowing.
>
> (Siemens 2005)

If learning is to be considered 'actionable knowledge', then certainly the distribution of information in a contemporary networked world gives teachers something to consider when making classroom decisions about facilitating the learning of today's pupils. The ongoing research of Sugata Mitra and his team into self-organised learning environments (SOLEs) (see, for example, Dolan et al. 2013) challenges many teachers' beliefs about learning and teaching (2013). SOLEs are defined as 'models of learning in which students self-organise in groups and learn using a computer connected to the internet with minimal teacher support' (Dolan et al. 2013).

Papert and Harel (1991) were early proponents of 'taking down the walls that too often separate imagination from mathematics' and proposed the term *constructionism* to describe 'learning by making' in tangible and purposeful contexts. Resnick was very much influenced by Papert's view that students should go beyond being consumers and become creators being able to design, create and express themselves with new technologies (2012a). Resnick and Rosenbaum (2013 p. 6) in their research at MIT sought collaboration with the LEGO Group to:

> ... develop the LEGO Mindstorms and WeDo robotics kits, which enable young people to build robotics devices that move, sense, interact, and communicate. In the process, young people learn important mathematical, engineering, and computational ideas. Even more important, they learn to think creatively and work collaboratively, essential skills for active participation in today's society.

Resnick et al. (1996) underline the importance that students learn effectively when they are working on 'personally meaningful projects'; therefore, personalisation is key. Similarly, the notion of tinkering implies reaction and response to 'the specific details of the particular situation' (Resnick and Rosenbaum, 2013, p. 3). Scratch enables learners to create artefacts that may involve importing and 'mixing graphics, animations, photos, music and sound' (Resnick, 2012a). Belshaw (2011), when defining digital literacies, identifies *constructive* and *creative* components. In relation to constructive, Belshaw discusses 'creating something new, including using and remixing content from other sources to create something original . . . .understanding how and for what purposes content can be appropriated, reused and remixed' (2011 p. 208–209). The creative dimension in Belshaw's definition is about 'doing something new in new ways' (2011 p. 12).

Apprenticeship model

Craft and Hall (2009) describe aspects of creative learning in an apprenticeship model including: dimensions which could carry forward into a computing context; the teacher modelling expertise and approaches; authentic tasks, locus of control being with the students and risk-taking. Teachers and curricular modelling is recognised as an effective approach within computer science also (National Research Council of the National Academies 2010). Further, the notion of presenting students with the idea that there are often additional and alternative ways of finding solutions and time is needed to incubate ideas seems very applicable in this context (Craft and Hall, 2009).

Playful kindergarten approach

> Tinkering as a playful style of designing and making. (Resnick and Rosenbaum 2013 p. 3)

Resnick (2012b p. 50–51), in proposing a *lifelong* kindergarten approach in education, expands on Papert's notion of constructionism, explaining 'why the activity of making is so important to the process of learning':

> When you make something in the world, it becomes an external representation of the ideas in your head. It enables you to play with your ideas and gain a better understanding of the possibilities and limitations of your ideas. Why didn't it work the way I expected? I wonder what would happen if I changed this piece of it? By giving an external form and shape to your ideas, you also provide opportunities for other people to play with your ideas and give suggestions on your ideas. Why didn't I think of that? How can I make it more useful for people?

Fundamentally, Resnick (2012b p. 51) is advocating that learning with a kindergarten approach is a spiral creative process:

> There is a constant interplay between making new things in the world and making new ideas in your head. As you make new things, and get feedback from others (and from yourself), you can revise, modify and improve your ideas. And based on these new ideas you are inspired to make new things. The process goes on and on, with making and learning reinforcing one another in a never-ending spiral.

On another occasion, Resnick and Rosenbaum (2013 p. 163) link the kindergarten approach and the Maker Movement, acknowledging that:

> … although most people involved in the Maker Movement are not focused explicitly on education or learning, the ideas and practices of the Maker Movement resonate with a long tradition in the field of education—from John Dewey's progressivism (Dewey, 1938) to Seymour Papert's constructionism (Papert, 1980, 1993)—that encourages a project-based, experiential approach to learning.

Resnick and Rosenbaum (2013) suggest key pedagogical points in relational to establishing a culture of designing and tinkering in educational contexts:

- *Emphasise process over product.* . . . . To engage people in thinking about the tinkering process, encourage them to document and discuss intermediate stages, failed experiments, and sources of inspiration.
- *Set themes, not challenges.*
- *Highlight diverse examples.*
- *Keep examples and documentation on display* for continuing inspiration.
- *Tinker with space.* Consider how you might rearrange or relocate, to open new possibilities for exploration and collaboration. For example, how can

the arrangement of tables and screens help people see each other's work? How can the arrangement of materials encourage clever and unexpected combinations?

- *Encourage engagement with people, not just materials.* Resist the urge to explain too much or fix problems. Instead, support tinkerers in their explorations by asking questions, pointing out interesting phenomena, and wondering aloud about alternative possibilities.
- *Combine diving in with stepping back.* While it is valuable for tinkerers to immerse themselves in the process of making, it is also important for them to step back and reflect upon the process.

Reflective questions

The College Board (2014) pose three pertinent questions in relation to creativity and computational thinking that are worthy of reflection:

1   How can a **creative development process** affect the **creation of computational artefacts?**
2   How can computing and the use of **computational tools** foster **creative expression?**
3   How can computing **extend traditional forms** of human **expression** and **experience?**

(p. 6)

Summary

Rather than computational thinking opposing creativity, it should be viewed as a deep, pure form of creativity. This view is embedded and amplified in Creative Computing (Brennon, Balch & Chung 2014). What is perhaps the key question is more about evolution in our cultural understanding of creativity being the preserve of 'the Arts' and not computer science. Similarly, there is a shift in cultural and popular understanding of computational thinking to one that emphasises its iterative and creative process. Resnick concluded that:

> ... one of the biggest challenges in realising Papert's dream are *sic* not technological but cultural and educational. There needs to be a shift in how people think about programming ... We need to expand the conception of digital fluency to include designing and creating, not just browsing and interacting.
> (2012a p. 46)

Resnick and Rosenbaum (2013) remind us that the success of our pupils in the future 'will depend not on what they know, or how much they know, but on their ability to think and act creatively—on their ability to come up with innovative solutions to unexpected situations and unanticipated problems' (p. 4).

Further reading and viewing-

Gershenfeld, N. (2007) Fab: *The coming revolution on your desktop – from personal computers to personal fabrication.* Basic Books: New Ed edition.

Peyton-Jones, S. (2014) *Teaching creative computer science* at TEDxExeter [online]. (Available from: https://www.youtube.com/watch?v=Ia55clAtdMs#t=85). Peyton-Jones argues that Computer Science is a foundational subject for all, he 'wants children not just to consume technology, but to be creative with it'. Further, he asks, 'What does that mean for teaching computer science in schools, and why is the rest of the world watching England?' (available from: https://www.youtube.com/watch?v=Ia55clAtdMs#t=85).

Honey, M., & Kanter, D. (eds.). *Design, make, play: Growing the next generation of STEM innovators.* London: Routledge, pp. 163–181.

References

Brennan, K., Balch, C., and Chung, M. (2014) *Creative computing: Scratch curriculum guide* [online]. Available from: scratched.gse.harvard.edu/guide/ [Accessed 15 July 2017].

Brennan, K., and Resnick, M. (2012) *New frameworks for studying and assessing the development of computational thinking: Using artifact-based interviews to study the development of computational thinking in interactive media design.* Paper presented at annual American Educational Research Association meeting, Vancouver, BC, Canada [online]. Available from: http://web.media.mit.edu/~kbrennan/files/Brennan_Resnick_AERA2012_CT.pdf [Accessed 13 December 2016].

Cohen, J.D., Jones, W.M., Smith, S., and Calandra, B. (2016) Makification: towards a framework for leveraging the Maker Movement in formal education. *In: Society for Information Technology & Teacher Education International Conference* Vol. 2016, No. 1, pp. 129–135.

Computing At School (2015) CAS computing progression pathways KS1 (Y1) to KS3 (Y9) by topic [online]. Available from: http://community.computingatschool.org.uk/resources/1692 [Accessed 13 December 2016].

Craft A., and Hall, E. (2009) Changes in the landscape for primary education (3rd ed.) *In: A/ Wilson (ed.), Creativity in primary schools.* Exeter: Learning Matters, pp. 7–18.

Csizmadia, A., et al. (2015) *Computational thinking: a guide for teachers* [online]. Available from: http://community.computingatschool.org.uk/resources/2324 [Accessed 2016].

Curzon, P., et al. (2014) *Developing computational thinking in the classroom: A framework* [online]. Available from: http://community.computingatschool.org.uk/files/3517/original.pdf [Accessed 13 December 2016].

Dede, C., Mishra, P., & Voogt, J. (2013) *Advancing computational thinking in 21st century learning. International Summit on ICT in Education* [online]. Available from: http://www.edusummit.nl/fileadmin/contentelementen/kennisnet/EDUSummIT/Documenten/2013/Advancing_computational_thinking_in_21st_century_learning.pdf [Accessed 13 December 2016].

Department for Education (DfE) (2013) *National curriculum in England: computing programmes of study.* London: DFE.

Department for Culture, Media and Sport (DCMS) and the Department for Education and Skills (DfES) (2006) *Nurturing creativity in young people: a report to government to inform future policy.* London: DfES.

Dolan P., et al. (2013) Self-organised learning environments (SOLEs) in an English school: an example of transformative pedagogy? *Online Educational Research Journal* [online] 2013, 1–19. Available from: http://www.ncl.ac.uk/ecls/research/publication/196125 [Accessed 13 December 2016].

Dougherty, D. (2011) *We are makers TED Talk* [online] Available from: https://www.ted.com/speakers/dale_dougherty [Accessed 13 December 2016].

Gershenfeld, N. (2006) *Unleash your creativity in a Fab Lab TED Talk* [online]. Available from: http://www.ted.com/talks/neil_gershenfeld_on_fab_labs [Accessed 13 December 2016].

Gove, M. (2012) *'Harmful' ICT curriculum set to be dropped to make way for rigorous computer science* [online]. Available from: https://www.gov.uk/government/news/harmful-ict-curriculum-set-to-be-dropped-to-make-way-for-rigorous-computer-science [Accessed 1 February 2013].

International Society for Technology in Education (ISTE) and the Computer Science Teachers Association (CSTA) (2011) *Operational definition of computational thinking for K-12. Education* [online]. Available from: http://www.iste.org/docs/ct-documents/computational-thinking-operational-definition-flyer.pdf?sfvrsn=2 [Accessed 1 August 2016].

Martin, L. (2015) The promise of the Maker Movement for education. *Journal of Pre-College Engineering Education Research (J-PEER)*, 5(1), Article 4.

Montessori, M. (1912) *The Montessori method*. New York, NY: Frederick Stokes Co.

Munro, J. (n.d.) *Insight into the creativity process: identifying and measuring creativity* [online]. Available from: https://students.education.unimelb.edu.au/selage/pub/readings/creativity/UTC_Assessing__creativity.pdf [Accessed 13 December 2013].

National Advisory Committee on Creative and Cultural Education (1999) *All our futures: Creativity, culture and education* [online]. Available from: http://sirkenrobinson.com/pdf/allourfutures.pdf [Accessed 19 July 2017].

National Research Council of the National Academies (2010) *Report of a workshop on the scope and nature of computational thinking*. Washington, DC: The National Academies Press.

OCR (2012) *Computing – J275 (from 2012)* [online]. Available from: http://www.ocr.org.uk/Images/72936-specification.pdf [Accessed 12 August 2016].

OCR (2015) *Computer Science (9–1) – J276 (from 2016)* [online]. Available from: http://www.ocr.org.uk/Images/225975-specification-accredited-gcse-computer-science-j276.pdf [Accessed 13 December 2016].

Papert, S., and Harel, I. (1991) *Situating constructionism from constructionism*. New York, NY: Ablex Publishing Corporation.

Pearson (2105) *Edexcel level 1/level 2 GCSE (9–1) in Computer Science (1CP1)* [online]. Available from: https://qualifications.pearson.com/en/qualifications/edexcel-gcses/computer-science-2016.html [Accessed 17 July 2017].

Peppler, K., Halverson, E., and Kafai, Y.B. (eds.) (2016) *Makeology: Makerspaces as learning environments* (Volume 1). London: Routledge.

Qualifications and Curriculum Authority (2004) *Creativity: find it, promote it. Promoting pupils' creative thinking and behaviour across the curriculum at key stages 1, 2 and 3*. London: Qualifications and Curriculum Authority.

Resnick, M. (2012a) Reviving Papert's dream. *Educational Technology, vol. 52, no. 4, pp. 42–46*.

Resnick, M. (2012b) Lifelong kindergarten. *Cultures of Creativity. p. 50–52*.

Resnick, M. (2013) *Teaching kids to code* [online]. Available from: https://www.edsurge.com/n/2013-05-08-learn-to-code-code-to-learn. [Accessed 1 August 2016].

Resnick, M., and Rosenbaum, E. (2013) Designing for tinkerability. *In:* M. Honey and D. Kanter (eds.), *Design, make, play: growing the next generation of STEM innovators.* London: Routledge. pp. 163–181.

Resnick R., Bruckman A., and Martin, F. (1996) Pianos not stereos: creating computational construction kits. *Interactions* 3, (5) 40–50.

Robinson, K. (2001) *All our futures: creativity, culture and education.* Sudbury: DfEE.

Savage, M., & Barnett, A. (2015) *Digital literacy for primary teachers.* St Albans: Critical Publishing.

ScratchEd (2011) *Creative computing: a design-based introduction to computational thinking* [online]. Available from: http://scratched.media.mit.edu/sites/default/files/CurriculumGuide-v20110923.pdf [Accessed 12 December 2016].

Scully, R.P. and Hind, E. (2015) *Biohacking the future.* B&T, (2813), p. 56.

Sentence, S., and Csizmadia, A. (2016) Computing in the curriculum: challenges and strategies from a teacher's perspective. *Education and information technology,* pp. 1–27.

Siemens, G. (2005) Connectivism: a learning theory for the digital age. *International Journal of Instructional Technology and Distance Learning* [online], Vol. 2 No. 1, Jan 2005. Available from: http://www.itdl.org/journal/jan_05/article01.htm accessed [15 July 2017].

Silver, J. (2013) *Hack a banana, make a keyboard!* TED Talk [online]. Available from: https://www.ted.com/talks/jay_silver_hack_a_banana_make_a_keyboard [Accessed 13 December 2016].

The College Board (2014) *AP computer science principles curriculum framework* [online]. Available from: https://secure-media.collegeboard.org/digitalServices/pdf/ap/ap-computer-science-principles-curriculum-framework.pdf [Accessed 1 August 2016].

Wilson, A. (ed.) (2009) *Creativity in primary education.* London: Learning Matters Ltd.

Wisconsin Task Force on Arts and Creativity in Education (Updated on Feb 19, 2010) *Towards a definition of creativity* [online]. Available from: http://www.education.com/reference/article/towards-definition-creativity/ [Accessed 1 August 2016].

Wing, J. (2006) *Computational thinking.* Communications of the ACM March 2006/Vol. 49, No. 3, 33–35.

Chapter 11

Bring your own device?

Paul Hynes and Sarah Younie

Bring your own device (BYOD) is a term used to describe a scheme whereby pupils bring their own devices into school to facilitate their learning. In reality, this allows pupils to bring a range of devices into school and use them to help in a variety of different ways. At the core of this is pupils (and their parents) taking responsibility for the purchase, maintenance, training, insurance and eventual replacing of the technology they use for learning both within and outside school.

A more accurate term would probably be bring your own technology (BYOT) or bring your own *devices*, as this incorporates the range of potential devices that pupils can bring into school, which can include mobile phones, smartphones, tablets, laptops, e-readers and MP3 players.

The debate for schools is whether they persist with the purchase, maintenance, replacement and disposal of school-bought technology or opt to accept the use of the pupil-bought technology to remove some of these issues. Schools also need to consider if and how classroom management and learning activities need to be developed. These are fundamental questions in the digital evolution of schools and will be critically examined in this chapter.

So why do schools opt for a BYOD scheme? Typically, a school

- may have no money available for wide-scale technology purchases, although they do believe in the power of mobile devices to help learning;
- may have uncertainty over the impact of a mobile device on learning;
- may have uncertainty over future funding that would lead to problems of creating a sustainable scheme with the current technologies in the school;
- may have uncertainty over what is the perfect device – tablet vs netbook vs. laptop, for example;
- can explore mobile learning without incurring any administration or technical support costs.

There may also be uncertainty over what future devices could be just around the corner – 'phablets' (part phone, part tablet; devices typically have a larger screen than is usually associated with a smartphone) and touchscreen ultrabooks could also become the device of choice.

With respect to BYOD, a useful first step towards the integration of learner-bought devices on a wide scale is to complete a survey that gives an overview of what devices the pupils own and what devices they already (or potentially could) bring into school. This can be a bespoke survey, perhaps designed by pupil digital leaders, or a more global survey such as the 'Your Own Technology Survey' (www.yots.org.uk).

A model scenario for open device usage

There are many different BYOD implementation strategies that may be adopted by a school. To further understand the key issues around such implementations, it may be useful to consider an example of what this looks like in practice through a model scenario.

Pupils are allowed to bring into school any device they want. If the device allows, they can connect to free, filtered wireless Internet access without the need of a password. This is a connection to the Internet and does not provide access to the school network unless it is through a web browser. This model means there are no technical or administration issues and it avoids the queue for technicians when pupils come back after the Christmas break wanting to connect their latest gadgets to the school wireless. The only downside to this approach concerns tracking of usage by individual pupils. Whilst at any point it is known what devices are connected to the network, which wireless access point they are using and what they are doing, what is not known is exactly which pupil the device belongs to. If a device should be caught accessing something inappropriate, then that device can be blocked using its unique identifier (MAC address).

The classroom use of the devices remains under the control of the teacher – they decide when and how the devices should be used. This flexibility fits comfortably with the nature of most lessons where multiple activities are employed. The device could be used solely for a five-minute starter activity, a mid-lesson progress-checking quiz or a plenary activity. The advantage of bring your own mobile technology here lies in the pedagogical flexibility it allows the teacher to deploy in ways that are most appropriate for each lesson and topic. In addition, also see Chapter 13 on the use of tablets in secondary classrooms.

What issues are there for BYOD and using mobile devices in schools?

There are a range of issues concerning mobile devices in schools, which pertain to: (1) classroom management concerning the use of devices in lessons; (2) understanding the pedagogical potential of new tools, which takes time to explore and develop for classroom implementation; (3) understanding the research and evidence base that indicates an impact on learning; and (4), justifying and defending the school's decision to move to a BYOD policy.

1. Classroom management

It takes time for teachers and learners to get used to how bring your own mobile devices can be used practically in a lesson. Some teachers make the transition easily, and phrases like 'screens down' replace the more traditional 'pens down'. Other staff find it more difficult and need to gain their confidence at their own pace. For this to happen, it is essential that the teacher is always seen as the key authority in the classroom and this position is supported by senior leaders. For some teachers, their starting point could be as simple as asking learners to take a photo of this week's homework from the whiteboard at the end of the lesson. The next key step in developing the classroom management of mobile devices is to separate behaviours from the device. A good mantra is to punish the behaviour, not the device. If a learner disobeys instructions, is not engaging or does not complete an acceptable amount of work in a lesson, then these should be effectively dealt with through appropriate sanctions. The crime is not using a mobile phone in a lesson, but rather not obeying the teacher's instructions.

2. Pedagogic potential of new devices and finding the uses that have impact

As new devices appear, so do new functions. Alongside this, new websites, software and apps are going live every day. How do schools and particularly individual subject teachers know what is out there and how to exploit it? One solution is to use a team of pupil digital leaders who have a role in investigating and trialling the potentiality of new tools and uses. These pupils can be linked to departments so they can exploit their specialist subject knowledge when evaluating new tools.

There is a range of apps for teaching with tablets; for example, see Caldwell and Bird (2015) for practical suggestions of how to devise meaningful learning activities that make the most use of apps. Below, Caldwell and Bird (2015) suggest the following tips for teaching with tablets:

- Select rather than collect: Put together a core set of content creation apps that you can reuse across topics.
- Find app smashing combos: Amplify learning by choosing apps that work well together to make and share multimodal digital artefacts.
- Make learning visible: Use online bulletin boards, whiteboard mirroring, learner response apps and polls as pit stops and respond to learning as it happens.
- Build in discovery time: Save yourself time by allowing learners to explore and demo their own tips and tricks and test apps.

Developing a pedagogic understanding of the potential affordances created through tablets and apps does take time. The time needs to be made available for teachers to examine new tools, trial them and prepare learning experiences around them.

How, then, can teachers update their knowledge regarding the uses of mobile devices for learning? This relates to continuing professional development (CPD), and we know from research (Leask and Younie, 2013) that formal CPD is patchy, underfunded and fragmented; however, exciting and emergent new forms of informal CPD are being generated by teachers. An innovative grass roots approach has evolved which utilises social media, such as Twitter, Google discussion groups and online blogs, to inform teachers of new applications concerning mobile technologies for learning. (See, for example, the Google discussion group 'Digital Evolution of Schooling' at www.digital-evolution-of-schooling@googlegroups.com or Tim Clark's blog 'BYOT Network: Transforming schools and classrooms into learning communities with personalized technology tools and digital content' at www.byotnetwork.com and Twitter @BYOTNetwork.) These are fast and effective communication channels, which inform teachers of evolving pedagogic uses, often written by teachers to share and disseminate ideas with other teachers.

3. Impact on learning and associated research evidence

Although there have been a number of research projects around previous generations of mobile devices (particularly laptops), few definitively show an improvement in attainment for learners using newer devices such as smartphones and tablets. There are some interesting examples and successful small-scale projects, but there is still a lack of a replicable model of mobile pedagogical implementation that is guaranteed to deliver results.

This is interesting given that the BESA (British Education Suppliers Association) 2015 survey reported that in the UK, around 75% of schools are using tablets for over 50% of lesson time, but finding research that substantiates that such use leads to improved learning outcomes is extremely difficult, as reported by Hennessy (2016). Similarly, Habler et al. (2015) found that research on mobile tablets was sparse with respect to identifying a replicable model for pedagogic use. Habler et al. (2015) conducted a critical, systematic review of the research literature on tablets to evaluate if, when and how using mobile devices impacts learning outcomes. Of the 103 studies examined, only 23 were found to be useful. Instead, the reviewers found that the research largely focused on motivational aspects of tablets, not learning gains, and that the majority of studies were small scale and lacked research rigour. Overall, the researchers reported that the published research to date was extremely limited and fragmented with respect to substantiating learning gains.

Although the research may be sparse in relation to mobile tablet uses to improve learning outcomes for children and young people, there is a wealth of research on other types of digital technologies that do demonstrate a positive effect in enhancing learning; see Younie and Leask (2013) for a summary of such research. This, however, raises another issue with respect to teachers engaging with research, which pertains to time and accessibility.

With respect to the limited research on tablets that does demonstrate effective outcomes, locating this research and finding the time to read it is challenging for busy classroom teachers. Academic research is not easily locatable for teachers due to a number of factors. First, educational research is published in academic journals, which are not accessible unless a teacher has access to a university library or research database, and unless teachers are registered at a university undertaking a specific program, then they are unlikely to have access. Alumni arrangements may exist in some cases, but this doesn't solve the second problem, which is that academic research papers are long, between five and eight thousand words, and very time consuming to read as reported by Jones et al. (2015).

This leads us to raise another key issue concerning teachers' access to the knowledge base of their own profession, which is to do with the timescale taken to publish academic research. The lead-in time regarding academic publication in journals is protracted and can take anywhere between one and two years for research to be published due to the time taken for peer review and the backlog of papers waiting to be published. It is not uncommon for journals to have an 18-month waiting list for publication even after reviews have taken place. This provides a very specific problem with respect to the fast-moving field of technology.

This may explain why some schools have gone ahead and purchased new devices without any research evidence to support their pedagogical use in the classroom, because that research was not yet published. Or, even if it was, it was not easily accessible, and difficult for the head teachers and senior staff to locate the research, read it and analyse it. However, it was not always thus. It used to be the case that a government agency specifically commissioned and published educational technology research in schools, which was disseminated in ways that were accessible for teachers regarding open access to the research and length, with short executive summaries of reports. This was the role and function of Becta (British Education Communications and Technology Agency), which was set up by the Labour government in 1998 and disbanded in 2010 when the coalition government came to power, and Becta was abolished during the 'burning of the quangos' in May 2010.

However, this public body arguably played an important civic service for the teaching profession by commissioning research to gather evidence on the effectiveness of digital technologies for learning, and publishing this research in digestible ways. In this sense, the knowledge base of the profession was being built and managed in a time when a proliferation of technology was entering the market and schools needed an evidence base to make decisions about purchasing such technologies. One may well ask: Where is that knowledge and advice now? With the demise of Becta as an advisory service, the space is now open to EdTech companies to market their wares directly to schools; but how are school leaders to know the difference between sales talk and proven effective pedagogical uses of such technologies? Again, there is a need for robust research into the effectiveness of technologies targeted for education use.

In terms of providing teachers with access to research on technologies, the coalition government assured the profession that all previous research undertaken for Becta was to be archived in 2010. However, should you try to use the national archive to locate publicly funded Becta research, you will most likely experience links that are broken and receive 404 errors stating that the page is no longer available. However, if this had been the physical destruction of resources that had cost taxpayers millions of pounds, given that the Becta budget for research was significant across its lifespan, then there would have been a scandal.

Arguably, if a research library was burnt down and had to be rebuilt, and it burnt down again and had to be built again, then serious questions would be asked of the government regarding the spending of public money in this way, yet with online research resources and archives this has happened. Another example is the TTRB (Teacher Training Resource Bank); again, this is archived, but many of the resources are no longer accessible – is this a silent crime? This is certainly one debate concerning educational technology research that could be more actively explored and publicly critiqued.

What the research did say with respect to tablet use, in the systematic review of the research literature conducted by Habler et al. (2015), was that of the 103 studies examined, only 16 found positive learning outcomes, five studies found that tablets made no difference and two studies reported a negative impact. The positive results were found in relation to tablets supporting learner-centred pedagogies, through utilising the user-friendly functions of tablets such as the touchscreen ease of navigation, which supported inclusion and use by SEN learners. Also, the portability and availability of multimedia information on mobile devices was found to be useful to learners. However, there were barriers to learning with tablets, too, which concerned limited curriculum content and lack of interactivity, as well as teachers reporting lack of professional development opportunities and problems with wireless connectivity in some cases (Hennessy, 2016). With respect to the debate about teachers' CPD requirements for BYOD, we are back to the debate concerning teachers' access to knowledge: how this had been previously supplied by government (Becta) and dismantled, and how now in the contemporary landscape is being filled ad hoc through social media networks.

With respect to the systematic review carried out by Habler et al. (2015), this is to be welcomed for its critical evaluation of the field and for providing an evidence base to inform teachers' practice. Habler et al. (2015) are to be commended for providing an insightful summary and analysis of the research on tablets. Not surprisingly, the reviewers concluded that more in-depth, rigorous research is required given that so few studies focused on learning outcomes. With regard to teachers reading systematic reviews, this still requires time. For busy classroom teachers, this is a challenge; however, Hennessey (2016) went one step further by summarising the key points of the research in a blog, which was significantly more accessible at only 800 words long.

Interestingly, as Jones et al. (2015, p. 555) observe, 'research alone does not inform practice, rather a process of knowledge translation is required to enable research findings to become meaningful for practitioners in their contextual settings'. To this end, teachers need access to the research, which is then translated into practice. In the field of knowledge management, this is known as translational research (see Burden et al., 2013) and is a term that is used to 'describe the movement of available research knowledge into active professional use' (Le Velle, 2015, p. 460).

A major project that is addressing the issue concerning teachers' access to knowledge and research to inform their practice is MESH (Mapping Education Specialist knowHow), which is a translational research project that provides summaries of research for teachers (see www.meshguides.org). The aim is to provide easy online access to summaries that can inform teachers' professional knowledge and enable them to support their professional judgements with evidence.

Given that Hennessy (2016, p. 1) makes the point that schools' procurement of tablet devices is based on very little evidence, and that 'purchasing rationales are extraordinarily vague', the case that access to research is more crucial than ever in guiding schools' technology adoption. One can see here how BYOD neatly sidesteps the issue of investing in mobile devices when the pedagogical advantage is yet to be guaranteed.

4. Defending the use of mobile devices

Many schools embarking on BYOD schemes find resistance and negative publicity aimed at them from parents and the local community. This is hard to combat without any tangible research to direct them towards. To counteract this, schools tend to ensure that all teachers and pupils can defend the policy and usage with real examples that have an undeniable impact on learning. It also raises the issue that the little research that has been done, which is positive (Habler et al., 2015), should be more widely publicised so that teachers can be armed with the research evidence to defend their professional decisions. In fact, the MESH tag line is exactly that: 'connecting educators with summaries and sources of educational research' (www.meshguides.org).

The MESH vision is to provide teachers with easily accessible research evidence that helps teachers justify their pedagogic choices based on informed judgement of that evidence. In the same way that the medical profession justifies its practice on research evidence, so, too, can education move to a position where this is possible. However, to realise this vision, the profession needs to establish a quality-assured knowledge base that can be accessed and interrogated by teachers and academics (see www.meshguides.org). Also, see the Education Endowment Fund (EEF at www.educationendowmentfoundation.org.uk/) and the Coalition for Evidence-Based Education (CEBE at www.cebenetwork.org/) as examples of other initiatives aimed at the development of a systematic knowledge base for education.

Issues with current tablet schemes in schools

At the time of writing, tablets are the most common device being rolled out in 1:1 schemes around UK primary and secondary schools (BESA Survey 2015). This ratio factor has an appeal, and tablets are incredibly popular as a piece of mobile technology. The enthusiasm for these devices has now been embraced by many schools. It has not all been plain sailing, however, especially for the early adopters. A series of issues have been identified that have led to the failure of many schemes, which has resulted in tablets sitting unused in cupboards. The lessons from these failings are useful for schools looking at developing mobile device use, whether it is through a BYOD scheme or a 1:1 rollout through school purchases. These issues are the lack of full functionality in tablets, the design of tablets for 'coffee table' rather than 'school desk', the tension between being able to personalise the tablet and locking down its features for consistency in the classroom, problems relating to updating, app creation, day-to-day logistics and the need for one device to fit all, saving and sharing work and strategies to deal with damage and replacement. These will be discussed in turn.

Lack of full functionality. People's definition of functionality varies, but at a base level, it can be an expectation that the tablet should do anything the previous device did. In most cases, people consider the tablet to replace an existing laptop. This leads to disappointment with certain features such as the lack of a proper keyboard, screen size, protective cases and the limited range of tools or apps available. Apps are limited by their size and their power. They do not replace the functionality of a full piece of software or powerful websites. They are also the enemy of a school trying to ensure equality of experience for learners using their own devices, as often certain applications are only available on one type of device – whether it is Android, Apple, Microsoft or Blackberry. Some people do think that apps are a fad. Apps have been marketed well to ensure they tie people into one brand of device and ultimately, people may buck against this. The majority of schools opting for BYOD put their focus on useful websites as, with the arrival of HTML5, they become more and more powerful. The web is the standard, and by focusing energies on using that as the main tool, means that any Internet-enabled device can access materials and functions whether it is a smartphone, laptop, desktop PC, tablet, gaming console or even a smart TV.

Tablet design is for coffee table not school desk. Many schools find that they are trying to shoehorn tablet technology into a role it was not designed for. The core of tablet use is for a single user to check their email, social networks, view streamed video and listen to music. The physical and operating system design is not focused at the typical learner and the type of support they need to help with their learning. Tablets may adequately cover the consumption of information through the use of video, eBooks, websites and so on, but fall short with the tools for creation (and particularly co-creation) for learning. Only recently have tools become available to allow online or app-based video editing, as an example, yet desktops and laptops have had this functionality for 20 years. Classroom usage was not the primary audience for the designers of tablets, and schools feel this as they push the devices towards uses that were not intended.

Personalisation vs. lockdown. This key debate has been happening for over 10 years with regard to the use of laptops in schools, and is still prevalent with the tablet schemes of contemporary classrooms. Most network managers would prefer devices to be school owned and locked down so pupils cannot alter software, apps, desktop background and so on. This is a valid perspective, as locking down does provide a situation that requires the least technical support time to maintain. The difficulty with this approach is that pupils do not feel ownership of the device. This frequently leads to frustration and, historically, to more damage to the devices. Schools that allow pupils to personalise their device and install their own software or apps report fewer instances of damage. Tools are arriving on the market that allow a halfway house situation, which may be a solution for some schools. These tools allow parts of the desktop/home screen to be locked whilst allowing the user some access to change themes, backgrounds, and add software.

Updating operating system software and apps. All mobile devices have regular updates pushed at them by software developers. Some have an automatic updating function, whereas others do not. If apps, in particular, are not updated, then they can be vulnerable to bugs and security issues. Many schools have found that they cannot rely on pupils to carry out the updating and so they periodically collect devices to be updated centrally. This has a large cost implication in terms of administration time, technical support time and also the loss of learning time whilst the pupil is without their device. New tools on the market, as well as developments in the operating systems of tablets, are making this process easier, but it can still cause anxiety with many network managers in schools.

App creation. One of the most exciting experiences for today's contemporary learners is when they design and create their own apps. With the revised Programme of Study for Computing (née ICT) coming into maturity, more and more schools are adding app development into their curriculum offering. As well as a useful tool for teaching programming and design principles, app generation is seen as cool and has a wow factor that engages and motivates learners. The availability and use of the app creation tools is not a problem, but the difficulty learners experience is publishing and sharing their apps once completed. In this case, iTunes' strength is also its weakness. Of all the app stores, iTunes probably has the highest quality assurance, which is a great benefit in not allowing poor quality and underdeveloped apps out on to the market. The downside for this is that many learners cannot see their finished product actually used on its intended device. This is not an issue with Android, where a learner can design and create an app before sharing it across their friends' devices.

Day-to-day logistics, and can one device fit all? A key challenge facing schools is how they support individual learner needs through the devices. With BYOD, the user selects their own device, although not with the educational functions at the forefront. The difficulty with 1:1 rollouts is that the usage is diverse.

Can one device meet the needs of a Year 13 mathematics learner as well as a Year 7 learner with literacy difficulties?

The issues of connecting tablets and other mobile devices to wireless networks are relatively straightforward, but difficulties are experienced by schools with connecting devices to displays (projectors, monitors, etc.). Again, the design of the technology does not help. There are solutions to wirelessly display a mobile device screen, but often they are designed for the home and not for different users to be connecting throughout a school day. Printing from devices is also an issue that few schools have solved to the satisfaction of the unconfident teacher.

Saving, backing up and sharing work. Mobile devices come into their own when used in conjunction with cloud storage and online applications solutions. Although reliant on reliable wireless network access, the idea of saving all your files to the cloud, trusting someone else to back the files up and then easily sharing work in a couple of clicks is desirable and easily possible. However, it is frequently the area that teachers and learners have little experience in, and often they are trying to gain that experience at the same time as learning how to use a new device. The Google Drive solution seems a favourite with schools for its ease of use, generous storage allowance and, most important, the opportunity to make key files available offline for use when outside the wireless range. However, another facet to this debate to consider concerns online ethics and ownership: how many teachers and learners have read the terms and conditions of such cloud-based storage options and fully understand who owns the IP (intellectual property) of the documents created and stored online? What ethical issues should learners be alert to concerning the saving, backing up and sharing of work online? (See Chapter 8 'Using Web 2.0 technologies to enhance learning and teaching' for further points of consideration.)

Damage and replacement. This is probably the least discussed topic when planning a 1:1 solution for learners in schools, and it is certainly not the top of suppliers' list of things to discuss with schools as they start their sales marketing pitch. The reality is a harsh one with some well-publicised examples of schools losing over a third of their devices to damage in the first year. To feel comfortable in the fact that the devices are insured is a false situation. It is a certainty that the insurance premiums for that school will rise, as will any other schools operating a similar scheme with the same insurer. The less noticeable impacts of damage include the extra administration costs and the potential loss of faith from parents, learners and teachers. The intangible cost of the loss of faith is not to be underestimated.

Such a loss of faith can be highly detrimental to school and its community. This is because schools are attempting to build a culture of digital evolution with mobile technologies and BYOD, which is built on trust; however, a loss of confidence in the devices can be damaging to the development of an emerging ecosystem. Interestingly, both Lee and Levins (2012 and 2016) and Canada's Alberta Ministry of Education (Province of Alberta, 2012) affirmed that schools have to be culturally and technologically ready to move to BYOT and be willing to embrace its underlying educational principles concerning personalised learning, and that this is an evolutionary process, with faith at its heart.

What are the funding possibilities for schools wanting to provide 1: 1 mobile devices?

Where a school does want to promote and support 1:1 provision for mobile devices, the debate to be had concerns who is responsible for buying the device and then paying for it. Does the school purchase the device and then own it, or does the school buy the device and then parents purchase it from the school? With respect to the latter option, a parental payment scheme is straightforward to organise, but many schools have had serious backlashes from parents if the scheme feels like it is not voluntary. With school-led leasing schemes, there is an extra administration burden and also a reputational responsibility that falls on the school. A supplier-led leasing scheme takes away some of this burden but does, of course, cost more, as the supplier takes on extra responsibility and accountability.

Using an e-learning foundation is one obvious solution for maximising the impact from parental contributions. With the school, parents and businesses paying into the charity, the benefits of gift aid make the scheme more cost effective. One issue that needs to be raised is the breaking of the direct link between people who pay in and direct benefit, as if this is not solved clearly, there could be issues regarding tax and gift aid that may need to be repaid.

The use of pupil premium funding to provide mobile devices for eligible pupils is an obvious solution and will become increasingly prevalent as the amount of pupil premium funding increases with time. A further solution is that the school pays itself from its own budget. This is not as crazy as it may sound at first. This removes equality issues, collection costs and so on. Schools that have done the costings of such an approach regularly cite the reduction in reprographic costs, electricity bills, desktop replacement costs and technical support, as these are areas where savings can be made and then these savings can be redeployed to fund such a scheme.

The key is getting the learning right

When moving to 1:1 provision for learners and mobile devices, the school teaching staff need confidence, comfort and ideas. There is a practical CPD issue here with regard to teachers using a device to support their classroom teaching. The confidence will come over time for all staff, but they are a diverse group and some will take longer than others. The key issue is having enough pedagogic ideas for using the devices to enhance learning. This is more difficult, as teachers do not always have the time to find, research and trial their ideas, although this is essential for teachers to be assured enough for the activities to be included in schemes of work.

One solution is for each department to come up with 10 'no-brainer' uses of mobile devices for classroom practice, which are negotiated and agreed as the way forward, and which teachers understand deliver better results and learning gains than previous traditional methods. Pupil digital leaders are a useful source of ideas and can also do much of the planning and trialling of new ideas. Simple ideas could include the following as well as the plethora of ideas shared over the Internet and social media under the banner of educational technology uses.

- Use the camera to record still images.
- Use the camera to capture video.
- Record audio notes/voice notes/podcasts.
- Browse the web.
- Listen to podcasts.
- Watch videos.
- Use QR codes to access documents, websites or audio/video content.
- Access the school's learning platform/virtual learning environment (VLE).
- Annotate a document.
- Complete a survey/quiz.
- Produce and use some online flashcards.

The key is keeping up to date with the possible pedagogic uses of mobile devices. As new tools are developed and current tools superseded, it is important that the uses continue to develop to maximise the learning. Also, see Chapter 13 on the use of tablets in secondary classrooms, which complements this chapter.

Where does this fit with e-safety?

It is a given that a school needs an acceptable use policy (AUP) that is agreed by staff, pupils, parents and governors. The best models for e-safety education use pupil leadership as a key element and are also open about the risks and dangers. It is often the case that the most inappropriate material is brought in from home on pupil mobile devices. This can be due to inadequate filtering and supervision at home but may also be as a result of filtering not being foolproof. Likewise, in any school there will be plenty of pupils with the technical know-how to bypass school web filters. That is why schools and teachers have an essential role to play in educating all learners to understand and minimise the risks involved. This can also help to prepare pupils for the workplace and understand key issues concerning digital literacy, including understanding one's own digital footprint and how to stay safe online and follow ethical work practices online. Increasingly, employers are allowing their employees to use social media during their working day – as long as the work is completed adequately then employers seem happy. It is an essential time management skill that pupils would need to develop and currently is not part of most schools, which raises the issue of how important it is to develop digital literacy skills in schools and digital citizenship.

Conclusions

With BYOD and 1:1 implementation, we need to be aware that often the focus can tend to be on the device and tools rather than on the learning. This is to do with school readiness, where the school culture (or ecology) has sufficient trust within its systems to go with BYOD. BYOD is a critical decision in a school's digital evolution (Lee and Broadie, 2015).

BYOD needs integrating into a whole school approach to technology, which has learning and pedagogical application at its heart. BYOD should not be reduced to a simple matter of technology and overcoming budget short-comings, but rather should be part of the digital evolution of schools where teacher and learner agency are seen as part of the dynamic that develops a school's digital maturity. To this end, BYOD has much to offer both learners and teachers as a way of negotiating contemporary technologies in traditional classrooms.

References

BESA (2015) 'Tablets and Connectivity' Annual Survey. London: British Education Suppliers Association.

Burden, K., Younie, S., and Leask, M. (2013) Translational research principles applied to education: the mapping of educational specialist knowhow (MESH) initiative. *Journal of Education for Teaching: International research and pedagogy,* Vol. 39, No.4, pp. 459–463.

Caldwell, H., and Bird, J. (2015) *Teaching with tablets.* London: Sage.

Clark, T. (n.d.) *BYOT Network: transforming schools and classrooms into learning communities with personalized technology tools and digital content* [online blog]. Available from: www.byotnetwork.com and Twitter @byotnetwork

Google Group 'Digital Evolution of Schooling'. BYOD discussions available from: https://groups.google.com/d/msgid/digital-evolution-of schooling/14653849574 61.37347%40cg.catholic.edu.au

Habler, B., Major, L., and Hennessy, S. (2015) Tablet use in schools: a critical review of the evidence for learning outcomes. *Journal of Computer-Assisted Learning,* 32 (2), 139–156.

Hennessy, S. (2016) *Tablets in schools: tools for learning or tantalising toys?* [online blog]. BERA (British Educational Research Association), 21 June 2016. Available from: https://www.bera.ac.uk/blog/tablets-in-schools-tools-for-learning-or-tantalising-toys [Accessed 19 July 2017].

Jones, S., Procter, R., and Younie, S. (2015) Participatory knowledge mobilization: an emerging model for translational research in education. JET *Journal of Education for Teaching,* Special Issue, Volume 41, No.5, pp. 555–574.

Leask, M., and Younie, S. (2013) National models for continuing professional development: the challenges of twenty-first-century knowledge management. *Journal of Professional Development in Education,* Vol. 39, No. 2, pp. 273–287.

Le Velle, L. (2015) Translational research and knowledge mobilisation in teacher education: towards a 'clinical', evidence-based profession? JET *Journal of Education for Teaching*, Special Issue, Volume 41, No.5, pp. 460–463.

Lee, M., and Broadie, R. (2015) *A taxonomy of school evolutionary stages* [online]. Broulee Australia. Available from: http://www.schoolevolutionarystages.net

Lee, M., and Levins, M. (2012) *Bring your own technology: the BYOT guide for schools and families*. Melbourne, Camberwell: ACER Press.

Lee, M., and Levins, M (2016) *BYOT and the digital evolution of schooling*. Armidale: Douglas and Brown. Available from: http://douglasandbrown.com/publications/

Province of Alberta (2012). *Bring your own device: a guide for schools* [online]. Available at http://education.alberta.ca/admin/technology.aspx (Accessed 19 July 2017).

Younie, S., and Leask, M. (2013) *Teaching with technologies: the essential guide*. Maidenhead: Open University Press.

Chapter 12

Technology and inclusion

Chris Shelton

Introduction

This chapter considers a number of different debates related to inclusive practice using technology, including how technology can be used to support the individual needs of pupils but also how it might contribute to excluding pupils through creating a 'digital divide' or perpetuating stereotypes.

While it is widely acknowledged that inclusion is a vital aspect of teaching, the term itself has been a subject of much debate. For example, as Fredrickson and Cline (2009) show, early discussions of inclusion focussed on the provision for pupils with special educational needs or disabilities and whether these pupils should be taught in mainstream schools or separately in specialist schools or units. However, over time, understandings of inclusion have broadened to encompass a much wider range of pupil characteristics, including, but not limited to, gender, ethnicity, first language, cultural and social differences. At the same time, the focus for teachers has moved from questions about *where* pupils should be educated to questions about *how* they should be educated and the quality of this education (e.g. Ekins and Grimes, 2009). In this context, Ainscow et al. (2006) distinguish between narrow conceptions of inclusion, for example, those that are only concerned with special educational needs or disciplinary exclusion from school, and broader understandings that see inclusion as an approach to education based on inclusive values (including equity, participation, compassion, respect of diversity and others). They suggest that inclusion is a process 'of increasing the participation of students in, and reducing their exclusion from, the curricula, cultures and communities of local schools' (p. 25). This chapter adopts this broader view and is therefore concerned with how we can ensure the inclusion of all learners.

In particular, it is concerned with how digital technologies may be used to help enable the inclusion of all pupils both when teaching computing and when using technology across the curriculum.

However, as this chapter shows, using technology can also raise challenges for inclusion; for example, does the use of technology in schools exclude pupils without access to technology at home or those who lack the skills to use it well?

The second part of the chapter looks at some of the ways that teachers have used different technologies to reduce exclusion and create a more inclusive learning environment in their schools. In particular, it discusses ways in which technology has been used to support learners with special educational needs or disabilities and the debates raised by the use of 'assistive technology'. The chapter then discusses some of the issues of diversity and prejudice raised by technology and concludes by discussing how teachers can develop an inclusive pedagogical approach to the teaching of computing.

Does technology increase inequality?

This distinction between those who can access digital technologies and those who cannot is often termed the 'digital divide'. This phrase first became popularised in the late 1990s and was particularly used to refer to the supposed 'divide' between those who had access to the internet and those who did not. Even from the start, this was a controversial issue. For some, internet access was seen as a luxury that not everyone needed: famously, US politician Michael Powell said in 2001, "I think there is a Mercedes divide. I would like to have one, but I can't afford one" (reported in Warschauer, 2004). However, as government and commercial services began to rely more heavily on the internet, by the start of the 21st century it became clear that internet access was no longer a luxury and that technology use had become "an integral element of thriving in 21st century society" (Selwyn and Facer, 2007, p. 10). In education, there were concerns that children and young people who did not have access to the internet and new technology would be unable to learn the skills needed for future employment. It was feared that, in turn, this would widen existing inequalities as disadvantaged pupils fell behind more privileged peers who could take advantage of the new opportunities offered by technology (Venezky, 2000).

Initially, responses to the digital divide focussed on how technology and internet access could be provided to those without it. However, later work acknowledged that a focus on providing equipment could only provide a short-term solution, as without continued investment this, too, would eventually become out of date and could lead to previously included groups becoming excluded from using digital technology (Seale, 2010).

Although access to the internet is now far more widespread, there are still very large differences in access. While 80% of households in the most developed countries can now access the internet, this falls to just 7% in the least developed countries (UNOHCHR, 2016). In addition, this does not mean that everyone who has access to the internet makes equal use of the opportunities afforded by this access. According to Warschauer (2004), the important issue is not the availability of computers but people's ability to make meaningful use of them.

In fact, despite the widespread access, even in the more developed countries there is strong evidence for a 'participation gap' (Jenkins et al., 2009) between the ways that children from different socio-economic and ethnic backgrounds use technology and participate in online activity. Despite developments in digital technology, this participation gap has remained consistent over time even in those places where internet access is most prevalent. According to OECD (2015):

> In countries/economies where the socio-economic gap in access to the Internet is small, the amount of time that students spend on line does not differ widely across socio-economic groups; but what students do with computers, from using e-mail to reading news on the Internet, is related to students' socio-economic background.
>
> (p. 124)

This suggests that rather than 'democratising' education by providing access for all children to worldwide resources and opportunities, access to the internet has reproduced the existing differences between socio-economic groups – while the more advantaged children have benefitted from opportunities to create and share online, less well-off children have a much more limited experience of working online. This is reflected not only in the choices that students make out of school but in the work that they are set in lessons. Research in the United States (see, for example, the review by Warschauer and Matuchniak, 2010), has demonstrated that schools with similar access to technology but catering for different socio-economic groups exhibit different learning opportunities and outcomes for pupils – children in disadvantaged schools are more likely to use computers for less challenging tasks.

Another barrier to access is the dominance of the English language on the internet (Warschauer, 2004). Although websites can be accessed internationally, the reliance on many of these on English excludes speakers of other languages. While automatic language translation of websites continues to develop quickly, it is not without limitations, particularly for an audience of children. In addition, language translation does not address cultural differences. As the UN Special Rapporteur on the right to education notes:

> Education should be tailored to the needs of students and the local context. It has been noted that massive open online courses reflect an overwhelmingly Western, Anglo- American method based on a particular academic experience, knowledge base and pedagogical approach. The vast majority of courses are offered in English, which by definition cannot be sensitive to the local values and cultures of all countries.
>
> (UNOHCHR, 2016, para. 56)

The continued presence of a participation gap and cultural divides serves as a reminder that just because internet access is more common, teachers cannot assume that their pupils are not excluded from the opportunities this access affords. It reminds us that the activities set in lessons and for homework can reinforce existing social inequalities if they are not designed to address these. In fact, schools provide a site to encourage participation from all pupils and to support less privileged pupils in starting to explore the opportunities available for them. In this way, teachers can work to attain some of the democratic ideals that early adopters of the internet hoped for by using it in ways that give children access to learning resources and opportunities that they would otherwise have been unable to encounter.

Using technology to meet pupils' individual educational needs

Although access to the internet does not automatically ensure that young people are fully included in online activities, it has been claimed that technology can help to reduce some of the barriers that hinder children from being able to engage with their education. There are many examples of technology being used to support a pupil's individual needs. For example, a range of different technologies have been used to help pupils for whom English is not their first language. Becta (2005) identified that technology offers the potential to reflect linguistic and cultural diversity in the classroom; to provide opportunities for learners to share their work; to encourage experimentation and independence; and to allow children to work at their own pace. Even for very young bilingual children, technology can provide a catalyst for talk in English for pupils working together on a game or computer activity (Brooker and Siraj-Blatchford, 2002). While with older children, Pim (2015) used immersive computer games to promote academic language and raise standards in writing amongst advanced learners of English as an additional language (EAL) who had attained a basic level of conversational proficiency but were not yet fully fluent in academic language. Another example of technology used to address a very specific individual need can be found in the Echoes project (Guldberg et al., 2010). This aimed to create a game that would help young people with autism to learn social skills, for example, how to understand non-verbal cues such as gaze. (For more details, see Lemon and Porayska-Pomsta, n.d.)

Another aspect of inclusion is the removal of barriers to learning or interaction for learners with physical needs through the use of 'assistive technology'. This term refers to "any product or service that maintains or improves the ability of individuals with disabilities or impairments to communicate, learn and live independent, fulfilling and productive lives" (BATA, 2013, p. 4). There is now a wide range of different assistive technologies that are used to support individuals with particular needs. For example, hearing aids, screen magnifiers, switches that can be controlled with different movements including eye gaze, speech synthesisers and many more are now commonly found in schools. Assistive technologies such as these have many potential benefits including enhancing the performance of functional tasks for people with cognitive disabilities (Scherer, 2005), making the curriculum more accessible for those with visual impairments (Nees and Berry, 2013) and supporting communication (McNaughton and Light, 2013).

However, although there is now extensive evidence of the benefits of assistive technologies for helping the inclusion of individuals with particular special education needs (e.g. see Florian and Hegarty, 2004), they alone are not a solution to problems of exclusion. In fact, research into the actual use of assistive technologies has shown that there are high levels of non-use with 30% of assistive technologies discarded by the user within a year (Scherer et al., 2005). Given that these are expensive technologies with seemingly proven effectiveness, it is important to consider why this happens.

An important factor to consider when trying to make sense of the non-use of assistive technologies is to consider the extent to which they actually 'include' an individual. For some users of assistive technology, the technology itself serves as a symbol and visual reminder of their difference from the others in their class or group. Nees and Berry (2013) describe the stigma attached to the use of assistive technologies in the classroom. This can appear in several different forms: other students may perceive the user of the technology as different, teachers can be intimidated by the technology and not know how to use it and in tests, peers may perceive that the use of the technology gives an unfair advantage to the user. This final issue is particularly important because such perceptions can intensify negative feelings towards those with disabilities. Another reason that assistive technologies may be abandoned is that the design of some technologies can function to minimise the user's interactions with others or create barriers to social activities (Scherer, 2005), thus the technology becomes another way in which the user feels excluded and made to stand out.

Another concern about assistive technology is that it can be used in ways that distract from tackling important underlying sources of exclusion. For some time now, schools have moved away from a process of integration, whereby an individual is supported to 'fit in' with the school environment, to one of inclusion, where the school environment, curriculum and methods are adjusted so that all can access them. This distinction between integration and inclusion is important because it recognises that need for society to include all individuals rather than put the emphasis on the individual to assimilate and change. As Light and McNaughton (2013) note, with assistive technology "there is a danger that people with complex communication needs will be forced to adapt to the demands of the technology, rather than ensuring that the technology responds to their needs, skills, and preferences" (p. 306).

This is not to say that assistive technologies do not have an important role to play in ensuring inclusion. As we saw above, there is ample evidence that using such technologies can have a transformative effect on the lives and education of children and young people. One way forward will be to ensure that assistive technologies are designed and chosen in ways that promote inclusion rather than exclusion. Foley and Ferri (2012) propose that rather than some technology being 'assistive', all technology should be designed to be inclusive and accessible for all. This is important because recent research into the use of iPads as an assistive technology suggests that they do not lead to the same stigma that was associated with some purpose-designed technologies (McNaughton and Light, 2013). However, future studies will need to consider if these are discarded less frequently than previous assistive devices.

McGhie-Richmond and de Bruin (2015) go further and suggest that there is a need to move away from focussing on how technology can support particular groups of children who cannot access classroom-learning opportunities to a focus on how technology can be used to improve the education for all pupils. Using a framework based on Universal Design for Learning, they suggest that technology can help teachers to achieve this through extending learning in three ways: through offering multiple ways to engage with subject content, through offering multiple means of representing the curriculum and multiple means of action and expression. For example, they suggest that one-to-one mobile computing allows pupils to access different approaches because they can determine their own route through the resources available according to their preference and need. Such devices may also allow access to rich multimodal resources and give pupils a range of options for presenting and sharing their work. They argue that such an approach provides a better quality of education for all pupils whether or not they have been identified as having a particular individual need.

Technology, ethnicity and representation

If teachers are going to use a range of technologies in the classroom and wish to take advantage of the opportunities afforded by technologies, such as websites and video games that were not designed for the classroom, then they need to select their technology carefully. In order to ensure that schools and classrooms are inclusive, teachers need to ensure that the websites and computer software they use are inclusive. However, this alone is not sufficient as students will frequently experience biased and prejudiced material outside of school, and when using digital technology, there is an opportunity to point out where inequalities persist outside the classroom.

One important aspect of the use of technology for learning is to ensure that pupils learn to be safe online. This, too, is an issue of inclusion: the EU Kids Online project found that pupils from homes with lower socio-economic status were less empowered to cope with online risk and more likely to be upset by online content or messages than more privileged children (Livingstone et al., 2011). While school internet connections should be filtered to block out the most blatant and offensive examples of online prejudice, pupils may access biased and discriminatory materials out of school. This can include racist or homophobic websites, sites that promote violence or encourage prejudice on the basis of religion or other characteristics (e.g. Islamophobic websites). While students should not access such sites at school, pupils do need to be taught the skills to read information on the internet critically, to identify bias and to report offensive materials online.

Another area where pupils may encounter racist and sexist portrayals of different groups is through computer games. While there is evidence that computer games can be used very productively in the classroom, outside of school, pupils may play games that encourage or reinforce negative stereotypes.

For example, Alexander (2007) notes that computer games can often be sexist and hetero-sexist. In discussing the game Neverwinter Nights, Alexander describes how homophobic language was accepted by many players but also how some players attempted to 'queer up' the game in response to the restrictions imposed on them.

Racist representations are also common in computer games. Blackmon (2007) analysed how computer games represented different groups, for example, the negative portrayal of females, black and Jewish characters in Grand Theft Auto or the ways in which players were limited to certain hairstyles and certain skin tones in Sims 2. She suggests that racist representations in games have become more negative as computer games have developed and compares her childhood experience of playing a black character in a boxing game to the negative, racist portrayal of a black boxer in more recent games. Blackmon comments that it disturbed her that the young black boys playing the game appeared not to notice this negative representation, but on asking them, she discovered that they believed these images to represent popular (white) opinion: "What every white man thinks of every black man who wasn't raised in a white neighbourhood. That's just what the game is" (p. 207).

Blackmon concludes that "the representations that populate video games are telling of the ways that game developers see women and minorities" (2007, p. 212). But Blackmon suggests that these representations give teachers an opportunity to challenge racist attitudes: "This is our teachable moment. This is the place at which we can meet our students to talk about race, rhetoric and representation" (p. 214).

According to Egenfeldt-Neilsen, the "problem of representation" can be both a strength and a weakness of games. If computer games are used for educational purposes, then a "game representation may miss important aspects of a topic or misrepresent aspects . . . This can ultimately lead to students learning the wrong things if they are not capable of seeing that a representation is skewed" (Egenfeldt-Neilsen 2007, p. 187). However, Squire (2011) argues that for educational purposes the bias in computer games is their 'biggest strength'. Squire discusses teaching history through the computer game, Civilisation. He used the examples of bias and historical inaccuracies that he and his pupils found in the game as opportunities to discuss where the game and reality differ. Similarly, obvious misrepresentations can raise questions about the reliability of other aspects of the game and encourage pupils to take a more critical approach.

The examples of bias in computer games and on websites are two examples of how pupils might encounter stereotypes and negative representation when using technology. These examples demonstrate the need for teachers to choose the online resources that they use carefully in order to present a positive and diverse image of society. While teachers cannot control pupils' access to biased material outside of school, they can help to prepare students to identify, critique and report such materials, and this should be a key aspect of the schools' curriculum for computing and digital literacy.

Developing inclusive pedagogies for computing

While each of the issues discussed in this chapter has implications across the school curriculum, we must also consider how teachers can promote an inclusive approach to teaching the subject of computing. In line with the issues discussed above, inclusive computing teaching should meet the needs of all learners, promote participation and provide opportunities to celebrate diversity and tackle prejudice. Computing lessons provide a clear opportunity to ensure that pupils are prepared for and have opportunities to participate in online activities and to help to overcome the participation gap.

While it is widely acknowledged that there is a need to attract a more diverse workforce into the computing sector and that this needs to start at school, many efforts have focussed on extra-curricular activities such as after-school clubs for under-represented groups. However, as Kafai and Burke (2014) point out, extra-curricular activities compete with pupils' other interests and will never reach all the pupils who may benefit from them. Therefore, schools have a vital role to play in ensuring all pupils have a positive and inclusive experience of computing and have the chance to encounter role models who can inspire them and remove barriers to achievement. Initiatives such as Black Girls Code, Google RISE or CAS #include provide advice and resources to help promote positive role models and to encourage diversity.

Teachers of computing also need to consider how they will support the wide range of levels of attainment typically found amongst pupils in a computing class. In designing lessons, Florian (2015) proposes an "inclusive pedagogical approach" as an alternative to forms of individualised and differentiated teaching that aims to remove the unintended negative effects of singling out pupils for interventions. In Florian's approach, individual differences between learners are seen as something to be expected, and the focus moves from providing activities that work for *most* pupils and allows additional interventions for *some* who cannot access these to rich learning opportunities that can be accessed by *all*. She describes this as a shift in thinking from 'most and some' to 'all'.

In computing, Shelton (2016) provides an example of how this can be achieved when teaching programming through setting a range of different learning challenges using Scratch. The 'studio' feature of Scratch allows teachers to group together sets of Scratch projects for pupils to access and remix. If these projects are carefully designed to demonstrate progression in the aspect of computing being taught, then children can themselves select the task that is at the most appropriate level for them. This allows all pupils to work at a suitably challenging level but without the 'most/some' distinction noted by Florian.

A focus on participation in computing also leads to a broadening of the aims and objectives of the Computing curriculum. Kafai and Burke (2014) propose that teachers of computing focus on 'computational participation', which expands the concept of computational thinking that is central to many computing curricula to include personal expression and social participation. Computational participation is "the ability to solve problems with others, design systems for and with others, and draw on computer science concepts, practices and perspectives to understand the cultural and social nature of human behavior" (Kafai and Burke, 2014). By thinking about the achievement of their pupils in terms of computational participation, teachers can focus on the differences between who is or is not participating and how they might be encouraged to do so.

Conclusion

This chapter has considered some of the key issues and debates in inclusive computing and ICT education. A recent United Nations report stated that "Technology in education provides important benefits but it can also impair the right to education" (UNOHCHR, 2016) and this chapter has shown that technology has the potential to be used in ways that reinforce existing inequalities or in ways that challenge inequality and provide fairer opportunities for groups and individuals. As the examples above have shown, it is not enough just to consider the devices or software being used or to take an approach that focusses on the technology itself. Teachers need to think carefully about *how* technology is used so that they can make choices about technology that promote inclusion and reduce exclusion. An inclusive classroom is one where technology is used to enable learning and participation for all pupils. It is also a classroom that recognises how digital technologies represent groups and individuals in a diverse society and equip pupils to identify and challenge these representations. In doing this, teachers can begin to use technology as a tool for inclusion.

References

Ainscow, M., Booth, T., & Dyson, A. (2006) *Improving schools, developing inclusion.* London: Routledge.

Alexander, J., with McCoy, M., and Velez, C. (2007) A real effect on the gameplay: computer gaming, sexuality and literacy. *In:* G.E. Hawisher and C.L. Selfe (eds.), *Gaming lives in the twenty-first century: Literate connections.* London: Palgrave Macmillan.

BATA (2013) Assistive technology in the UK – baseline review 2013. British Assistive Technology Association.

Becta (2005) *Using ICT to support students who have English as an additional language: guide for EMA coordinators and teachers* [online]. Available from: http://www.naldic. org.uk/Resources/NALDIC/Teaching%20and%20Learning/Documents/EAL DocumentGuideforEMAGCoordinators.pdf

Blackmon, S., with Terrell, D. (2007) Racing toward representation: an understanding of racial representation in video games. *In:* G.E. Hawisher and C.L. Selfe (eds.), *Gaming lives in the twenty-first century: Literate connections.* London: Palgrave Macmillan.

Brooker, L., and Siraj-Blatchford, J. (2002) Click on miaow!: how children of three and four years experience the nursery computer. *Contemporary Issues in Early Childhood,* 3(2), 251–273.

Egenfeldt-Nielsen, S. (2007) *Educational potential of computer games.* London: Continuum.

Ekins, A., and Grimes, P. (2009) *Inclusion: developing an effective whole school approach.* Maidenhead: Open University Press.

Florian, L. (2015) Conceptualising inclusive pedagogy: the inclusive pedagogical approach in action. *In:* J. Deppeler, T. Loreman, R. Smith, and L. Florian L. (eds.) *Inclusive pedagogy across the curriculum (international perspectives on inclusive education, volume 7).* Bingley: Emerald Group Publishing Limited, pp.211–234.

Florian, L., and Hegarty, J. (2004) *ICT and special educational needs: a tool for inclusion.* London: McGraw-Hill Education.

Foley, A., and Ferri, B.A. (2012) Technology for people, not disabilities: ensuring access and inclusion. *Journal of Research in Special Educational Needs,* 12 (4), 192–200.

Frederickson, N., and Cline, T. (2009) *Special educational needs, inclusion and diversity. 2nd Edition.* Maidenhead: Open University Press.

Guldberg, K., Porayska-Pomsta, K., Good, J., and Keay-Bright, W. (2010) ECHOES II: the creation of a technology- enhanced learning environment for typically developing children and children on the autism spectrum, *Journal of Assistive Technologies,* 4 (1), 49–53.

Jenkins, H., et al. (2009) *Confronting the challenges of participatory culture: Media education for the 21st century.* Boston: MIT Press.

Kafai, Y. B., and Burke, Q. (2014) Connected code: Why children need to learn programming. Boston: MIT Press.

Lemon, O., and Porayska-Pomsta, K. (n.d) *Echoes* [online]. Available from: http://echoes2. org [Accessed July 2016].

Light, J., and McNaughton, D. (2013) Putting people first: re-thinking the role of technology in augmentative and alternative communication intervention. *Augmentative and Alternative Communication,* 29:4, 299–309.

Livingstone, S., Haddon, L., Görzig, A., and Ólafsson, K. (2011) *Risks and safety on the internet: The perspective of European children. Full Findings.* LSE, London: EU Kids Online.

McGhie-Richmond, D. R., and de Bruin, C. (2015) Tablets, tweets and talking text: the role of technology in inclusive pedagogy. *In:* J. Deppeler, T. Loreman, R. Smith, L. Florian (eds.) *Inclusive pedagogy across the curriculum (international perspectives on inclusive education, volume 7).* Bingley: Emerald Group Publishing Limited, pp. 211–234.

McNaughton, D., and Light, J. (2013) The iPad and mobile technology revolution: Benefits and challenges for individuals who require augmentative and alternative communication. *Augmentative and Alternative Communication,* 29(2), 107–116.

Nees, M.A., and Berry, L.F. (2013) Audio assistive technology and accommodations for students with visual impairments: Potentials and problems for delivering curricula and educational assessments. *Performance Enhancement & Health,* 2(3), 101–109.

OECD (2015) *Students, computers and learning: making the connection* [online]. Paris: OECD Publishing. DOI: 10.1787/9789264239555-en

Pim, C. (2015) *Developing the writing of advanced EAL learners through the use of 3D immersive adventure games.* British Council.

Seale, J. (2010) *Digital inclusion: a research briefing by the technology-enhanced learning phase of the Teaching and Learning Research Programme* [online]. London: London Knowledge Lab. Available from: http://www.tlrp.org/docs/DigitalInclusion.pdf

Scherer, M.J. (2005) Assessing the benefits of using assistive technologies and other supports for thinking, remembering and learning. *Disability and Rehabilitation,* 27(13): 731–739.

Scherer, M.J., et al. (2005) Predictors of assistive technology use: the importance of personal and psychosocial factors. *Disability and Rehabilitation*, 27(21), 1321–1331.

Selwyn, N., and Facer, K. (2007) *Beyond the digital divide: Rethinking digital inclusion for the 21st century*. Bristol: Futurelab.

Shelton, C. (2016) 'Beyond lesson recipes: first steps towards a repertoire for teaching primary computing' In *Proceedings of Constructionism 2016*, Bangkok.

Squire K. (2011) *Video games and learning: teaching and participatory culture in the digital age*. New York, NY: Teachers College Press.

UNOHCHR (2016) *Report of the Special Rapporteur on the right to education – issues and challenges to the right to education in the digital age* [online]. Human Rights Council, United Nations General Assembly. Retrieved from: http://ap.ohchr.org/documents/dpage_e.aspx?si=A/HRC/32/37

Venezky, R. (2000) The digital divide within formal school education: causes and consequences. *In: Learning to bridge the digital divide* [online]. Paris: OECD Publishing. Available from: DOI: 10.1787/9789264187764-en

Warschauer, M. (2004) *Technology and social inclusion: Rethinking the digital divide*. Cambridge: MIT press.

Warschauer, M., and Matuchniak, T. (2010) New technology and digital worlds: Analyzing evidence of equity in access, use, and outcomes. *Review of Research in Education*, 34(1), 179–225.

Part III

Classroom applications

Debates in the use of tablets in secondary classrooms

Jon Audain, Emma Goto and Tim Dalton

> The students of the future will demand the learning support that is appropriate for their situation or context. Nothing more. Nothing less. And they want it at the moment the need arises. Not sooner. Not later. Mobiles will be a key technology to provide that learning support.
>
> (Specht, 2009)

The use of mobile devices and tablet technology is becoming ubiquitous and, for better or worse, becoming wedded to modern life, whereby communicating, connecting and collaboration are all changing. Many of us now expect 24/7 access, and current approaches to teaching and learning are challenged when placed into the hands of learners. By its interactive and tactile nature, tablet technology has the potential to have an effect on the user when placed in their hands. Gardner and Davis (2013:3) comment that in a range of subtle and sometimes blatant ways, the use of technology is reconfiguring three aspects of life for us as a species: "our sense of personal identity, our intimate relationships to other persons, and how we exercise our creative and imaginative powers". It is within this culture that schools now find themselves under pressure to embed technology into the fabric of the classroom. However, with the speed at which technology changes, this can be problematic. This debate will consider whether these tablet technologies will, by virtue of their mobility, make a positive difference to our learners.

Heppell argues that, "the pace of change lays down some significant challenges to traditional systems, and to our wonderful generations of teachers" as well as reminding us that our children, "only get one chance at their childhoods, one chance for the joy of learning to take root firmly enough to last them a lifetime" (Heppell, 2014:vi). With this in mind, should secondary schools encourage their use of mobile technology rather than lock or block these devices? The process of using mobile tablets in a secondary school setting can be fraught with issues and debates about their use in the classroom, how they support learning and often the operational debates surrounding the daily maintenance and systems.

The chapter will explore the debates concerning:

- How does the use of mobile technology change the nature of learning in the classroom?
- What are the different implementation approaches to consider when contemplating a deployment of tablets?
- How is the implementation of tablet technology to be managed?

Tablets and PDA-type handheld devices have been used in schools for many years, but until recently, their use has not been widespread. Twining et al. (2005) recognised that early tablet computers could increase ICT use and improve the integration of ICT across the wider curriculum. However, these devices were costly and take up was minimal. Then in 2010, Apple introduced the iPad. This was a new type of device with a multi-touch interface that came running a mobile OS with a rapidly evolving app store to provide a range of mobile applications, more commonly known as 'apps', that could be used to personalise the device to the user's needs (Clark and Luckin, 2013). The iPad sold prolifically, with Windows, Google, Amazon and many more producing alternative tablets to compete within a growing and competitive market.

This has led to rapid uptake of this kind of technology in schools. Apple reported in February 2013 that they had sold more than eight million iPads to education customers (Etherington, 2013), and BESA (2013) forecasted that by the end of 2015, there will be 370,000 tablets in secondary schools in the UK. However, research on the benefits of this technology, whilst growing, is still limited. Whilst some may hail this technology as the new future of education, others might debate whether this is little more than an expensive distraction. There have been large procurements of tablet technology with some proclamations of great success, alongside a few well-publicised failures (Murphy, 2014). Do we have the evidence base required to justify the vast expenditure in schools in the UK and around the world?

How does the use of mobile technologies change the nature of learning in the classroom?

Whilst one could focus on the technology and its use, the insightful question is whether it will strengthen the learning. Beauchamp and Hillier (2014) remind us that when choosing whether to use a tablet within an educational context, the key consideration is how well the use of mobile technology helps learners to achieve the learning outcome at the appropriate time and place.

Engaging with the school's learning culture. There may also need to be a change in terms of learning culture. For example, Twining (2014) reports that pupils were often supporting teachers in their use of technology, where schools were using iPads. The traditional model where the teacher is the expert to impart knowledge and the pupil is there to learn is being challenged with an approach that is more akin to a learning community. The use of tablet technology can be organised to strengthen the links between formal and informal learning, allowing learners to influence the ways they are taught. Beauchamp and Hillier (2014) and Burden et al. (2012) also report a similar change in culture, with the teacher's role often becoming more about facilitation, with learners taking more of a lead and pupils and teachers working in a more collaborative way. In terms of learning how to use the technology, Heinrich (2012) also reports positive feedback to the introduction of iLeaders (expert pupils) to provide support and advice. This approach ensures pupils can learn from each other.

Creation versus consumption. The ability to create content rather than just to consume content is seen as a key pedagogical strength of tablet technology (Cochrane et al., 2013; Caldwell, 2015). However, many of the reported uses of tablets are about being able to access information. Often the practice which is observed involves the use of the Internet for research: the use of YouTube or apps so specific to subject matter that their use is limited to an individual lesson or short sequence of lessons. If an implementation of tablets is to gain momentum and success, then it is important to explore different ways to use the devices incorporating and playing to their strengths. There is a range of apps that could be seen as more powerful because of its ability to support knowledge creation and its organisation and presentation across the wider curriculum. Screencasting apps, mind mapping apps, video editing apps and podcasting apps are all examples of software with a wider curriculum application. Therefore, are schools really using tablets to their full creative potential?

There are considerations about what can actually be created easily on a tablet, as they are more appropriate for some tasks than others are. It may be simple to take a photograph or capture video using a tablet, although other tasks, for example writing, can be a challenge with such technology. The lack of a keyboard means that touch-typing is difficult and a relatively small screen size means navigation of text can be more cumbersome than on a desktop computer.

Tablet technology and assessment. Tablet technology can be used to capture learning (Grantham, 2015) and can support learners in assessing their work in various ways: the art pupils developing a portfolio of photographs of their work, the English pupils writing blogs for purpose and the PE pupils using film and apps to improve performance and form in sport. However, whilst our approaches to teaching and learning with technology may be changing in the UK to become more creative and learner centred, we are still wedded to an examination system that tests learners' ability to remember facts and write about them using pen and paper in a timed activity. Heinrich (2012) shared one parent's comment about how their child's handwriting had deteriorated since starting to use the iPad, and the teachers and parents were worried about the impact of this in examinations. The key debate, then, is do we have the flexibility to really conduct assessment differently in the 21st century?

Engagement versus distraction. Learner engagement is widely reported as one of the benefits of tablet technologies (Alberta Education, 2011; Heinrich, 2012; Beauchamp and Hillier, 2014; Benham et al. 2014). For example, Friedman and Garcia (2013) discuss how an iPad app provided multimedia content that brought to life primary sources in history lessons focused on the events of 11 September 2001 in New York. They found learners who were able to hear the voices of survivors in this way were more interested in the lesson than those who read transcripts of the survivors' accounts. However, an equally wide number of sources assert that a key challenge for educators is the potential distraction that tablet technology can provide (Sheppard, 2011; Karsenti and Fievez, 2013; Beland and Murphy, 2015). Furthermore, many question whether any increase in student engagement will stand the test of time or whether it is due to novelty, as there is still a limited amount of research and the technology is still relatively new (Friedman and Garcia, 2013). Is there a place for technology to draw the learner in, or will it distance them further?

Access to resources where the learning is happening. The mobile nature of this technology which promotes instant engagement by allowing access to learning tools where they are needed is reported as a benefit of tablets (Melhuish and Falloon, 2010; Heinrich, 2012). Certainly in a one-to-one setup (see Figure 13.1 – Definitions of different whole school approaches) such as that described by Heinrich (2012), there will be a far greater number of devices to connect to the

---

Department/Roaming sets of tablets

Class sets or a smaller number of devices are purchased. These sets are available for staff to borrow to use within lessons or curriculum projects. Alternatively, sets are purchased to support departments, or for a specific role i.e. the ability to collect data in science or the ability to paint and draw digitally.

One-to-one Provision

Students have their own personal use of a device for their learning. The school usually specifies the device, which may be purchased by the school or with parental contributions. This approach ensures uniformity of devices, making maintenance, upgrading and staff training easier.

Bring Your Own (BYO) Approaches - Bring Your Own Device (BYOD) / Bring Your Own Technology (BYOT)

Bring your own approaches allow students to make use of the technology they may well already own. They can usually bring a wide variety of different devices, such as, mobile computers, tablets or mobile phones. The devices can be connected to the school network, but usually this involves a pre-registration of some sort so users can be identified on the network. The students are then able to browse the Internet with the restrictions normally applied by the school Internet filters. Pre-defined lists of apps could also be provided, although often these deployments rely more on cloud-based software.

Pick and mix combinations – Banks + One-to-one + BYO

These methods allow schools to slowly scale up the implementation of tablets and technology. Schools with smaller budgets may adopt this approach as it allows schools to scale up provision as budget allows. This approach often means that implementation is slow and sporadic or diluted as everyone is doing different things.

Figure 13.1 Definitions of different whole school approaches

Internet than in a traditional ICT suite set up where teachers will be dependent on access to the Internet via sets of laptops or desktop machines. This can, in the right culture, lead to greater integration of ICT across the curriculum. Burden et al. (2012) identified that an increased number of tablet devices with access to the Internet changed the classroom dynamic increasing the diversity of learning activities. However, we should not forget that one-to-one set ups could be based around any type of technology. Would schools with one-to-one access to laptops or learners using their phones not report the same benefits? Or would the tablet, with its greater portability, still show advantages over even the lightest laptop computer?

Home access: issues of inclusion. When there is a one-to-one approach, this is likely to facilitate home access. This can enable teachers to set homework to be completed via the tablet. Heinrich (2012) found this to be the case, although a small, but significant, set of teachers were not yet setting homework in this way. In this school, the take up of the one-to-one scheme was dependent on parents' leasing an iPad. Whilst there was a high proportion who bought into the scheme, there was not 100% uptake. This could be a barrier to teachers setting homework to be completed electronically using the iPads. If not all learners have access to tablets, alternative homework will be necessary. Furthermore, if households do not have Wi-Fi this will further limit what can be achieved at home. Would a more powerful approach be to set homework that can be presented in a range of different ways to match the interests of the learner? That would allow those learners with a preference to use tablets to create and present learning to do so.

Impact on progress and achievement. McFarlane (2015) makes tentative claims about a link between frequent use of mobile devices and positive academic attainment. Heinrich (2012) finds limited evidence of teachers believing learners are making better progress when using iPads, and little or no evidence that teachers believe the one-to-one deployment of iPads has increased achievement. However, Beland and Murphy (2015) find that where learners are allowed access to mobile phones within school, there is a negative impact on learner achievement particularly for low-attaining pupils. Whilst we need to be cautious about drawing parallels between the use of mobile phones and tablet technology within schools, the implications of this study seem to warrant careful consideration. Impact on progress and achievement still remains an area where significantly more research is needed.

It could be argued that the use of tablets does change the nature of the classroom environment by its physical introduction. Evidence from the classroom describes learners as more aware of how to navigate technology as well as produce content for a given purpose. Respecting their use of technology promotes a trusting collaboration in the same way that they value the teacher's knowledge and passion for their curriculum subject. There are case studies (Apple, 2015; Galloway and McTaggart, 2015) of successful schools that have implemented mobile technology. Many of the more successful schools appear to start with a strong reputation for use of technology in the classroom, or they have made the decision to make large whole school changes with the support from all stakeholders. This isn't to say that other schools wouldn't be able to transition to one-to-one provision, merely that significant preparatory work may need to be undertaken.

What are the keys for decision-making for school leaders?

The process of large adoption is complex, involving decisions pre-, during and post-adoption of the equipment itself. Therefore, implementing tablet technology requires careful consideration. One can draw a comparison to the uptake of interactive whiteboards in schools. These are seen in classrooms across the country, but how well embedded into practice are they? How often are they used as a medium to facilitate interactivity and dialogue with learners? Do lessons need to be learnt from the ancestry of this adoption? Should a school 'jump on the bandwagon', or is this just hype and due to come to an end?

Fenn and Raskino (2008) indicate that the take up of technology often follows a set pattern. A product is launched and marketed with great promises of the impact this new gadget will have. This creates an initial interest, with a sharp peak of sales and use. However, there is typically then a dramatic drop in sales as the item fails to live up to the hype. As early adopters start to uncover the real benefits of the technology and share their findings more widely, sales will rise again and eventually plateau. This commercial model may also be mirrored in educational settings as the research suggests (Younie and Leask, 2013). Applications of this model to school technology integration were explored by Younie (2007), whose longitudinal research demonstrated that teachers' adoption of technology followed a pattern that had been identified earlier by Rogers' (1983) models of innovation. In addition, Younie (2007) found that levels of integration were higher where teachers were part of a community of practice with other colleagues who engaged in pedagogical debates about the affordances of the technology. Where teachers and departments generated new knowledge about how technology supported subject pedagogies, there were greater levels of embedded use.

For tablets, as with other technology, perhaps there is a case for waiting and learning from the lessons of others. As the technology becomes more fully understood, we can reflect on where other schools found the benefits to be and consider how well these benefits match to our needs. However, if everyone waits we are unlikely to learn anything new and education practice will always stand still. Innovators and early adopters (Rogers, 1983) are essential in order to see new ways teaching and learning can develop.

The implementation of a mobile tablet solution takes cautious consideration, decision-making and a whole school drive that is rooted in the belief of the difference tablets will make in the school and the students' learning. School leaders, governors, parent groups, students and teachers must be involved to gain the thoughts and opinions of all stakeholders, although it should be noted that there is a delicate balance to strike through the consultation process, as people may have views based on personal knowledge of the devices but may find it much more difficult to envisage what use will be like on a daily basis across a school and for classroom practice. Leaders must be prepared to justify their decisions on needs within the school and evidence from consultation. Deciding to implement tablet technology is no quick process and often takes longer than anticipated. Everyone in the school community is likely to need the opportunity to settle, reflect, adjust and be supported in the decision to implement a tablet solution. It is important to identify success criteria for the project in these early stages. Galloway and McTaggart (2015) remind us of the need to go back to these original requirements later on in order to evaluate the impact of the implementation. What was the aim when introducing the tablets? Has the aim been met?

Several different models of implementation are observed across schools, with different models suiting different contexts and settings:

- Department/roaming sets of tablets;
- One-to-one provision;
- Bring your own device (BYOD)/bring your own technology (BYOT);
- Pick and mix combinations: banks + one-to-one + BYOD.

Department/roaming sets of tablets. Class sets or a smaller number of devices are purchased. These sets are available for teachers to borrow to use within lessons or curriculum projects. Alternatively, sets are purchased to support departments or for a specific role, that is, the ability to collect data in science or the ability to paint and draw digitally.

Devices have to be set up for a standard user. Therefore, they are more difficult to personalise to the user's needs and approach to learning. Burden et al. (2012) found that students' ownership of the devices and ability to personalise were crucial for tablet technology to be effectively used in schools.

One of the problems you are likely to face if you try to introduce tablet technology into a secondary school is that this technology is generally designed for the individual (Crichton et al. 2012). Consideration has to be given to how the students will manage their data. If, for instance, they are working on a project over several lessons, where will they store their files at the end of each lesson? Transferring data from one device to another can be difficult, as when working within certain apps it simply is not possible to export data until a project has been completed. In a study of the use of iPads for reading with 11 to 13 year olds, Sheppard (2011) reports having encountered many issues with running a group of iPads; these included problems with synchronising and charging the iPads. There are companies now who will offer charging and synchronising solutions, although these may not solve all problems. Clearly, there are cost savings to be had with reduced sets of tablets; however, does this warrant the sacrifice of personalisation this approach is likely to entail?

One-to-one provision. An increasing number of schools are providing one-to-one access to tablets or computers. Some of these schools provide the technology for the children, whereas others encourage parents to buy devices through the school (Twining, 2014). The school usually specifies the device, which may be purchased by the school or with parental contributions. This approach ensures uniformity of devices, making maintenance, upgrading and staff training easier. One-to-one access to tablet technology reflects more closely the way the technology is currently designed to be used. This helps to overcome some of the technical issues such as devices being set up to use a single email account or being linked to an individual account in an app store. One-to-one provision clearly also allows devices to be personalised to reflect the learning needs of the individual user (Alberta Education, 2011). However, having one device per pupil creates a significant cost to either schools or families. Is it likely that these devices will be used widely enough to warrant such outlay, and how would we start to quantify the cost of academic gain?

Bring your own device (BYOD)/bring your own technology (BYOT).
'Bring your own' approaches allow learners to make use of the technology they may well already own. They can usually bring a wide variety of different devices, such as mobile computers, tablets or mobile phones. The devices can be connected to the school network, but usually this involves a pre-registration of some sort so users can be identified on the network. The learners are then able to browse the Internet with the restrictions normally applied by the school Internet filters. Pre-defined lists of apps could also be provided, although often these deployments rely more on cloud-based software.

Ofsted (2011) reports that by the end of their survey in 2011, a small number of schools were allowing children to bring their own devices in to school to learn with.

> This was seen as a more sustainable strategy for the longer term which would reduce the pressure on school budgets while also fostering the engagement of pupils and their parents in learning at school and at home.
>
> (Ofsted, 2011:46)

In order to enhance access and equity, ETAG – the Education Technology Action Group (2015) – urges schools to develop their digital technology strategies to include bring your own (BYO) approaches to technology. BESA (2013) reports a strong shift towards schools supporting learners bringing in their own technology, stating that only 19% of secondary schools who responded to their research would not consider this option.

When learners are bringing their own technology, there is likely to be some diversity. Some may bring tablet technology, others may bring computers but for many this will mean using their smartphone. However, this raises the debate as to how equitable BYO approaches. Are we strengthening the digital divide by creating a system where those that can afford their own technology are advantaged over those that cannot? If schools are to adopt these approaches, it seems crucial that they find strategies to ensure access for all.

Some see BYOD approaches as more flexible and therefore more likely to match the wants and needs of the individual user (Freedman, 2012). However, whilst some see this personalisation as a benefit, others warn of the potential pitfalls of this more divergent approach. Traxler (2010) warns that providing teaching materials in a variety of formats, which are accessible to all, may become problematic in an environment where students are allowed to access learning on an endless range of devices.

Where schools are taking a BYOD approach, they may become less involved in any technical support, with users being responsible for managing their technology (Twining, 2014). However, if learners are having technical issues with their device, how effectively will they be able to use them for their learning? Can we be sure that just because the learners have them, the devices will be working? This issue is discussed further in Chapter 11 by Hynes and Younie.

Pick and mix combinations – banks + one-to-one + BYOD. These methods allow schools to slowly scale up the implementation of tablet technology. Schools with smaller budgets may adopt this approach as it allows schools to scale up provision as budget allows. This approach often means that implementation is slow and sporadic or diluted, as it increases the likelihood of people doing different things.

Budget considerations

Investment in technology is expensive, especially on an enterprise scale. The implementation of tablets in a secondary school is a major investment, possibly with the same parity as a new school building. It can be agreed that the largest spend of implementing a tablet solution is at the beginning, whilst equipment and infrastructure are purchased and staff undergo initial training. However, there are often significant on-going costs to ensure that the infrastructure is up to date, broken tablets are replaced, old stock replaced, software apps purchased and staff training levels maintained. However, there may also be some savings in the long term, such as purchasing textbooks and technical support, as well as reduced expenditure on one-to-one support (Apple, 2015; Galloway and McTaggart, 2015). See Chapter 11 on BYOD.

Other aspects that need to be considered in the deployment of tablets.

Network infrastructure. In order to introduce or extend the use of tablet technology within a school, the network infrastructure needs to be of sufficient quality to cope with any increase in the number of devices. This will often require the wireless network to be updated (Twining, 2014). Schools should also consider their Internet connection. Sheppard (2011) undertook a research project using iPads, and after the project had begun, found that the school's infrastructure was not of a sufficient standard to allow a full class set of iPads to connect to the Internet at the same time. Similarly, Heinrich (2012) reported that one common complaint was due to occasional problems with connecting to the Internet because of poor network coverage. Upgrading the infrastructure may not be a popular choice of expenditure; after all, some may view money spent on something they cannot see, such as improved wireless access, as less desirable than expenditure on more devices. However, if a school fails to address these issues at the outset, how likely are they to bring about change in practice and embed this technology? Imagine the frustration for a teacher who is not confident with technology when they brave using tablet technology in a lesson, only to have the technology fail them at the first hurdle. How likely is it that they will brave using the technology when planning a similar lesson in the future?

Day-to-day management. Lai (2012) claims that two common reasons as to why the deployment of tablet technology can fail are damage and theft. Certainly, the portability of these devices could increase the risk of them being dropped or stolen. Therefore, can schools afford to cut costs in terms of protective cases and secure physical storage solutions?

One-to-one and BYOD approaches are dependent on students charging their own devices. Heinrich (2012) reported some issues with students failing to do this or running down the batteries at lunchtimes playing games. How will the school ensure students turn up with their device ready to learn? Will there be sanctions for students who fail to do this?

Careful consideration also needs to be given to who is responsible for content on the devices. Traditionally, backup of school-owned devices has been the responsibility of the school, but the move to BYOD or one-to-one may shift that responsibility to the user. In light of this, will schools need to update guidance and training? Even after you have provided for access of tablet technology, there will be a range of issues regarding the day-to-day management and upkeep of the devices. Galloway and McTaggart (2015) stress the need to consider technical management. For example, who will be in charge of deploying apps? Is this something that will be done by technicians, support staff, teachers or students? If a student device needs to be handed in for repair, is a replacement available?

It is vital that consideration is given to these basic issues around the day-to-day maintenance of the devices. It seems sensible to explore these issues at the planning stage, writing expectations into policies and procedures from the outset.

Acceptable use policy – AUP. There has been a long-recognised need to ensure the safety of all those involved in schools by the definition of expected behaviours and inappropriate conduct through the use of an acceptable use policy (AUP). However, Traxler (2010) warns that the traditional AUP will not be fit for purpose when faced with the challenge of a wider range of devices in schools, particularly if devices are student owned, as schools will have less control over the devices. AUPs need to evolve to meet the growing challenges brought into schools and the need for schools to teach students to stay safe with digital technologies. Another point to address within the AUP is how the devices will be used without causing a classroom distraction. The teacher must be empowered to use the technology whilst at the same time have the appropriate and correct sanctions, which can be applied for misuse.

Teacher professional development. Although recognition of the need for teacher development when introducing tablet technology is widespread

(Crichton et al. 2012; Clarke et al., 2013; Karsenti and Fievez, 2013), this is often an area that is neglected, which can lead to real problems integrating the technology into classroom practice (Conlon, 2004; Smith et al., 2005). Clearly, as well as technical know-how, teachers will need training to develop pedagogical awareness, helping them to explore the benefits of the technology and also the limitations within the classroom setting.

Fullan (2013) highlights the importance of progress within change management. Staff will be more likely to continue with development if they experience regular wins. One of the ways we can support this is to help staff to identify small, achievable goals that will help them to progress. Recognition and celebration of teacher success is also vital. Strategies such as short show-and-tell sessions within staff meetings can provide opportunities to celebrate success and share good practice.

Teachers are likely to benefit from time to play with the technology, enabling them to develop expertise and identify apps and activities that can be beneficial to learning (Burden et al., 2012). On top of their existing workload, there is likely to be a need for teachers to explore apps which may be relevant to student studies. This enables teachers to have a vested interest in how the app will assist their teaching pedagogy. If procurement of apps is largely based upon teachers trying apps out in their own time, will there be a budget to purchase single copies of apps for a trial?

Students and parents. Karsenti and Fievez (2013) urge schools to help raise parental understanding of the benefits and limitations of tablet technology. This would certainly seem prudent if schools want parents to buy into an implementation of tablet technology and contribute financially. Students and parents come to this technology in most cases with different experiences. Could putting tablet technology into the hands of students at home help to engage parents? Some report finding parents keen for children to bring home tablet technology, with them wanting to learn and find out more about what and how their children are learning (Alberta Education, 2011; Burden et al., 2012; Beauchamp and Hillier, 2014). However, whether parental engagement will increase when students take tablet technology home may well depend on how the students are using the technology. Heinrich (2012) reported that 87% of students in a one-to-one deployment of iPads said they used their iPads for playing games and social networking. Some would question whether this is positive in a world where cyberbullying and obesity are becoming increasingly problematic. If we have appropriate education about how to use technology in a healthy and responsible way, this would seem to be less of a concern. However, will schools be able to address this aspect fully? This raises the debate about digital citizenship and the role of schools to address these issues.

Conclusion

The implementation of the use of tablets in the secondary school can bring major change to the way the classroom traditionally functions. It challenges traditional teaching methods, confronts students' use of a device for learning purposes and opens up the expectations students readily have about the way they should be able to access technology. Schools cannot hide from the pervasive use of tablet and mobile devices students now have access to. If schools have a responsibility to educate students in methods to enhance their learning and ultimately their future employability, should they not be doing more to investigate the tablet's potential and application to the classroom given that this technology is only set to increase?

The use of tablets in secondary schools is on the rise, and as teachers, we have high expectations for learning. Where schools are moving into the arena of mobile technology, it is important to get the approach right to avoid tablet technology spiralling into an expensive distraction. Where schools get this balance right, it may go some way to ensure students enter the workforce with a confidence to express to their future employer an intent: an intent that I am skilled, I am knowledgeable, I embrace new technologies I am introduced to and I have the ability to rise to the challenges you set me in a flexible, global and mobile way.

References

Alberta Education (2011) *iPads: what are we learning? Summary report of provincial data gathering day* [online]. Available from: http://education.alberta.ca/media/6684652/ipad%20report%20-%20final%20version%202012-03-20.pdf [Accessed 8 May 2015].

Apple (2015) *Apple in education: real stories.* Available from: https://www.apple.com/uk/education/real-stories/ [Accessed 07 February 2015].

Beauchamp, G., and Hillier, E. (2014) *An evaluation of iPad implementation across a network of primary schools in Cardiff* [online]. Cardiff Metropolitan University. Available from: http://www.cardiffmet.ac.uk/education/research/Documents/iPadImplementation 2014.pdf [Accessed 17 December 2014].

Beland, L. P., and Murphy, R. (2015) *CEP discussion paper no 1350 May 2015 Ill communication: technology, distraction & student performance* [online]. Available from: http://cep.lse.ac.uk/pubs/download/dp1350.pdf [Accessed 5 June 2015].

Benham, H., Carvalho, G., and Cassens, M. (2014) Student perceptions of the impact of mobile technology in the classroom. *Issues in Information Systems* [online].15 (2), 141–150. Available from: http://iacis.org/iis/2014/101_iis_2014_141-150.pdf [Accessed 17 December 2014].

BESA (2013) *Tablets and apps in schools: full report* [online]. Available from: http://www.besa.org.uk/sites/default/files/tab2013_0.pdf [Accessed 17 December 2014].

Burden, K., et al. (2012) *iPad Scotland evaluation* [online], University of Hull. Available from: https://www.academia.edu/3197012/iPad_Scotland_Evaluation [Accessed 27 April 2015].

Caldwell, H. (2015) Manipulating media. *In:* H. Caldwell and J. Bird (eds.), *Teaching with tablets.* London: Sage, 1–16.

Clark, W., and Luckin, R. (2013) *What the research says: iPads in the classroom* [online]. Institute of Education, University of London. Available from: https://www.lkldev.ioe.ac.uk/lklinnovation/wp-content/uploads/2013/03/2013-iPads-in-the-Classroom-Lit-Review-1.pdf [Accessed 17 December 2014].

Clarke, B., Svanaes, S., and Zimmermann, S. (2013) *One-to-one tablets in secondary schools: an evaluation study* [online]. Tablets for schools. Available from: http://tabletsforschools.org.uk/wp-content/uploads/2012/12/FKY-Tablets-for-Schools-Stage-2-Full-Report-July-2013.pdf [Accessed 17 December 2014].

Cochrane, T., Narayan, V., and Oldfield, J. (2013) iPadagogy: appropriating the iPad within pedagogical contexts. *International Journal of Mobile Learning and Organisation* [online]. 7(1), 48–65. Available from: http://www.inderscience.com/storage/f116829121753410.pdf [Accessed 27 April 2015].

Conlon, T. (2004) A failure of delivery: the United Kingdom's New Opportunities Fund programme of teacher training in information and communications technology. *Journal of In-service Education* [online]. 30 (1), 115–140. Available from: http://www.tandfonline.com/doi/pdf/10.1080/13674580400200229 [Accessed 17 December 2014].

Crichton, S, Pegler, K., and White, D. (2012) Personal devices in public settings: lessons learned from an iPod touch/iPad project. *The Electronic Journal of e-Learning* [online]. 10 (1), 23–31. Available from: www.ejel.org

Education Technology Action Group (2015) *Education Technology Action Group: our reflections* [online]. Available from: https://drive.google.com/file/d/0B_4FnLyL2BFvMjBOVFY4ZnhRVTA/view [Accessed 6 February 2015].

Etherington, D. (2013) Apple has sold over 8M iPads direct to education worldwide, with more than 1B iTunes U downloads. *TechCrunch* [online]. Available from: http://techcrunch.com/2013/02/28/apple-has-sold-over-8m-ipads-direct-to-education-worldwide-with-more-than-1b-itunes-u-downloads/ [Accessed 06 May 2015].

Fenn, J., and Raskino, M. (2008) *Mastering the hype cycle: how to choose the right innovation at the right time.* Boston: Harvard Business School.

Freedman, T. (2012) *BYOD case study: Wildern School* [online]. Available from: http://www.ictineducation.org/home-page/2012/11/30/byod-case-study-wildern-school.html [Accessed 19 December 2014].

Friedman, A., and Garcia, E. (2013) "People with real experiences:" using mobile devices in high school social studies. *Social Studies Research and Practice* [online], 8, (3) 115–127. Available from: http://www.socstrpr.org/wp-content/uploads/2013/11/06489-Friedman-et-al.pdf [Accessed 19 December 2014].

Fullan, M. (2013) *Stratosphere.* Toronto: Pearson

Galloway, J., John, M., and McTaggart, M. (2015) *Learning with mobile and handheld technologies.* Abingdon: Routledge.

Gardner, H., and Davis, K. (2013) *The app generation: How today's youth navigate identity, intimacy, and imagination in a digital world.* New Haven: Yale University Press.

Grantham, S. (2015) Visible learning. In: H. Caldwell and J. Bird (eds.), *Teaching with tablets.* London: Sage, 29–44.

Heinrich, P. (2012) *The iPad as a tool for education: a study of the introduction on iPads at Longfield Academy, Kent.* Nottingham: NAACE. Available from: http://www.naace.co.uk/publications/longfieldipadresearch [Accessed 27 April 2015].

Heppell, S. (2014) Foreword. *In:* J. Audain (ed.), *The ultimate guide to using ICT across the curriculum for primary teachers: web, widgets, whiteboards and beyond!* London: Bloomsbury, vi.

Karsenti, T., and Fievez, A. (2013) *The iPad in education: uses benefits and challenges – a survey of 6,057 students and 302 teachers in Quebec, Canada* [online]. Montreal:

CRIFPE. Available from: http://karsenti.ca/ipad/pdf/iPad_report_Karsenti-Fievez_EN.pdf [Accessed 17 December 2014].

Lai, E. (2012) *Four reasons why school tablet rollouts can stumble or fail* [online]. Available from: http://www.zdnet.com/article/four-reasons-why-school-tablet-roll-outs-can-stumble-or-fail/ [Accessed 17 December 2014].

McFarlane, A. (2015) *Authentic learning for the digital generation*. Abingdon: Routledge

Melhuish, K., and Falloon, G. (2010) Looking to the future: M-learning with the iPad. *Computers in New Zealand schools: learning, leading, technology* [online], 22 (3). Available from: http://researchcommons.waikato.ac.nz/bitstream/handle/10289/5050/Looking%20to%20the%20future.pdf [Accessed 17 December 2014].

Murphy, M. (2014) Why some schools are selling all their iPads. *The Atlantic* [online]. Available from: http://www.theatlantic.com/education/archive/2014/08/whats-the-best-device-for-interactive-learning/375567/ [Accessed 7 May 2015].

Ofsted (2011) *ICT in schools 2008–2011* [online]. Manchester: Ofsted. Available from: https://www.gov.uk/government/uploads/system/uploads/attachment_data/file/181223/110134.pdf [Accessed 21 December 2014].

Rogers, E.M. (1983). *Diffusion of innovation*. New York: The Free Press.

Sheppard, D. (2011) Reading with iPads – the difference makes a difference. *Education Today*. 11 (3), 12–15. Available from: Document1http://www.minnisjournals.com.au/articles/ipads%20et%20t3%2011.pdf [Accessed 21 December 2014].

Smith, H., Higgins, S., Wall, K., and Miller, J. (2005) Interactive whiteboards: boon or bandwagon? A critical review of the literature. *Journal of Computer Assisted Learning* [online]. 21(2), 91–101. Available from: http://onlinelibrary.wiley.com/doi/10.1111/j.1365-2729.2005.00117.x/full [Accessed 17 December 2014].

Specht, M. (2009) Learning in a technology enhanced world: context in ubiquitous learning support. Available from: http://dspace.ou.nl/bitstream/1820/2034/1/Oratio_Specht.pdf [Accessed 2 February 2015].

Traxler, J. (2010) Will student devices deliver innovation, inclusion, and transformation? *Journal of the Research Center for Educational Technology* [online]. 6 (1), 3–15. Available from: http://www.rcetj.org/index.php/rcetj/article/view/56/177 [Accessed 27 April 2015].

Twining, P. (2014) Redefining education: one-to-one computing strategies in English schools. *Proceedings of the Australian Computers in Education Conference* [online], Adelaide, September 30–October 3 2014. Adelaide: Australian Council for Computers in Education, 448–457. Available from: http://acec2014.acce.edu.au/sites/2014/files/2014ConfProceedingsFinal.pdf [Accessed 19 December 2014].

Twining, P., et al. (2005) *Tablet PCs in schools: case study report: a report for Becta by the Open University*. Coventry: Becta. Available from: http://oro.open.ac.uk/6407/1/BTE_case_study_print.pdf [Accessed 17 December 2014].

Younie, S. (2007) *The integration of ICT into teacher's professional practice: the cultural dynamics of change*. Thesis (Ph.D), De Montfort University, Leicester, UK.

Younie, S., and Leask, M. (2013) Teaching with technologies: the essential guide, Maidenhead: Open University Press.

Chapter 14

Does Facebook have a place in the school classroom?

Exploring risks and opportunities

Angelos Konstantinidis

The central goal of this chapter is to shift the focus of the debate about the integration of Facebook in the classroom from questions of safety and distraction from learning to those of opportunities to rethink the teaching process and engage learners, with the hope that doing so will help teachers to consider how new modes of communication and interaction might be applied to their teaching practice and how to move beyond teaching paradigms that focus on the acquisition of information by learners. Facebook is taken as one example of a social network site (SNS); however, this chapter will critically examine the use of a range of such sites.

Introduction

Consider this scenario. After watching a short educational video, the teacher posted it in the class Facebook group along with the questions that the learners had to investigate. Then, learners worked together in small groups to gather articles, videos and photos that would help them answer the questions posed by the teacher. They shared the results of their investigation on the group wall and got feedback from their teacher and peers. Later, when learners went home, they used the chat tool to discuss the task within their group and continue their work. From time to time, they posted an update to the group wall or asked for directions and clarification from their teacher, while other learners popped in offering help. Finally, learners published their work on Facebook and other Web 2.0 services, and got recognition and readership from a much wider and diverse audience than that of their classroom.

The above description is just an imaginary scenario; nonetheless, it is not far from the reality of several schools around the globe. There are numerous anecdotal stories related to using Facebook for educational activities and learning purposes; just type the terms "Facebook" and "education" on Google, and you will get more than two billion results. Dozens of websites demonstrate and guide teachers on how to use Facebook for classroom teaching, offering practical tips and different teaching ideas, account the benefits and pitfalls from employing Facebook as a teaching tool and discuss why teachers should or should not use Facebook (e.g. Burt, 2011; Davis, 2015; Pappas, 2013; Walsh, 2011). Educators post articles on their blogs sharing their own experience of incorporating Facebook in the classroom and giving advice to other teachers, while others criticize Facebook, or Web 2.0 tools in general, and emphatically argue against their use for educational purposes (e.g. Barnwell, 2012; Conley, 2011; Joselow, 2015; Leicht & Globe, 2014; Shirky, 2014). But why so much debate and dialogue around Facebook use in the classroom?

At the core of this debate lie technological advances and more specifically, the emergence of social media. The term "social media" is used in this chapter as an umbrella term that refers to SNS like Facebook, Google+ and Myspace, as well as to blogging and media-sharing sites such as Twitter, Tumblr, Scoop.it and Instagram. The unprecedented growth and application of social media (Duggan et al., 2015; Perrin, 2015) has triggered long and vigorous debates on several issues, such as whether children who have grown up immersed in digital technologies have different skills and thinking from previous generations (Prensky, 2001), whether education practice should be changed to accommodate 'digital natives' (ibid.), whether new learning theories arise because of the ubiquitous use of Web 2.0 applications among young people (Downes, 2005; Siemens, 2005) and so on. In a similar way, the reactions of using SNS for educational purposes are mixed. Concerns are often couched in terms of e-safety and distraction from learning, while advocates emphasize the new literacy practices that learners need to succeed in a digital and highly connected world, and ask for a different education model that responds to the frequent use of social media by young people. From whatever side of the debate one approaches the use of social media in educational contexts, the reality remains the same: social media *are* an integral part of young people's lives. At the same time, educators are hesitant to adopt them for they are often constrained by exaggerated fears about e-safety (Sharples et al., 2009) and a lack of confidence and pedagogical knowledge about integrating social media in the classroom in appropriate and meaningful ways.

The aim of the chapter is not to solely discuss Facebook in relation to these issues, but rather to embrace all SNS in the discussion; nonetheless, Facebook is recognized as the primary venue for online communication among young people (Lenhart, 2015) and, as such, is the exemplar of the chapter. To open up this debate we start by examining e-safety issues that arise from the use of social media by children and consider whether social media use in the classroom would help to mitigate cyber-risks. Next, we explore how Facebook may act as a distraction from learning and discuss its potential to act as a catalyst for rethinking teaching practice. Finally, we explore a handful of practical guidelines for teachers who want to integrate Facebook or other SNS in meaningful ways into their classroom pedagogic practice.

Facebook in the classroom and e-safety: could they go together?

> At a public swimming pool we have gates, put up signs, have lifeguards and shallow ends, but we also teach children how to swim.
>
> (Byron, 2008, p. 2)

Given the widespread adoption of Facebook and the vast array of information that can be shared on it, children's safety is a recurring issue among educators and parents (Ofcom, 2008b; Sharples et al., 2009). Indeed, online networking offers enormous potential opportunities, but it also presents particular risks to children and teenagers, including exposure to inappropriate content, being bullied or bullying others and contact with strangers. Although Facebook sets a minimum age of 13 for its users, children start creating profiles on Facebook and other SNS from the age of eight (Ofcom, 2010; Livingstone et al., 2013) – sometimes with the help of their parents (Boyd et al., 2011; BBC, 2012) – more than one in five 9 to 12 year olds have a Facebook account (Livingstone et al., 2011), while the number of children who use SNS is increasing during adolescence (Ipsos MORI, 2007; Lenhart et al., 2010; Livingstone et al., 2013; Madden et al., 2013; Sharples et al., 2009). Additionally, as teenagers grow up, they tend to login to Facebook more frequently, have broader and more diverse online networks (including people they have never met in person) and share a wider range of information on their profile (Madden et al., 2013).

What are the actual risks of using Facebook?

Against this backdrop, it might seem irrational to incorporate Facebook in educational settings or employ it as an additional tool for engaging learners beyond the classroom's spacial/temporal constraints. Indeed, one might argue that using Facebook for educational purposes might further encourage its use from children and adolescents, which in turn would increase their exposure and vulnerability to online risks. However, this is barely the case.

Research shows that while it is clear that potential online risks are qualitatively different and even possibly more damaging in some cases (as in cyberbullying, for instance) from offline ones (Byron, 2008), it seems that there are no fundamental risks inherent to SNS and that online risks are often paralleling or an extension of the offline world (Dredge et al., 2014; Kwan & Skoric, 2013; Sharples et al., 2009; Vandoninck et al., 2012; Wolak et al., 2008). Despite the widespread fear that inappropriate adults could take advantage of information that children post about themselves online to locate and stalk them, it is evidenced that "online molesters have not changed their tactics as a result of the advent of social networking sites" (Wolak et al., 2008, p. 117). Has the media exaggerated the image of adults masquerading as younger people to trick naïve and innocent children into sexual contact? In the vast majority of cases victims are adolescents, they are aware of the real identity, age (usually no more than six years older than the victims themselves are) and sexual interests of the offenders, and they meet them face-to-face expecting to engage in sexual activity (Wolak et al., 2008). In fact, when the discussion comes to physical risks from contact with dangerous people, online public spheres appear to be a much safer place than the offline world for children under the age of 12 (Wolak et al., 2008). To conclude, several nation-wide reports show that research deals more with the *risk* of harm rather the *actual* harm imposed to SNS users (Millwood Hargrave et al., 2006; Ofcom, 2008a).

As regards cyberbullying, although the likelihood of being involved either as victim or as harasser in such actions is often predicted by the time spent online (Brandtzæg et al., 2009; Hinduja & Patchin, 2008; Staksrud et al., 2013), several studies have shown that it is largely associated with traditional bullying experiences (Dredge et al., 2014; Hinduja & Patchin, 2008; Kwan & Skoric, 2013) and school problems (Hinduja & Patchin, 2008; Vandoninck et al., 2012), while some studies have revealed that SNS are not a particularly favoured avenue among teenagers for cyberbullying activities (Brandtzæg et al., 2009; Staksrud et al., 2013; Ybarra & Mitchell, 2008). As with fears about risks from online child molesters, it seems that cyberbullying dangers are fewer than "school fears and policies seem to imply" (National School Boards Association, 2007, p. 5). Traditional bullying is still more prevalent in young people's lives and as such, constitutes a greater problem than cyberbullying (Bullying UK, 2014; Byron, 2008). Nevertheless, it should be also taken into account that the qualitatively different characteristics of the online networked spaces, that is persistence, visibility, spreadability and searchability, add "a new dimension to how bullying is constructed and understood" (boyd, 2014, p. 133), which may augment the intensity of harm caused by bullying and greatly expand its negative ramifications.

In addition, even though there are several studies which suggest that the mere ownership of an account on SNS increases the likelihood of online risks (Staksrud et al., 2013), it is evidenced that posting personal information online is not by itself a particularly risky behaviour, and it seems that what actually increases risk are certain types of online interaction (Wolak et al., 2008). It is interesting that even studies which argue that simply the use of a Facebook account increases risk concur that risky online practices or interactions are far more predictive for actually encountering online dangers (Staksrud et al., 2013), or as Staksrud et al. put it: "*How* one uses SNS matters, therefore, even more than *whether* one uses SNS" (2013, p. 48; author's emphasis). So, what are the practices that put young people into danger? It seems that having an active Facebook profile and sharing some personal info (such as the real name of the owner and personal photos) does not significantly increase risk, rather risky practices include: having a public profile (instead of a private one), providing contact information on it (phone number and/or home address), having an expanded network of friends (more than 100), having unknown people on friends list, interacting with unknown people and sending personal information to them, talking online to unknown people about sex, seeking pornography online and being rude and/or nasty online (Dredge et al., 2014; Staksrud et al., 2013; Wolak et al., 2008). The odds of encountering online dangers increase as young people engage in more types of these interactions (Staksrud et al., 2013; Wolak et al., 2008). As previously mentioned, children under the age of 12 can safely enjoy the benefits of the online world for they use the internet in simpler, less interactive ways, whereas when they enter adolescence they tend to experiment with and expand the use of the internet to pursue their interests in music, games and so on (Livingstone, 2006) – an attitude that renders them more vulnerable to online risks. Of course, it is not the internet or Facebook in particular to blame, rather the growing independence and sexual curiosity that young people experience during adolescence (Wolak et al., 2008). In fact, beyond the age of 12, several and complex factors have a bearing on Facebook use, including personality (Amichai-Hamburger & Vinitzky, 2010; Ross et al., 2009), digital literacy (Staksrud et al., 2013), homosexuality and abuse history (Wolak et al., 2008), social norms and influence (Cheung & Lee, 2010; Currie et al., 2009), daily needs and preferences of the individual (Vrocharidou and Efthymiou, 2012), and perhaps others not yet investigated.

Why Facebook integration into the classroom might serve e-safety

As it has been shown, SNS use does not hide significant dangers for both children and adolescents, so risks *do* exist. Most children have competent internet skills, but do they understand the risks and how to protect themselves from harm? For the more children use the internet the more they need to know on safer use. Adolescents are sharing more personal information on SNS than they did in the past. If SNS are banned from classrooms, as is the current practice in most school districts (National School Boards Association, 2007), then teachers can only lecture about internet safety without being able, for instance, to help learners in adjusting privacy settings or to advise them about the information they share. Byron's (2008) swimming pool metaphor is successful for it helps us understand that solely imposing prevention measures without appropriate guidance is not an effective strategy. And if teachers are to "guide" learning about internet safety, they must be *there* to guide it.

Facebook in the classroom: is it beneficial for learning or not?

High quality education is shaped by changes in the characteristics of student learners and the ways in which they use new technologies to exchange information. One thing is clear: the convergence of social networking technologies and a new "always on" pedagogy is rapidly changing the face of education.

(Baird & Fisher, 2005–2006, p. 6)

Technological innovations are often seen either as opportunities for transforming teaching and learning or as having deleterious effects on the education of the young (Sefton-Green, 2006). The latest revolution of the web, often called Web 2.0 or the social web, has radically changed the way people communicate, share knowledge, and absorb information. In essence, Web 2.0 marks a change in the dynamics of the web, from one-way top-down to many-to-many communication, which made user-to-user interaction and collaboration possible on the web, information sharing the norm and creation of web content a reality. During the last decade, Web 2.0 technologies have exploded in number, features and applications while their audience has increased exponentially across all cultures and ages, but especially among young people. See Chapter 8 on Web 2.0 for more information on how teachers can utilize this type of technology for pedagogical practice.

Today's learners have grown up completely immersed in the digital world, and social web tools use is an inherent part of their life (Prensky, 2001). They have their own mobile phone from the age of 10, and they feel so closely related to it that they regard it as a "body part" (Oksman & Rautiainen, 2003). Similarly, they view computers and the web not as disconnected from their daily activities, but as an assumed part of their everyday lives (Oblinger, 2003). Most children have a computer with internet access in their bedrooms or access to the internet at home. They use internet as both consumers (e.g. download music and videos) and producers (e.g. upload photos and videos, maintain websites) of content (Green & Hannon, 2007; National School Boards Association, 2007; Project Tomorrow, 2010). While adults are concerned about how children are using digital technologies, for children, using them is "completely ingrained in their lives" (Green & Hannon, 2007, p. 16) and they "simply use . . . [them] as tools to make their lives easier" (Green & Hannon, 2007, p. 10). Among all Web 2.0 services, SNS and especially Facebook have greatly attracted young people. One of the reasons for this is that they view SNS as a key socialization space where they can stay in contact with their friends, talk about the day's events and meet new people (Lenhart & Madden, 2007; Project Tomorrow, 2010).

Facebook, commercialism, and distraction from learning

The proliferation of SNS provokes educators to debate how they can harness their power for engaging and enhancing learning, yet many educators are quite sceptical and posit that social media should not be adopted just because of availability. The most important issues against the use of social media for learning purposes that are raised in the research literature can be broadly categorized into two categories: (a) SNS were designed for commercial rather for learning purposes and (b) most often SNS hinder learning performance by distracting learners.

Friesen (2010) and Friesen and Lowe (2012) question the educational role of social media and argue that in the centre of these services are corporate interests, which sell their product, namely users' attention, to advertisers. Rather than aiming at connecting learners with teachers and peers, the structure, design and content of these services are informed by advertising interests rendering the learning process subordinate and minimizing learners' control over his/her experience. While it is beyond dispute that Facebook and other SNS are, above all, commercial in form and that profit is their first priority, quite paradoxically, the fact that commercialism literally invaded schools a long time ago (Sukarieh & Tannock, 2009) is overlooked. Arguably, if educators wish to address the perils of consumerism and commercialization, then a more effective way would be to grow informed and responsible citizens, rather than stand by while children are bombarded with advertisements. Surely, it is more logical to educate children on how to protect themselves from advertisements' impact while they are already using Facebook for educational purposes than through preaching and lecturing alone.

Educators have often related learners' time spent on Facebook with lower academic performance and task switching, which increases cognitive load and reduces attention to the primary task. At this point it should be noted that the research studies discussed in this paragraph were applied mostly in higher education contexts, as research investigating the impact of SNS in learning performance in school settings is scarce (Hew & Cheung, 2013), and as such, the results should be approached with caution as regards their application to non-adult learners. Several studies have found that overall time spent on Facebook as well as using Facebook during class were negatively associated with learning performance (Junco, 2012b; Junco & Cotten, 2012; Kirschner & Karpinski, 2010; Wood et al., 2012), and that Facebook users are less likely to stay focused on a task during self-study (Judd, 2014), while they are more likely to multitask during lectures (Judd, 2014) and to spend fewer hours per week studying (Junco, 2012a; Kirschner & Karpinski, 2010). However, it seems that literature is not conclusive on how Facebook use affects academic performance as it was also found that not only is there no difference in grades between Facebook users and non-users (Kolek & Saunders, 2008; Pasek et al., 2009), but that learners who multitask may have higher grades than their peers who do not (Karpinski et al., 2013). What is more interesting for our discussion in this chapter, however, is to examine further the conditions under which Facebook use might deteriorate learning performance. Gupta and Irwin (2016) investigated whether the level of interestingness of the primary learning task has an effect on learners' attention and focus on task, and it was found that learners were more susceptible to distractions on Facebook when it was of low interest. Thus, Facebook use might not be the distraction, because learners who experience low arousal levels are more inclined to resort to coping strategies like daydreaming, doodling, texting, chatting and passing notes to their friends (Mann & Robinson, 2009). From another point of view, Junco (2012a) found that the way Facebook is used better predicts academic performance than time spent on site. Thus, activities like gathering and sharing information increase learners' engagement with their study field, while increased frequency of using the Facebook chat tool results in lesser time spent preparing for class.

Facebook as a tool for learning

While most young users confirm that they use Facebook mostly for entertainment and socializing, learning also occurs in, most often, an intuitive and informal way. For example, Greenhow and Robelia (2009) found that high school learners are engaged in several communicative and creative practices within SNS, while in a recent study on adolescents it was revealed that Facebook use had a significant positive impact on their verbal abilities, working memory, and spelling (Alloway et al., 2013). In addition, adolescents who use SNS are more computer literate, nurture a more positive attitude towards computers, and have less computer anxiety compared to their peers (Appel, 2012). What might be surprising is that learners' online discussions are revolving around educational and learning topics. In a nationwide survey on US learners aged 9 to 17 years old, it was revealed that one of the most common topics of conversation on SNS was education, while one in two learners talk specifically about schoolwork (National School Boards Association, 2007). Add to this, in the study of Greenhow and Robelia (2009), it was found that SNS provided high school learners with opportunities for school task-related support and appreciation of creative work. Thus, social media not only play a crucial role in helping children socialize and learn, but its role is becoming more and more important as children grow up.

The significance of social media in student life does not necessarily ensure that their integration in the school classroom would be beneficial for teaching or for learners' learning. In other words, it could be argued that there is and there should be a distinct difference between the out-of-school and in-the-school spheres, and that what is acceptable or even beneficial in the former would not necessarily hold the same affordances or effects in the latter. Although this is true to some extent, this way of thinking hinders teachers from taking benefit of the real-life experiences and knowledge that learners may bring to the classroom and of all the learning contexts that they are involved in, while also depriving learners from knowledgeable adults in their learning with technology (Hsin et al., 2014). Learners' experience of using social media in classroom settings lags far behind their experience outside school, which demotivates them and generates a sense of 'digital dissonance' for the learners (Clark et al., 2009). Contrarily, if we adopt the view that boundaries between learning settings can be permeable (Barron, 2006) and, thus, what is learned in school can stimulate learners' interest for out-of-school learning and, accordingly, what is learned out of school can shape what is learned in school, then it is reasonable to think of using SNS in the classroom as an effective method for enabling a kind of permeability between school and social life.

Thus, the greatest potential of integrating Facebook in classroom settings lies in helping teachers to figure out how to integrate the online and offline experiences of their learners and how learning in school can lead to learning activities outside school walls. If Facebook is to be incorporated in the classroom merely to replicate the traditional way of doing things without questioning the teaching practices, then it would become just a "fancy" add-on. Or, even worse, it might have negative effects on learning as discussed above. Instead, teachers should investigate ways of employing Facebook to extend learning outside the classroom's walls and guide learners in using it constructively and in a safe manner. For example, learners may use Facebook to share photos and videos from local events, run a class poll or contest for something related to their studies, create a Facebook page for their school/class, and so on. In addition, participation in online activities, such as wall discussions and search for information online, gives learners the opportunity to acquire practical knowledge and skills in using the web in a safe way and for meaningful purposes in a more relaxed, informal manner. In this way, teachers can support young people to develop digital skills and an awareness of the advantages and disadvantages/dangers of online activities. For a further discussion on developing digital citizenship skills, see Chapter 6 on this.

Next steps and way forward

> Luckily, the fundamental role of a teacher is not to deliver information. It is to guide the student in the social process of learning.
>
> (Muller, 2014)

Teachers are interested in finding ways of integrating Facebook into their classroom practice to leverage its learning potential without, exposing learners, themselves or their school to unwanted risks and negative side effects. However, keep in mind that the use of SNS within the classroom context is still fairly new and as such, research into the integration of Facebook with formal lesson activities is still very limited. Taking into account that Facebook was not designed for educational purposes, it is especially important to design and develop carefully your teaching goals and pedagogical strategy before integrating Facebook into your classroom. Although there is no method that can be equally effective for all subject areas and learners' grade level, below is a list containing five guidelines that may help you start:

1   **Discuss your idea.** Do not forget that SNS use in the school classroom is still a sensitive and controversial topic. Many parents have strong convictions about SNS and the safety issues schools have rules against their use, while learners may not be willing to use SNS either. It is better to discuss your idea about integrating Facebook or other SNS with all stakeholders and get their consent before actualizing your plan.
2   **Create a separate account.** It is especially important to know how to regulate information disclosure on Facebook. If you are uncertain how to do it, then it is better to create a separate Facebook account for connecting with learners and parents. In fact, creating a separate account strictly for teaching purposes may be the best course of action, as it would help you keep your private online life separate and protect your learners from questionable online posts and contacts from your personal network (Sumuer & Yildirim, 2014).

3   **Understand your new role**. Your main role online is to facilitate rather than orchestrate learning through SNS. Capture learning opportunities missed in the classroom and initiate discussions. Encourage learners and facilitate reflection about learning.

4   **Promote self-directed learning**. Start discussions for topics that interest learners (it does not necessarily have to be lesson content or even school-related topics). Through discussion, help learners assess their current level of knowledge and set their own goals. Let learners choose their own topics for discussion.

5   **Develop an online community**. Teach learners how to communicate online, promote empathy and develop an atmosphere of trust. Organize activities that depend on collaboration and group work. Give roles to the more competent learners and encourage them to support their weaker peers.

With the proliferation of social media in young people's daily lives, new challenges for teachers have emerged. While educators raise concerns over e-safety and learning risks that accompany Facebook use in the class, many worldwide have embraced its potential for enhancing learning and engaging learners. In this chapter, instead of approaching these risks in a one-dimensional way, as problems that should be solved or completely avoided, a more holistic approach has been adopted that examines the risks in their context and questions whether it is time to rethink the teaching process to both address the risks and engage learners in learning.

References

Alloway, T., Horton, J., Alloway, R., and Dawson, C. (2013). Social networking sites and cognitive abilities: do they make you smarter? *Computers & Education, 63,* 10–16.

Amichai-Hamburger, Y., and Vinitzky, G. (2010). Social network use and personality. *Computers in Human Behavior, 26,* 1289–1295.

Appel, M. (2012). Are heavy users of computer games and social media more computer literate? *Computers & Education, 59,* 1339–1349.

Baird, D.E., and Fisher, M. (2005–2006). Neomillennial user experience design strategies: utilizing social networking media to support 'always on' learning styles. *Journal of Educational Technology Systems,* 34 (1), 5–32.

Barnwell, P. (2012). Why Twitter and Facebook are not good instructional tools. *Education Week Teacher* [online]. Retrieved from: http://www.edweek.org/tm/articles/2012/05/30/fp_barnwell.html

Barron, B. (2006). Interest and self-sustained learning as catalysts of development: A learning ecologies perspective. *Human Development, 49,* 193–224. doi: 10.1159/000094368

BBC (2012, April 26). Facebook: parents 'help children break age limits'. *BBC News* [online]. Retrieved from http://www.bbc.com/news/education-17853498

boyd, d. (2014). *It's complicated: the social lives of networked teens.* New Haven: Yale University Press.

boyd, d., Hargittai, E., Schultz, J., and Palfrey, J. (2011). Why parents help their children lie to Facebook about age: unintended consequences of the 'Children's Online Privacy

Protection Act'. *First Monday* [online], 16 (11). Retrieved from http://firstmonday. org/ojs/index.php/fm/article/view/3850

Brandtzæg, P.B., Staksrud, E., Hagen, I., and Wold, T. (2009). Norwegian children's experiences of cyberbullying when using different technological platforms. *Journal of Children and Media, 3* (4), 349–365.

Bullying UK (2014). Bullying UK National Survey 2014. *Family Lives* [online]. Retrieved from http://www.bullying.co.uk/anti-bullying-week/bullying-uk-national-survey-2014/

Burt, R. (2011). The why and how of using facebook for educators – no need to be friends at all! *The Edublogger*. Retrieved from http://www.theedublogger.com/2011/05/11/ the-why-and-how-of-using-facebook-for-educators-no-need-to-be-friends-at-all/

Byron, T. (2008). *Safer children in a digital world: The report of the Byron Review.* Nottingham: DCSF Publications.

Cheung, C., and Lee, M. (2010). A theoretical model of intentional social action in online social networks. *Decision Support Systems, 49,* 24–30.

Clark, W., et al. (2009). Beyond Web 2.0: mapping the technology landscapes of young learners. *Journal of Computer Assisted Learning, 25*(1), 56–69.

Conley, D. (2011). Wired for distraction: kids and social media. *TIME* [online]. Retrieved from http://content.time.com/time/magazine/article/0,9171,2048363,00.html

Currie, P., Lewis, J., and West, A. (2009). Learners' Facebook 'friends': Public and private spheres. *Journal of Youth Studies, 12*(6), 615–627.

Davis, M. (2015). Social media for teachers: guides, resources, and ideas. *Edutopia.* Retrieved from http://www.edutopia.org/blog/social-media-resources-educators-matt-davis

Downes, S. (2005, October). E-learning 2.0. *eLearn Magazine.* Retrieved from http:// elearnmag.acm.org/featured.cfm?aid=1104968

Dredge, R., Gleeson, J., and Garcia, X. (2014). Presentation on Facebook and risk of cyberbullying victimisation. *Computers in Human Behavior, 40,* 16–22.

Duggan, M., et al. (2015). Social media update 2014. Pew Research Internet Project [online]. Retrieved from http://www.pewinternet.org/2015/01/09/social-media-update-2014/

Friesen, N. (2010). Education and the social Web: Connective learning and the commercial imperative. *First Monday* [online], *12*(6). Retrieved from http://firstmonday.org/ ojs/index.php/fm/article/view/3149/2718

Friesen, N., and Lowe, S. (2012). The questionable promise of social media for education: Connective learning and the commercial imperative. *Journal of Computer Assisted Learning, 28,* 183–194.

Greenhow, C., and Robelia, B. (2009). Old communication, new literacies: Social network sites as social learning resources. *Journal of Computer-Mediated Communication, 14,* 1130–1161.

Hinduja, S., and Patchin, J.W. (2008). Cyberbullying: an exploratory analysis of factors related to offending and victimization. *Deviant Behavior, 29,* 129–156.

Hew, K., and Cheung, W. (2013). Use of Web 2.0 technologies in K-12 and higher education: the search for evidence-based practice. *Educational Research Review, 9,* 47–64.

Ipsos MORI (2007). *Student Expectations Study: Key findings from online research and discussion evenings held in June 2007 for the Joint Information Systems Committee.* JISC.

Green, H. and Hannon, C. (2007). *Their space: Education for a digital generation.* London: Demos.

Greenhow, C., and Robelia, B. (2009). Old communication, new literacies: Social network sites as social learning resources. *Journal of Computer-Mediated Communication*, 1130–1161.

Gupta, N., and Irwin, J.D. (2016). In-class distractions: The role of Facebook and the primary learning task. *Computers in Human Behavior*, *55*, 1165–1178.

Hsin, C.-T., Li, M.-C., and Tsai, C.-C. (2014). The influence of young children's use of technology on their learning: A review. *Educational Technology & Society*, *17*(4), 85–99.

Joselow, M. (2015). Digital distraction: How phones are taking over the classroom. *Forbes* [online]. Retrieved from http://www.forbes.com/sites/maxinejoselow/2015/06/25/digital-distraction-how-phones-are-taking-over-the-classroom/#5a7a85f02ce1

Judd, T. (2014). Making sense of multitasking: The role of Facebook. *Computers & Education*, *70*, 194–202.

Junco, R. (2012a). Too much face and not enough books: The relationship between multiple indices of Facebook use and academic performance. *Computers in Human Behavior*, *28*, 187–198.

Junco, R. (2012b). In-class multitasking and academic performance. *Computers in Human Behaviour*, *28*, 2236–2243.

Junco, R., and Cotten, S. (2012). No A 4 U: The relationship between multitasking and academic performance. *Computers & Education*, *59*, 505–514.

Karpinski, A., et al. (2013). An exploration of social networking site use, multitasking, and academic performance among United States and European university learners. *Computers in Human Behavior*, *29*, 1182–1192.

Kirschner, P., and Karpinski, A. (2010). Facebook® and academic performance. *Computers in Human Behavior*, *26*, 1237–1245.

Kolek, E. A., and Saunders, D. (2008). Online disclosure: An empirical examination of undergraduate Facebook profiles. *NASPA Journal*, *45*(1), 1–25.

Kwan, G., and Skoric, M. (2013). Facebook bullying: An extension of battles in school. *Computers in Human Behavior*, *29*, 16–25.

Leicht, G., and Globe, D. (2014). Should teachers be using social media in the classroom? *Public Broadcasting Service (PBS)* [online]. Retrieved from http://www.pbs.org/newshour/updates/social-media-valuable-tool-teachers/

Lenhart, A. (2015). Teens, social media & technology overview 2015. *Pew Research Internet Project* [online]. Retrieved from http://www.pewinternet.org/2015/04/09/teens-social-media-technology-2015/

Lenhart, A., and Madden, M. (2007). Teens, privacy and online social networks. *Pew Research Internet Project* [online]. Retrieved from http://www.pewinternet.org/2007/04/18/teens-privacy-and-online-social-networks/

Lenhart, A., Purcell, K., Smith, A., and Zickuhr, K. (2010). Social media & mobile internet use among teens and young adults. *Pew Research Internet Project* [online]. Retrieved from http://www.pewinternet.org/Reports/2010/Social-Media-and-Young-Adults.aspx

Livingstone, S. (2006). Drawing conclusions from new media research: Reflections and puzzles regarding children's experience of the Internet. *The Information Society*, *22*, 219–230.

Livingstone, S., Ólafsson, K., and Staksrud, E. (2011). *Social networking, age and privacy* [online]. EU Kids Online, London: LSE. Retrieved from http://eprints.lse.ac.uk/35849

Livingstone, S., Ólafsson, K., and Staksrud, E. (2013). Risky social networking practices among "underage" users: lessons for evidence-based policy. *Journal of Computer-Mediated Communication*, *18*, 303–320.

Madden, M., et al. (2013). Teens, social media, and privacy. *Pew Research Internet Project* [online]. Retrieved from http://www.pewinternet.org/Reports/2013/Teens-Social-Media-And-Privacy.aspx

Mann, S., and Robinson, A. (2009). Boredom in the lecture theatre: An investigation into the contributors, moderators and outcomes of boredom amongst university learners. *British Educational Research Journal, 35*(2), 243–258.

Millwood Hargrave, A., Livingstone, S., and Brake, D. (2006). *Harm and offence in media content: updating the 2005 review* [online]. Ofcom's Submission to the Byron Review, Annex 6: Literature Review. Retrieved from http://stakeholders.ofcom.org.uk/binaries/research/telecoms-research/annex6.pdf

Muller, D.A. (2014). *This will revolutionise education*[online]. Retrieved from https://www.youtube.com/watch?v=GEmuEWjHr5c

National School Boards Association (2007). *Creating and connecting: research and guidelines on social – and educational – networking* [online]. Grunwald Associates. Retrieved from http://www.nsba.org/sites/default/files/reports/CREATING-CONNECTING-Research-and-Guidelines-on-Online-Social-and-Educational-Networking.pdf

Oblinger, D. (2003). Understanding the new learners: Boomers, gen-xers, and millenials. *Educause Review*, 37–47.

Ofcom (2008a). *Ofcom's submission to the Byron Review – Annex 5: the evidence base-the views of children, young people and parents*[online]. Retrieved from http://stakeholders.ofcom.org.uk/binaries/research/telecoms-research/annex5.pdf

Ofcom (2008b). *Social networking – a quantitative and qualitative research report into attitudes, behaviours and use* [online]. Ofcom Report. Retrieved from http://news.bbc.co.uk/2/shared/bsp/hi/pdfs/02_04_08_ofcom.pdf

Ofcom (2010). *A quarter of internet users aged 8–12 say they have under-age social networking profiles* [online]. Ofcom Report. Retrieved from http://media.ofcom.org.uk/news/2010/a-quarter-of-internet-users-aged-8-12-say-they-have-under-age-social-networking-profiles/

Oksman, V., and Rautiainen, P. (2003). "Perhaps it is a body part": How the mobile phone became an organic part of the everyday lives of Finnish children and teenagers. *In:* J. Katz (ed.), *Machines that become us: the social context of personal communication technology*. New Brunswick, NJ: Transaction, pp. 293–308.

Pappas, C. (2013). The Facebook guide for teachers. *eLearning Industry* [online]. Retrieved from http://elearningindustry.com/the-facebook-guide-for-teachers

Pasek, J., More, E., and Hargittai, E. (2009). Facebook and academic performance: Reconciling a media sensation with data. *First Monday* [online], *14*(5). Retrieved from http://firstmonday.org/ojs/index.php/fm/article/view/2498

Perrin, A. (2015). Social media usage: 2005–2015. *Pew Research Internet Project* [online]. Retrieved from http://www.pewinternet.org/2015/10/08/social-networking-usage-2005-2015/

Prensky, M. (2001). Digital natives, digital immigrants. *On the Horizon, 9*(5), 1–6.

Project Tomorrow (2010). Creating our future: learners speak up about their vision for 21st century learning. *Project Tomorrow* [online]. Retrieved from http://www.tomorrow.org/speakup/pdfs/su09NationalFindingsLearners&Parents.pdf

Ross, C., et al. (2009). Personality and motivations associated with Facebook use. *Computers in Human Behavior, 25*, 578–586.

Sefton-Green, J. (2006). Youth, technology, and media cultures. *Review of Research in Education, 30.* 279–306.

Sharples, M., Graber, R., Harrison, C., and Logan, K. (2009). E-safety and Web 2.0 for children aged 11–16. *Journal of Computer Assisted Learning, 25,* 70–84.

Shirky, C. (2014). Why I just asked my learners to put their laptops away. *Medium* [online]. Retrieved from https://medium.com/@cshirky/why-i-just-asked-my-learners-to-put-their-laptops-away-7f5f7c50f368#.64c5jupuz

Siemens, G. (2005). Connectivism: A learning theory for the digital age. *International Journal of Instructional Technology and Distance Learning* [online], *2*(1). Retrieved from http://www.itdl.org/Journal/Jan_05/article01.htm

Staksrud, E., Ólafsson, K., and Livingstone, S. (2013). Does the use of social networking sites increase children's risk of harm? *Computers in Human Behavior, 29,* 40–50.

Sukarieh, M. and Tannock, S. (2009). Putting school commercialism in context: A global history of Junior Achievement Worldwide. *Journal of Education Policy, 24*(6), 769–786.

Sumuer, E. and Yildirim, S. (2014). Teachers' Facebook use: Their use habits, intensity, self-disclosure, privacy settings, and activities on Facebook. *Educational Studies, 40*(5), 537–553.

Walsh, K. (2011). Facebook in the classroom. Seriously. *EmergingEdTech* [online]. Retrieved from http://www.emergingedtech.com/2011/03/facebook-in-the-class room-seriously/

Wolak, J., Finkelhor, D., Mitchell, K.J., and Ybarra, M.L. (2008). Online 'predators' and their victims: Myths, realities and implications for prevention and treatment. *American Psychologist, 63,* 111–128.

Wood, E., et al. (2012). Examining the impact of off-task multi-tasking with technology on real-time classroom learning. *Computers & Education, 58,* 365–374.

Vandoninck, S., D'Haenens, L., De Cock, R., and Donoso, V. (2012). Social networking sites and contact risks among Flemish youth. *Childhood, 19*(1), 69–85.

Vrocharidou A., and Efthymiou I. (2012). Computer mediated communication for social and academic purposes: Profiles of use and University students' gratifications, *Computers & Education, 58,* (1), Pages 609–616

Ybarra, M.L., and Mitchell, K.J. (2008). How risky are social networking sites? A comparison of places online where youth sexual solicitation and harassment occurs. *Pediatrics, 121*(2), E350-E357.

Chapter 15

Using video for assessment practices inside classrooms

Chris Dann and Tony Richardson

The chapter debates the place of video in teachers' assessment practices of learners' work in classrooms. The chapter examines the following issues: the ethics of using video in classrooms; the storage implications; how the use of video may affect formative and summative assessments; and how video may support learner achievement through providing a mechanism for feedback.

Teachers are expected to have a voice in debates concerning pedagogical issues in their classrooms. One of those debates centres on the use of mobile devices and video capture inside classrooms. The real issues are, first, that the ethics of recording and storing video of children and young people must be considered. Second, how should video capture be used inside the classroom? Third, how is the video data going to be shown or shared? Fourth, will the video be streamed over the Internet, stored as is or edited and/or altered to meet educational needs? And finally, are there restrictions and expectations of how, where, when and for what purpose video can be used for learning inside classrooms?

As a teacher working in this environment, your input will be highly valued given your knowledge for leading learning and teaching. However, given that the technology is always evolving, some teachers are less familiar with mobile devices, which allow for instant video recording. You may be surprised to learn that the proportion of secondary school teachers who are over 50 years of age has increased by 4% across the OECD countries to 36% (OECD, 2014). To this end, there is much to gain from exploring emerging assessment practices that utilise the use of new generation mobile devices that allow for easy video capture inside classrooms.

This is not a debate we can ignore given that there are 350 to 400 different mobile devices in the market today and that mobile devices have overtaken fixed Internet devices, such as desktop computers (Morgan Stanley Research, 2014). This debate over how mobile devices, such as mobile phones and tablet devices with video capture, can be used to pedagogical effect is just getting started. The implications for you as a teacher are reflected in the increasing forms of mobility which are being presented to the market. According to CISCO (2017) 69% of mobile data traffic will be video by 2019, with global traffic from wearable devices expected to grow 18-fold from 2014 to 277 petabytes per month by 2019. Whether you wish to take up new mobile capabilities, or not, will depend on many factors, but first, you will need to consider your position on the current mobile video-enabled technologies and their role in the assessment of learning outcomes.

The ethics of using video in classrooms

Whilst there are ethical concerns with the use of video in the classroom, these concerns can be addressed through establishing relationships built on trust.

One of the major challenges facing the use of video is the ethical concern that it poses with respect to the learners in the classroom. The next section argues that these concerns can be addressed through establishing relationships built on trust.

When it comes to the ethical challenges facing teachers using video-captured data on mobile devices, there are a number of areas of concern. One of the key concerns is in the changing relationship between learners and teachers. A classroom is a place where relationships are established between learners and teachers (Hattie, 2009). These form the foundations by which learners and teachers connect and, as a result, learners engage (Richardson, 2014). One of the concerns of the use of video within the classroom is: How does video impact on the learner and teacher relationship? This concern has an ethical dimension with the use of video potentially impacting the way in which teachers and learners interact. Whether such impact is negative or positive is a moot point, but to maximise the chances of beneficial outcomes is to ensure that these relationships, and the use of mobile video technology within them, are built on trust, openness, honesty and transparency. This is evidenced through learners and teachers engaging in the learning and the exchange of ideas based on collaboration and negotiation.

The concern associated with videos, within the classroom, is focused by not what will be used, but rather how it will be used. If the video captured shows a failure to learn, might this result in blame or demoralisation of the learners? One way this concern could be placated is through learners and teachers focusing on the collaboration and negotiation of learning outcomes from the curriculum documents. Although there are ethical concerns with the use of video in the classroom, those concerns can be addressed through establishing learner and teacher relationships built on trust. This may include signing a policy, which explicitly outlines a code of conduct that is followed regarding video use inside classrooms, whereby all learners and the teacher agree to abide by the policy.

An alternative to the simplistic view of mutual trust taken above on the ethical use of mobile video capture is presented below and is premised on the understanding that technology is changing and teachers and learners need to recognise the complexities of the emerging technologies.

Arguably, trust as a basis of ethical use of mobile video-enabled devices in classrooms presents a simplistic view of the practice. Trust is a concept that is used, interpreted and constructed in different ways by individuals and needs to be considered as a context-specific phenomenon (Rousseau et al., 1998). If we were to rely solely on the development of trust and the feedback received and given in the relationship between learners and the teacher, this would be a major mistake. The trust element is premised on the relationship between the person being videoed and the person videoing. This shallow view fails to recognise that the video taken by a person using a mobile device may provide data to others, by mistake or purposefully, and that the 'others' may or may not be involved in the learning process.

Analysis of the real issue is required if we are to explore the ethical implications of using mobile video-enabled devices in classrooms. To outline a much more serious view, you need to consider the following issues in this debate: first, the ethics of recording and storing video of children and young people. Second, how should video capture be used inside the classroom? Third, how is this going to be shown or shared? Fourth, will the video be streamed over the Internet, stored as is or edited and/or altered to meet educational needs? And finally, are there restrictions and expectations of how, where, when and for what purpose video can be used for learning?

Video captured on a mobile device will automatically be stored on the device itself and possibly on a remote server accessed by the device. Any mobile device that can capture video and transmit the video across a network needs to be handled by individuals who are cognisant of the implications of their actions. To transmit the video from a mobile device across a network involves initial capture of the video in the device, storing of the video on the device and then transferring it to either a cloud or personal physical drive. Either way, the video images leave the device and are available for others to possibly access. Physically losing the hard drive is very different to storing the video data in a cloud. Both have different access issues.

As researchers in mobile video feedback, the authors were required to take ethical responsibility for the security of the video data during its travels. First, to conduct research about the impact of mobile video capture, ethical consideration required us to ensure that the video was not stored on the device after the application had used it, and it was stored elsewhere. Second, the application needed to be capable of only transmitting the video over a locked wireless network and not over a 3G network. These restrictions on video location and transmission were supported by password protection. Password requirements ensured that the video on the device could not be accessed and the system would time out if a teacher left the device open on their desk. To prevent unauthorised access, password entry to the application on the mobile device and password protection on the web portal serving the application containing the video for individual users was also required. Further to this, each mobile device had to be linked to a cloud-based instance, and each instance had to be secured differently to any other school instance.

Even with each of these securities catered for in the ethical approval process, there were further requirements. These included all users signing a code of conduct that ensured that they would not share their personal login details with any other user or individual. Clearly, education ethical bodies have expected procedures to follow. Examples of ethical bodies are: the country or state education department; schools and school districts; and universities. These will require greater ethical considerations around the use of video in classrooms than simply trust. Their concerns in our case study in Australia rested with the privacy of leaners in classrooms due to their vulnerability, focusing on people who cannot be trusted.

If you are to explore the use of video, you will need to gain knowledge of the ethical requirements of the state/government and managers of your school. Internationally, these restrictions vary. Sometimes there are variations within countries where, for example, in Australia, each state has a separate ethical approval process and various standards. The critical documents required to obtain ethical clearance that, in an Australian example, you will need to consider include: the Child Protection Act for your teaching location, the Information Privacy Act and Professional Codes of Conduct.

As a teacher, it is possible to use video within the classroom, but the reality is that the ethical implications associated with its use are predicated on more than simply trust.

Video storage implications

As will be discussed later in this section, the use of evidence in determining the level of academic success of learners is becoming increasingly more significant. This significance is the result of finding ways in which learners' outcomes can be clearly defined and measured (McLaughlin & Talbert, 2006; Hattie, 2009). As a consequence of this, schools are now required to obtain and store more 'evidence' on learner outcomes. It will be argued that the use of video can decrease the need for physical storage space required by schools to evidence learning outcomes.

The collection of evidence, by schools, on learners has increased over time for some countries, though not all. When compared to the 'Asian educators', countries like the United States and Great Britain have fallen behind in their capacity to address the educational outcomes of learners (Asian Society, 2011). In order to address this, there has been an emphasis on *high-stakes testing* (McLaughlin & Talbert, 2006), whereby learners are subjected to a battery of tests that are used to determine outcomes linked to standards. The greater the demand placed on procuring more and more evidence on learners, the more enhanced the need for schools to store that evidence. Given the emphasis that schools have on 'paper', the impact on storage is reflected in a school's capacity to locate or purchase storage space to house this evidence. Added to this is the security associated with ensuring that the evidence is safe from tampering, theft or damage. One way in which this situation could be addressed is by using video digital files.

The most important aspect of the use of video is that the evidence is collected and stored in a digital format. What this means is that there is no need to store excessive quantities of paper, for example, teacher assessment books or folders. Within the context of an assessment piece, a teacher, when learning outcomes suit this method, could, for example, simply video that learner and add verbal comments to the digital capture instead of having to write down copious amounts of notes on a student. When this has been completed, the evidence can then be saved in a digital format either to an external hard drive or to a secure server. In this way, a teacher would be able to collect evidence on several learners and not be required to store individual documents or folders on, for example, 30 learners. Instead, all the evidence would be stored in digital format requiring much less storage space.

Video storage would also have a spin-off in that there would be a greater ease of access to the evidence for both the teacher and learner. Instead of the teacher or learner having to rummage through numerous folders, there would be quick access to the evidence by simply accessing it via the external hard drive or a secure server. Hence, the use of video will decrease the need for storage space required by schools and the time teachers and learners use to access the data.

Whilst the debate here focuses on storage capacity, cost and the intent of providing evidence for accountability purposes, the real controversy here is the focus on the storage of evidence. This focus is being driven more by management and accountability factors rather than the pure element of what we need for improved learning. The controversy is that storage of evidence is being considered to measure the overall student cohort's progress. Evidence of this type is stored because it is used by a school to justify its learning outcomes and teachers can justify their pedagogical approach. In the current climate, it would appear naïve to suggest that storage requirements of assessment were defined by the data's usefulness to the learner in the learning process.

If we can assume that learner assessment data is only needed to inform program and student learning, then we can begin to explore the implications of storage for pure educational purposes and not an imposed political accountability-driven purpose. If we need to ensure the accountability and governmental requirements of storage, then we must consider a different set of requirements. The space required to house data, that is useful to the learner and the educators involved with that learner, will take some digital space, and this will be less than the cluttered back rooms and storerooms of yesteryear.

A learner-centred focus creates a greater focus on access to the stored evidence for both the teacher and learner. Instead of the teacher or learners having to hunt through folders, there would be quick access to the evidence by simply accessing pre-defined database reports that draw data from its external hard drives or a secure server.

However, digital video can take up large spaces on hard drives and servers. But the word 'space' requires definition. If we are concerned with digital space, then video storage will take up less space than hard copies of work, but video files without compression applied can be much larger than other forms of digital files. Regardless of the above details, the key factors are:

- the cost of the storage space
- the location of the storage space
- access to the storage space
- the governing laws of your country of education district
- ownership of the data being stored.

The cost is reducing for online digital space as the evolution of technology increases the size of files. My first classroom computer had less memory than my current phone, and it held the school's records for the year and all my planning and all student digital files. Not only are the files sizes changing, but also the life of the files is decreasing in social networks. To be clear, the relevance to the viewer of the images has a shorter life (where this is defined as the length of time one could view the video). For example, a viral video can be transmitted worldwide and be viewed by millions on the 1st of October. However, by the 3rd or 4th of October, the video may well be so buried in the social network of the millions of individuals who accessed it that it is no longer relevant to their daily life.

Schools and departments carried the initial cost of digital storage when the first networks were introduced to schools. The rapid rate of change in technology has now introduced cloud storage and bring your own device (BYOD) programs, as schools realise they do not have the physical or digital capability to store the required information. Whilst the cloud may seem to be the answer to the financial costs of physical storage, there are other costs.

Costs associated with physical storage could include the time in training for the organisation to incorporate cloud computing, reorganisation of organisation as they accommodate external storage options and the social cost of information exposure. Cloud storage is now expanding to accommodate one's desktop so that you can log onto a computer anywhere and your desktop and files can be accessed in the same way you would from your personal computer. Risks to privacy and highly sensitive data need to be considered if this type of storage is to be considered. Cloud storage can have other implications and is being broadly adopted now, with the 2013 NMC Horizon Report (K–12 Edition) identifying it for adoption. Cloud storage has the ability to house files collected via mobile devices when they are being used for assessment purposes.

These files can be reviewed, edited and only small amounts of the video actually used, and often to assist the teacher in their practice rather than assisting learners. Critical analysis of what should be videoed and how much should be videoed needs to be thought through. Apart from the physical storage of the video, schools embarking on a video capture for feedback have a raft of new issues to consider. How much do they spend on the video equipment? Cameras are expensive. Do they set up a video editing suite? Do they purchase video editing software for learners and teachers to use? If the systems are for specific learner-centred outcomes, then these purchases may be justified, but given the cost and time it takes for a software package to be upgraded, this may also need to be placed in the equation.

To summarise the storage debate you will first need to decide what you will store, what you are going to do with it and why it is important to you. Once you have answered these questions, ask yourself, how sustainable over time is your solution to your needs? How will you protect the learners whom you are charged to protect and teach? Mobile devices, as they become part of the learning environment, can capture an assortment of perspectives for the enhancement of learning at a reduced cost to the school.

Formative and summative assessment implications

The use of video can assist in the development of formative assessment and may assist in the decline of summative assessment.

It could be suggested that one of the main areas in which education is undergoing a significant change is in assessment (McLaughlin & Talbert, 2006). A mainstay of educational outcomes has for many years been the use of summative assessment, whereby a student's end-of-term, end-of-semester or end-of-year result reflects that student's capacity to meet the criteria of a course or unit of work. It will be argued that the use of video will assist in the development of formative assessment and could assist in the decline of summative assessment.

If one of the important jobs of education is about improving the quality of a learner's capacity to understand and, therefore, achieve at school, then embedded in that job is a cogent need to ensure that learners are presented with effective feedback (Hattie, 2009). Clearly, the continual use of summative assessment as a tool to facilitate this does not fall within the boundaries of an effective system. The focus of providing learners with feedback at the end of a task seems rather odd because the learners are not capable of addressing any shortfalls in the learning during the learning process. In a sense, a student is told at the end of the assessment why they did not receive an A+ for their assessment piece instead of being guided to achieve an A+ on their assessment piece. It is here that video could assist in providing learners with effective feedback during the learning process as opposed to allocating a result at the end of the task. Video can achieve this in a number of ways. First, video can capture in real time (Dann & Richardson, 2015) the events surrounding the use of the learning process.

A teacher can capture what a learner is doing as it happens and provide feedback to that learner on any aspect of their learning that may require further elaboration. Second, video will enhance the ability of the teacher to help learners address instantaneously any gap in knowledge (Dann & Richardson, 2015) that the learner may have encountered in the learning process. A gap in knowledge represents the distance between a learner's capacity to achieve planned specified learning outcomes *with* teacher support and *without* teacher support (Dann & Richardson, 2015). Consequently, video feedback provided to the learners, by the teacher, is highly effective due to its reliability and real-time delivery. This is so because the teacher can provide valuable video evidence to support learners, and learners in turn can view and reflect on the video evidence to assist them in locating gaps in knowledge. The learner achieves this by comparing what they (the student) demonstrated, without teacher support, to the comments from the teacher. The difference in the comparison reflects a learner's gap in knowledge.

There is enough research to suggest that the quality of the teacher has a direct impact on the outcomes of learners (Hattie, 2009), which includes the quality of a teacher's feedback (Hattie, 2009). With this being the case, the use of video evidence to supply real-time feedback to learners, that assists in addressing gap(s) in knowledge, will facilitate enhanced learning.

With respect to the balance between formative and summative assessment, first we need to understand that there has always been an imbalance between these, with formative assessment having been described as invisible in documentation (Jessop et al., 2012). If we are to try to provide real-time feedback and tip the balance in the favour of formative assessment, then there needs to be consideration given to the process and its impact on the learning process. The addition of video feedback and collection for evidence of learner achievement can directly impact this imbalance. The ability to effectively use tools, including video, to increase student learning outcomes will be one opportunity to decrease the imbalance. Video is being used as part of feedback to students (Dann & Richardson, 2015). Research into the effectiveness of video used as feedback used to commonly refer to video collected using a video camera and manual digital storage. Once stored, it then needed to be transferred. This manual and time-consuming process is not needed now with current technologies. What is a shame is that educators appear not to be investing time and effort into the application of these current technologies. This is not to say that research into the phenomenon is not occurring, but if we are to use the Nike slogan 'Just do it', we would be further down the track in effectiveness and usage than we find ourselves today.

Summative assessment is characterised by the measurement of learning outcomes at the end of a unit of work and to ensure that students have achieved a particular learning outcome. Increasingly, the curriculum outcomes are reflecting the 21st century skills that require ongoing development by the learner and increased opportunities for formative assessment. Increasingly, assessment for learning (Earl, 2013) has become an important part of assessment of curriculum outcomes. Video, when used as feedback, can form part of formative assessment processes.

For example, the use of video in a physical education (PE) lesson, which utilises motion analysis, can enable the learner and the teacher to immediately analyse a performance and make improvements. This is potentially a very powerful use of video to enable critical reflection on skill development. This example was drawn from Mallen's (2014) research, which demonstrated that when video analysis technology is used in PE settings, learners' skill acquisition and understanding of that skill increased. Using this feedback technology also increased learners' engagement, which in turn enhanced learners' motivation. The potential of video to turn around disaffected learners was also supported by the research of Casey and Jones (2011), who undertook a study in New South Wales, Australia using video analysis in a variety of ways in PE lessons. A key finding was that technology engaged learners in a way where they became facilitators of their own learning through reflecting on the video. Specifically, the video analysis in lessons created an environment in which disaffected learners developed a more concise understanding of throwing and catching.

For generations, teachers have collected evidence of student progress and have tried to provide evidence of student progress towards their learning goals – mostly for the school, the parents and the wider educational system itself. Why is it that teachers and the educational profession continue to resist opportunities to improve their practices now that video and mobile devices are available? Changes in education are slow if not tedious, and the slowness of educational change is recognised as a trademark of our profession. Research over decades has called for changes to teacher habits, and yet classroom practice is practically unchanged (Fullan, 2007). Mobile technology has impacted Allied Health and numerous other professions, including nursing. Large multinational organisations use and integrate mobile technologies into their workflow. When a new technology appears to have benefits to student learning, the profession spends time considering the benefits, researching the process, labelling and exploring the possible impact, and when all is said and done, the technology is rarely used and becomes outmoded. The rate of technological change will require decision makers to act and work on the best information they have at the time. Educators are so often concerned with the impact of something and, as such, they fail to implement a system and lose the opportunity to allow the system to have the impact.

If you are going to provide students with exceptional curriculum outcomes, you, too, will have to assume responsibility for the speed of your decisions and your pedagogical adaptability. Will you take on board new technologies and become a learner or become so focused on the processes and management that have been entrenched in educational practice that you will exclude innovations such as mobile video-enabled devices from playing a role in formative assessment?

For many years, summative assessment has been given a bad name. Viewing the use of mobile technology and the collection of video as part of the assessment process can be beneficial and create a summative picture of the student's current capability. Capturing video for feedback does not necessarily change the fact that we need to report to parents and the system where the students are at a given point of time. What we need to consider is the detail of the summative picture. If a summative picture is created with a single test result, this has a certain value to the students', the parent and the system. If the summative picture is created from the same test, plus the sum total of the students' attempts to acquire the knowledge or skill, then we have a summative picture that provides a richer and more detailed view of the students' learning. We would argue that if we add to this the formative outputs, captured during the time a student has spent learning the skill or knowledge, then the result is an even more fine-grained assessment statement.

The power of video evidence in classrooms

The use of video can enhance the recording of evidence to assist teachers in the classroom and thereby address a learner's gap in knowledge.

For a teacher to be in a position to diminish a learner's gap in knowledge, effective feedback will become a vital tool. Therefore, the use of video can enhance the recording of evidence to assist teachers in the classroom by addressing an individual student's gap in knowledge (Dann & Richardson, 2014).

With increased use of formative assessment, there will be a greater emphasis on teachers being able to provide learners with effective feedback, as feedback plays a key role in learners' outcomes (Marzano, 2007; Hattie, 2009). The issue for teachers will relate not to the effectiveness of the feedback to the class but rather a capacity to deliver effective feedback to individual learners. There may, of course, be similarities with respect to converging areas in learners' gap[s] in knowledge; however, the teacher will need to be able to quickly ascertain and then prove to a learner or learners where their gap in knowledge exists. It is suggested that video evidence will have a critical part to play in this process.

Teachers need to provide evidence to parents and students of a student's leaning. In most cases, it is a teacher's inability to provide the evidence that can lead to challenges. These challenges may be associated with the student, parent or student/parent. Video evidence of the application of the task to either the student or parent would be one cogent way in which effective feedback could be provided.

The challenge for the teacher is that their feedback may be useful to the learner but the learner may not believe what the teacher has to say. If this is the case, then the effectiveness of the feedback is limited to the points that the learner accepts. A failure on the part of the learner to understand the full meaning of the teacher's feedback could result in very little diminishment in a learner's gap in knowledge. By providing a learner with video evidence of their task, in real time, it would be very difficult for the learner to question the validity of that evidence, as it is an honest, open and transparent representation of what the learner presented.

Consequently, the use of video can enhance the delivery of effective evidence to assist teachers in the classroom by addressing a learner's gap in knowledge.

The use of video for feedback that is collected on a mobile device brings with it concerns founded in the misuse of mobile phone cameras by individuals (Wickel, 2013). This concern is highlighted by, for example, selfie becoming Oxford Dictionary's word of the year in 2013 (Day, 2013). So why would we as educators introduce the opportunity to post videos and provide feedback, possibly negative and harmful, to our learners who have put themselves into potentially vulnerable positions by being videoed? How can this be seen as a responsible act? Is this taking it too far? Is it possible that the education community is overreacting? Serious consideration is required to ascertain whether the risk of the technology being used inappropriately might outweigh the educational benefit that may come with the technology.

It could be argued that the benefits of video feedback can far outweigh the risk associated with its use. There were risks and fears when the Internet, tripod video cameras and use of MP3 players and DVD players was introduced in classrooms. Using these devices in formative and summative assessment processes can be part of the assessment of curriculum outcomes. The use of video as feedback and evidence to inform assessment judgements is an important point to consider here, and it is important to note that we do not advocate for the application of video for all curriculum outcomes but rather for curriculum outcomes that require students to demonstrate 21st century skills.

A separate point to consider is that the teacher's pedagogy can be interrupted, disrupted and derailed by the intrusion of the technology. Most teachers will have trouble defining their pedagogy and dismiss intrusions into their daily routines without offering extended evidence of the possible improvement. This dismissal is due to the pressure of curriculum accountability and the increasing responsibilities being placed on teachers in school communities. The disruption to a teacher's pedagogy is critical in the learning process for the teacher, and digital technologies are uniquely placed to stimulate disruption (Younie and Leask, 2013). The potential for change does not lie in the technology itself but in the appropriation of that technology by the teacher, who has the agency to create pedagogical change. Pedagogy is the art of teaching and revolves around the decisions that teachers make when guiding and directing the teaching and learning process.

Separate to this is your ability to keep the learning process focused on the learning outcomes. In the current accountability climate for education, the learning process requires teachers to record both formative and summative assessment, and we argue that video offers an opportunity to provide evidence to inform teachers' assessment of learners' achievements, supporting learner achievement using video as a basis for feedback.

Video feedback as support for learners leading to higher achievement

The final section of this debate centres on the use of video as a tool for increasing learner achievement via improvement in feedback. It will be argued that by using video, a teacher will be able to provide learners with highly effective feedback, which will culminate in higher learner achievement.

There is sufficient research (Hattie, 2009; Hanushek, 2010; Richardson, 2014) to suggest teachers can influence learner outcomes. The manner in which teachers influence learner outcomes is specifically through providing teacher feedback (Hattie, 2009). The more effective the feedback the more effect it could have on learners. Vygotsky's seminal work on the zone of proximal development (Latham et al., 2007) emphasises the importance of establishing a cogent link between what the learner knows and does not know. Vygotsky's work suggests that it is the difference between what a learner can and cannot do without support that will diminish their zone of proximal development. It is here that the use of video could be introduced to assist learners, through an increased level of support, via video feedback, to improve learner achievement.

Arguably, the genesis to effective feedback stems from a teacher's capacity to capture learner understanding of a task in real time. Based on Vygotsky's work to assist learners in diminishing their lack of understanding, it is important that learners are able to undertake tasks and be successful in those tasks without a great deal of assistance from the teacher. Clearly, the more a learner can perform a task without teacher intervention the better the chance that the learner will complete that task. Consequently, by a teacher using video evidence to substantially prove a learner's understanding or lack of understanding, the teacher is increasing their level of support for the learner. This increased level of support is provided by the highly effective feedback supplied by the teacher through the use of video. This would culminate in enhanced levels of learner achievement because there is a direct association between learner outcomes and teacher quality. The quality of the teacher (Hattie, 2009) is reflected in their ability to effectively communicate with learners, and one way in which this occurs is via the effectiveness of the teacher's feedback in addressing learners' lack of understanding. Consequently, if the teacher's feedback can be improved, then there should be a commensurate level of success associated with the level of achievement of learners.

However, the use of video can be more distracting and potentially threatening when attached to assessment. Research by Willis et al. (2012) has identified that there is increased pressure associated with the presence of video. However, if used to provide feedback that allows for continued and focused growth, it can be accepted. Yet, some learners may find it all very challenging and difficult in the beginning.

The psychological impact of videoing the learner should not be underestimated. In past years, learners may have been affected by a memory of a teacher's words, especially if they were negative. Now they can be reminded of these words, with the added images of the teacher's facial expression, their tone, the reaction of their peers and the location being held for longer and impacting the learner in much greater ways, both good and bad. This highlights the need for teacher sensitivity with respect to giving feedback to learners.

Conclusion

The debate concerning video use for classroom practice is challenging you to explore your willingness to experiment with this technology. Are you willing to engage with mobile video collection systems in classroom assessment? The arguments for and against their use create a significant dilemma for you in your professional practice. Your professional judgement will be called on as will your knowledge of your own pedagogy. Knowing your own pedagogy is critical to your decision because it will only be you who knows how you will approach the technology and how you can integrate it into your assessment processes, whether it be for summative or formative assessment. This chapter has outlined five specific areas that you might need to consider before embarking on the use of video-enabled technologies in your assessment of curriculum learning outcomes. Some learning outcomes lend themselves to various forms of assessment and only some of these may be appropriate for video feedback and assessment.

Globally, the increase of mobile devices is outstripping purchases of desktop computers, and new technologies will continue to develop. In terms of mobile devices, they have become prevalent in society and have pervaded schools and educational settings despite the resistance of some. This chapter has focused the debate on current technologies, but you will be faced with the ethical dilemmas that are embedded in the use of mobile technologies like wearable devices, such as Internet-enabled watches, Google Glass® and so forth. Will you face the challenge and innovate or simply repeat old pedagogic practices? The choice is yours.

The ethical use of technology, storage implications, assessment practices and the opportunity for video evidence to support learner achievement has been debated, and it raises some important issues for teachers to consider. Over the past few years, the increased presence of mobile technology has been growing in the teaching profession. Understanding that new devices and new approaches will be presented to you, over the course of your career, is the first step to ensuring a considered approach to their implementation. The second requirement is for you to be prepared to debate the issues involved and be actively engaged in the introduction of devices so that you can play a proactive role in their successful appropriation for pedagogic purposes.

References

Asian Society. (2011) *Improving teacher quality around the world* [online]. The International Summit on the Teaching Profession, March 16 and 17, 2011. Available from: http://www2gov/about/inits/ed/internationaled/teaching-summit-2011.html.ed. [Accessed 10 October 2016].

Casey, A., and Jones, B. (2011) *Using digital technology to enhance student engagement in physical education* [online]. *Asia-Pacific Journal of Health, Sport and Physical Education*, Vol 2, Issue 2, pp. 51–66.

CISCO (2017) *Cisco visual networking index: global mobile data traffic forecast update, 2016–2021 white paper* [online]. Available from: http://www.cisco.com/c/en/us/solutions/collateral/service-provider/visual-networking-index-vni/mobile-white-paper-c11-520862.html [Accessed 15 July 2017].

Dann, C., and Richardson, T. (2015) Improving the work integrated learning experience through mobile technologies. *In:* J. Keengwe and M.B Maxfield (eds.), *Advancing higher education with mobile learning technologies: cases, trends, and inquiry-based methods*, IGI Global, pp. 154–69.

Day, E. (2013) How selfies became a global phenomenon. *The Guardian* [online], 13 July 2013. Available from: https://www.theguardian.com/technology/2013/jul/14/how-selfies-became-a-global-phenomenon [Accessed 20 July 2017].

Earl, L. (2013). *Assessment as learning: using classroom assessment to maximize student learning, 2nd edition*. Thousand Oaks, CA: Corwin Press.

Fullan, M. (2007). *The new meaning of educational change*. London: Routledge.

Hanushek, E.A. (2010) Waiting for "Superman" How we can save America's failing public system. *In:* K. Webber (ed.), *The difference is great teachers*. New York: Participant Media Guide. pp. 81–100.

Hattie, J. (2009). Visible learning. *A synthesis of over 800 meta-analyses relating to achievement*. London: Routledge.

Jessop, T., McNab, N., and Gubby, L. (2012) Mind the gap: an analysis of how quality assurance procedures influence programme assessment patterns. *Active Learning in Higher Education*, 13 (3) pp. 143–154.

Latham, G., et al. (2007). *Learning to teach, new times, new practices.* Oxford: Oxford University Press.

Mallen, G. (2014) *Evaluating the benefits of using video motion analysis when teaching Physical Education in a secondary school setting.* Thesis (unpublished Master's), Leicester: DeMontfort University.

Marzano, R.J. (2007). *The art and science of teaching.* Alexandria, VA: ASCD.

McLaughlin, M.W., and Talbert, J.E. (2006). *Building school-based teacher learning communities – professional strategies to improve student achievement.* New York: Teachers College Press.

Morgan Stanley Research (2014). *Internet and media: bringing it all together.* New York, NY: Morgan Stanley.

OECD (2014) *Education indicators in Focus 20* [online]. Organisation for Economic Co-Operation and Development, March 2014. Available from: https://www.oecd.org/education/skills-beyond-school/EDIF2014No.20(eng).pdf [Accessed 15 July 2017].

Richardson, T. (2014) *Early career teacher conceptions of a quality teacher – a phenomenographic approach.,* The University of the Sunshine Coast, Queensland, Australia.

Rousseau, D. M., Sitkin, S. B., Burt, R. S., and Camerer, C. (1998). Not so different after all: a cross-discipline view of trust. *Academy of Management Review*, 23, 393–404.

Wickel, T.M. (2013), Narcissism and social networking sites: the act of taking selfies. *Elon Journal of Undergraduate Research in Communications* [online], Vol. 6, No. 1, Spring 2015. Available from: https://www.elon.edu/docs/e-web/academics/communications/research/vol6no1/01WickelEJSpring15.pdf [Accessed 13 December 2016].

Willis, M., et al. (2012) *Designing mobile information systems to support WIL experiences.* In: OZCHI 2012: Conference of the Australasian Computer-Human Interaction Conference, pp. 653–656.

Younie, S., and Leask, M. (2013) *Teaching with technologies: the essential guide.* Maidenhead: Open University Press.

Chapter 16

Developing reflective practice in the classroom using ICT

Helen Boulton

Introduction

This chapter highlights the debates and controversies concerning developing reflective practice in the classroom and the use of ICT to support reflective practice. The chapter presents an overview of the place of reflective practice in the professional development of teachers, and then debates whether reflective practice has a place in the classroom and whether technologies are able to advance current practice.

Purpose of reflection

Reflective practice has been a key element of teacher education and the professional development of teachers for several decades. Boulton and Hramiak (2012a) trace the origins of reflective practice back to Aristotle and the Nicomachean ethics. However, reflective practice in teaching and learning is usually seen as developing from Dewey's (1933) notion of reflective attitudes and Schön's (1983) notions of 'reflection on action' and 'reflection in action', which now proliferate teacher professional practice.

However, there is criticism of reflection in action. For example, Carr and Kemmis (1986), Day (1993) and Solomon (1987) argue that reflection can result in a narrowness of focus and a failure to acknowledge the social processes requiring dialogue with others in similar situations, thereby developing more criticality of reflection.

Reflective practice was initially aligned to organisational learning in business by Argyris and Schön (1978) who identified three types of learning, each of which is associated with reflective practice in teaching and learning:

- Single-loop learning where learning takes place which does not impact on policy and practice across the organisation;
- Double-loop learning where learning impacts on the organisation in terms of changes to policy or practice; and
- Deutero-learning whereby the organisation creates an environment for reflection and learning and recognises that new processes or policy are needed, such as through seeking feedback from staff and students.

There is now a growing literature related to discourses on reflection drawing on Schön's (ibid.) seminal text to illustrate how the literature developed in the 1990s from reflection per se to aligning reflection with the development of teachers and other professions such as nursing (Dymoke and Harrison, 2008).

Alignment between reflective practice and practitioner action research is increasingly illustrated in the literature (Bengtsson, 1995; McNiff and Whitehead, 2009). Action research developed in classrooms by advocates such as Stenhouse (1975), Carr and Kemmis (1986), Elliott (1993) and McNiff and Whitehead (2009), provides a methodology for teachers to research their own practice in a cyclical process involving observation of practice, reflection, development of revised practice and implementation of the revised practice through action, as illustrated in Figure 16.1. Action research is often cyclical in nature with one cycle leading to the next until the reflective cycle is completed. Bandura (1991) added a further dimension to the notion of reflection through aligning self-reflection to the social cognitive theory of self-regulation leading to self-efficacy.

Towler and Broadfoot (1992) recognised the significance of professionals reviewing and reflecting:

> In an effort to understand what has taken place and to gain a clear idea of what has been learned or achieved is to use language in such a way that knowledge and thought processes become available for introspection and revision. If we know what we know then we can change it.
>
> (ibid., p. 137)

Drawing on Munby et al. (1989), Towler and Broadfoot (ibid.) aligned reflection to self-assessment, defining this as the process of reflecting on past experience and understanding what has been learnt or achieved. However, simply reviewing practice will have little value unless it is aligned to planning and target setting to identify new patterns and knowledge, and making sense of new practice by relating to previous practice, thus reflecting a constructionist approach to learning. Brockbank and McGill (1998) developed this notion further by suggesting that through this reflective process, you are able to make choices often informed by others, through dialogue, enabling creativity. Through the use of technology to reflect, reflections can be opened to others beyond those in the practitioner's community of practice, thus facilitating a wider audience and arguably, a deeper level of reflection.

Figure 16.1 Action research cycle.

In more recent literature, the reflective professional is discussed in terms of an accepted process of becoming and being a teacher, with teacher education globally incorporating the development of reflective practice (Hramiak and Hudson, 2014). There is continuing debate in the literature around whether reflection can be learnt and whether the language of reflection should be taught (Moon, 2007). Discussion of reflective practice has moved the professional beyond someone who reflects on their own practice to becoming a professional with a language of critical reflection and practitioners developing a 'reflective, evidence-based approach to realising and improving teaching and learning' (Light et al., 2009, p. 274). This process positively challenges the traditional format of the apprentice style of professional development where 'teachers as learners are seen as passive recipients of knowledge' (McMahon et al., 2011, p. 79) to one where the complexity of teaching is recognised as situated within individual classrooms with dialogue between teachers/mentors as essential and emphasising engaging with others through communities of practice (Wenger, 2009). Reflective practitioners who then draw on literature to develop their understanding and inform their reflections critically demonstrate a deeper level of reflection leading to reflexivity to continually improve classroom practice. This relates closely to Vygotsky's (1978) identification of the zone of proximal development, which identified the distance between the developmental level of learning and what could be learnt through 'collaboration with more capable peers' (ibid. p. 86), continually improving their classroom practice.

Light et al. (2009) identify three features for effective reflective practice for teachers in higher education which are applicable to teachers in schools: space, which relates to the teaching environment and knowledge which is discipline based; time, which includes reflecting back on practice and forward on developing practice critically, that is, dialogue with students and colleagues and educational/research literature in seeking improvement to practice; and matter, which incorporates the previous features and acknowledges that learning for the professional needs to be active and based on research and evidence to develop a higher level of reflection. Thus, teaching is transformed through reflection into a 'process of inquiry' with the teacher becoming an active researcher into their own practice.

Moon (2007, p. 115) adds to the debate around depth of reflection, viewing reflective practice as 'holistic and organic', moving through different levels of reflective writing from mere description of an event to the deepest level involving dialogue with relevant others or research literature, and a development of metacognition in reviewing one's own practice.

Reflective practice for the teacher is generally related to critically improving teaching and learning and improving student progression. Hence, there needs to be recognition that reflection should lead to improvement in practice. It can be argued that an improvement in practice should impact the classroom, that is, on learning outcomes and student achievement. Guskey (2002) developed a framework for professional development with five levels of impact which could arguably be applied to reflective practice:

- Level 1: Participants' reactions
- Level 2: Participants' learning
- Level 3: Organisations' support and change
- Level 4: Participants' use of new knowledge and skills
- Level 5: Student learning outcomes.

To consider this further, reflective practice involves reflection on action (Schön, 1983), which will normally result in developing practice leading to learning. Engagement at a critical level, that is through dialogue with others or informed by learning through the experiences of others, will lead to the development of new knowledge or skills which can then be applied to classroom practice, leading to an impact on student learning outcomes. It could therefore be argued that Guskey's framework provides a reflective scaffold which moves the teacher beyond merely evaluating a lesson. It could be argued that this also reflects the action research cycle set out in Figure 16.1, that is, the delivery of a lesson, following planning, and critical reflection on that lesson will lead to learning which will result in changes in the delivery the next time the lesson is taught, or in following lessons, which will impact on student learning outcomes.

Zwozdiak-Myers (2012, p. 25) provides a simplistic framework for reviewing practice and argues that this will help teachers to develop their epistemology of practice:

- What was taught?
- How was it taught?
- Did pupils achieve the intended learning outcomes?
- What teaching strategies were effective or ineffective?
- How do I know?
- What does this mean?
- How does this make me feel?
- How might I do things differently next time?

However, it could be argued that this framework ignores the dialogic- and research-informed critical depth of reflection argued by others as important for engendering a more critical and deeper level of reflection.

We now move to consider the place of reflection in the school classroom before discussing technologies that could be utilised to support reflective practice.

Reflective practice in the classroom can encompass self-assessment, scaffolding pupils in developing a deeper level of learning using a framework which scaffolds this development through questions such as the following based on a critical incident framework to help them to develop their reflective writing:

- What happened?
- How did you feel about it?
- What was good or bad?

- How could you develop this for the future?
- What did others have to say? This may be dialogue with peers or feedback from the teacher.

Hramiak and Hudson (2014) argue that when used in classrooms, reflective practice can be applied as a way of problem-solving, while Price et al. (2012) align reflection in the classroom to a form of self-assessment, suggesting that this can impact on the teaching and learning styles of both teacher and pupils. Indeed, Price et al. (2012) argue that there is evidence that self-assessment has beneficial effects on pupil's awareness, motivation and involvement in their work. While Munby et al. (1989) suggest that students will require support to develop self-assessment and skills in reflective practice, Stefani et al. (2007, p. 62) identify that reflection can help students to learn how to be 'honest about themselves and open to criticism' while learning to provide feedback to their peers which is positive and constructive. This has the potential be a motivational and exciting experience for learners. However, carefully structured development of reflection is essential in your classroom to encourage an open and reflective environment.

Developing Price et al.'s (2012) suggestion of aligning reflective practice in the classroom through self-assessment may assist pupils in developing an ability to reflect and become self-critical, while encouraging motivation by giving them responsibility for their own learning and by implying that their opinions matter. This could help students to identify and be aware of their own weaknesses as well as set targets to develop these into strengths, leading to increased pride in positive achievement and confidence building.

Pupil reflection on the lesson and their progress towards learning outcomes would provide essential feedback on how your teaching is received, thus aiding classroom management and emphasising the notion of partnership in the learning process. Begun at the age of five and continued throughout the period of formal education, reflection would provide continuity between phases of education.

Towler and Broadfoot (1992, p. 139) suggest that children as young as five are able 'to remember and review activities, differentiate the enjoyable from the tedious, the easy from the more difficult and to communicate their opinions', thus suggesting that reflection may be appropriate from Year 1 through to Year 13.

While reflective practice can be verbal, reflections are normally recorded in a format that can be revisited. Alterio (2004, p. 321) suggests that reflective practice should 'enable individuals to comprehensively and systematically clarify ideas and expectations'.

Having highlighted the debates in reflective practice for teachers and whether reflection has a place in the classroom, we now move to identify and debate whether technologies are able to advance current practice in reflective practice. The technologies discussed are not intended to be exhaustive, and it is recognised that other technologies can be engaged to support reflection. However, the technologies below have all been tried and tested to support reflective practice by the author, or observed in practice by the author.

Technologies

Technologies can provide new and exciting platforms for reflective practice. There has been a longstanding argument over the last decade as to whether teachers are 'digital immigrants' and their students 'digital natives' (Prensky, 2001), while others suggest new generations coming through education are the 'net generation' (Tapscott, 1999) or the 'millennials' (Howe and Strauss, 2009), suggesting a lower level of digital literacy for teachers. However, whether or not you have grown up with technology and consider yourself a confident user of technology platforms, they can offer a place for reflective practice and are becoming increasingly simple to use and easily accessible via the Internet. This section introduces a range of simple platforms which provide a virtual space to enjoy the freedom of reflecting on practice. As technologies continue to develop, platforms are increasingly offering cloud storage, providing the reflective practitioner with the opportunity to reflect anywhere, anytime, moving from one mobile technology to the next, enabling continuity of reflective practice rather than carrying around a handwritten reflective log.

The platforms critiqued below all require an investment of time to learn to use them and also develop reflective writing, using technology which is a different experience to handwriting reflections. However, developing the skills in reflecting online, linked to the Internet to quickly find research to support your reflections and thus increasing the criticality of your reflective practice, will prove time saving. It is equally important that the technology does not take over from the purpose of using it, that is, to reflect. The technologies included in this chapter are mainly intuitive, so they are simple to learn and use for the purpose of reflective practice. As you become more confident, you can start to explore the technology and identify features appropriate for your reflections. For example, you can add pictures, drawings and other media such a video clips to remind you of your lesson, enhance your reflective practice and provide authentic evidence of the experiences you are reflecting on.

Debates around each of the technologies will be explored. We will also provide a brief overview of how you might prepare to use each technology and provide examples of each technology for reflecting. Reflection online has been termed 'E-flection' by Boulton and Hramiak (2012a). There are many benefits to using online technologies for reflection such as the potential to move reflections beyond being private and enable peer feedback, either within your community of practice or beyond, and potentially globally (ibid.). Many of the technologies also provide the facility to share specific reflections rather than all reflections, thus you can ask for feedback from others whom you choose to share you reflections with, providing not only another level of criticality but also the 'social' element discussed earlier. Boulton and Hramiak (2012b) make reference to the change in language that is often adopted when using online tools, of which you may need to be aware if you intend to share your reflections with others.

ePortfolios

ePortfolios have potential in terms of supporting reflective practice and a space for recording professional development. Other technologies such as wikis and blogs, now freely and easily available, can provide additional opportunities for reflection, peer feedback, discussion and sharing of artefacts and reflections. You may want to incorporate the views of your students in your reflections and might want to consider using other technologies, such as Etherpad, Padlet and CorkBoardIt with your classes to inform your reflections; each of these technologies can be incorporated into ePortfolios, wikis and blogs. Each of these technologies is debated below. An often-hidden benefit of reflecting online is that it can help increase your digital literacy. You may want to explore a range of technologies that can provide a virtual reflective space to find the one that suits your reflective practice.

ePortfolios are an excellent tool to encourage reflective practice (Roberts et al., 2005; Boulton, 2014). The Joint Information Systems Committee (JISC, 2008, p. 6) defines ePortfolios as 'created by the learner, a collection of digital artefacts articulating experiences, achievements and learning'; thus, an ePortfolio makes an excellent space for developing reflections. You may have developed an ePortfolio as part of your initial teacher education/pre-service course such as PebblePad, Mahara or a bespoke ePortfolio platform. It is, however, recognised that the purpose of an ePortfolio changes to be more goal focussed as teachers qualify and progress through their careers (Conway 2001; Boulton, 2004).

ePortfolios provide a space where you can showcase the development of your practice, adding artefacts to support your reflections, exploring how to improve your work and, where appropriate, linked to targets which may relate to threshold competencies. They also provide a space for you to develop your professional identity (Stenberg, 2010).

ePortfolios can be accessed 24/7 and generally work on PCs, Macs and tablets, and so can extend your opportunity to develop your reflections from anywhere. Most ePortfolios provide a facility so that you can share either the whole ePortfolio or selected reflections with others, thus enabling dialogue with peers, mentors and appropriate others. However, as argued by Vernazza et al. (2011) it can be time-consuming to learn to use ePortfolios.

A key benefit of an ePortfolio for reflections is that once set up it can be developed throughout your professional life (Heinrich et al., 2007). Choosing the right ePortfolio is important. Most schools provide an ePortfolio for students which may provide an easily accessible space for teachers to reflect; however, a limitation is that it may not be available if you leave the institution, which does not facilitate the notion of a reflective space for lifelong learning (Boulton, 2014).

Wikis

A wiki can provide a platform for sharing reflections, providing an opportunity for peer-to-peer learning and co-constructing knowledge. The term wiki originates from the Hawaiian word wiki-wiki, which means quick. A wiki is a collaborative software platform which allows authors to create and edit, thus developing ideas, concepts and understanding. Richardson (2010) aligned a wiki to being able to publish on the web. The key benefit is that you are able to publish or share your reflections with others. It may be that you want to reflect collaboratively, such as on a project or new pedagogy, and a wiki will facilitate this; thus, the wiki supports the constructivist paradigm of learning referred to earlier. Using the wiki to reflect collaboratively also supports Vygotsky's (1978) notion of the zone of proximal development; that is, by sharing and developing critical reflections you may move beyond the zone of individual knowledge. The downside is that most wikis do not provide opportunity to select the content to be shared with others; either the whole wiki is shared or it remains private to the owner.

Blogs

Blogs allow reflections, sharing opinions and discussions in the form of an online journal. The term blog originated from the ship's log where entries were made in chronological order. Caldwell and Honeyford (2015, p. 24) describe blogs as being 'powerful' as they allow authors to define their own spaces, which can lead to more creative reflections using different multimedia. Blogs can be private, opened by the owner to their community of peers or shared globally, thus enabling feedback from others and potentially resulting in a more critical approach to reflective practice. Alterio (2004) suggests that sharing reflections via a blog can increase motivation and enable a wider network of feedback, thus providing opportunities for multiple perspectives to develop reflections at a deeper and more global level.

The multimedia element of blogs can provide a richer environment for students' reflections; they can add text, video, voice, music and artefacts, thus encouraging greater creativity in their reflective practice.

Within a wiki, pages can be created enabling you to organise your reflections into different elements of practice rather than a more chronological approach as outlined for a blog. You can also add multimedia artefacts and ask others for their feedback. Some authors enjoy having a professional and personal space to reflect; through creating new areas, a wiki could provide such a space.

As part of their reflective practice, teachers frequently listen to, and encourage, their students to evaluate their teaching and provide feedback, which can then inform reflective practice. Increasingly, technologies can be used in class, or beyond the classroom, to encourage input of reflections by students. Examples of these include Etherpad and Padlet, both of which enable text to be added electronically via tablets or other mobile technology; the whole pad holding student contributions could form an artefact to reflect on, or specific comments could be copied into a journal to provide a deeper level of reflection. If students are not able to create text, a technology which simulates a corkboard could provide a mechanism for images or other artefacts to be presented as if posted on a corkboard, thus providing stimulus to reflective practice.

Conclusion

In this chapter, we have highlighted the key debates surrounding the place of reflective practice in professional development and identified different levels of reflective writing, drawing on key proponents of reflective practice and providing frameworks that can be adopted to scaffold a deeper level of reflection. We have suggested moving from a low level of reflection through mere description of an event to the deepest level involving dialogue with relevant others and/or research literature, as well as a development of metacognition in reviewing one's own practice. Thus, we have developed the notion of social reflective practice and presented some of the debates around widening reflective practice beyond personal reflections and sharing more widely, inviting comment on practice, arguing that this can lead to a deepening of reflective practice.

We have suggested how technologies can provide a virtual space for reflective practice, facilitating a wider range of authentic multimedia evidence, suggesting that this could lead to a deeper level of reflection by sharing virtual reflections within a community of practice, or to a global audience inviting feedback to advance current practice. As with all technologies, careful thought has to be given to using the right technology, and this will differ depending on personal style of reflective practice. We have identified that moving from a pen-and-paper process of reflective practice to reflecting electronically can take time to accomplish, but the benefits of having access 24/7 from anywhere can be stimulating, and the notion of adding multimedia can be exciting and provide a new level of reflective practice.

References

Alterio, M., 2004. Collaborative journaling as a professional development tool. *Journal of further and Higher Education*, 28, 321–332.

Argyris, C., and Schon, D., 1978. Organizational learning: A theory of action approach. *Reading, MA: Addision Wesley*.

Bandura, A., 1991. Social cognitive theory of self-regulation. *Organizational Behavior and Human Decision Processes*, 50 (2), 248–287.

Bengtsson, J., 1995. What is reflection? On reflection in the teaching profession and teacher education. *Teachers and Teaching: Theory and Practice*, 1 (1), 23–32.

Boulton, H., 2014. ePortfolios beyond pre-service teacher education: a new dawn? *European Journal of Teacher Education*, 37 (3), 374–389.

Boulton, H., and Hramiak, A., 2012a. E-flection: the development of reflective communities of learning for trainee teachers through the use of shared online web logs. *Reflective Practice*, 13 (4), 503–515.

Boulton, H., and Hramiak, A., 2012b. Writing in the Virtual Environment. *In:* L. Clughen, and C. Hardy, eds., *Writing in the disciplines: Building supportive cultures for student writing in UK higher education*. Bingley: Emerald Group Publishing, 2012, pp. 99–121.

Brockbank, A., and McGill, I., 1998. *Facilitating reflective learning in higher education* Buckingham: SRHE and Open University Press.

Caldwell, H., and Honeyford, G., 2014. Blogging to support digital literacy in schools and universities. *In:* S. Younie, M. Leask and K. Burden, eds., *Teaching and learning with ICT in the primary school.* London: Routledge, 2014, pp. 24–38.

Carr, W., and Kemmis, S., 1986. *Becoming critical education knowledge and action research.* London and Philadelphia: The Falmer Press.

Conway, P.F., 2001. Anticipatory reflection while learning to teach: From a temporally truncated to a temporally distributed model of reflection in teacher education. *Teaching and Teacher Education,* 17 (1), 89–106.

Day, C., 1993. Reflection: a necessary but not sufficient condition for professional development. *British Educational Research Journal,* 19 (1), 83–93.

Dewey, J. 1933. How we think. A restatement of the relation of reflective thinking to the educative process (Revised edn.), Boston: D. C. Heath.

Dymoke, S., and Harrison, J. (eds.), 2008. Reflective teaching and learning: a guide to professional issues for beginning secondary teachers. London: Sage.

Elliott, J., 1993. *Reconstructing teacher education.* London: Falmer Press.

Guskey, T.R., 2002. Professional development and teacher change. *Teachers and Teaching: Theory and Practice,* 8 (3), 381–391.

Heinrich, E., Bhattacharya, M., and Rayudu, R., 2007. Preparation for lifelong learning using ePortfolios. *European Journal of Engineering Education,* 32 (6), 653–663.

Howe, N., and Strauss, W., 2009. *Millennials rising: The next great generation.* London: Random House LLC.

Hramiak, A., and Hudson, T., 2014. *Understanding learning and teaching in secondary schools.* London: Routledge.

Joint Information Systems Committee, 2008. *Effective practice with e-portfolios: Supporting 21st century learning.* JISC.

Light, G., Cox, R., and Calkins, S., 2009. *Learning and teaching in higher education: The reflective professional.* London: Sage.

Lortie, D., 1975. *Schoolteacher: A sociological study.* London: University of Chicago Press.

McMahon, M., Forde, C., and Martin, M., 2010. *Contemporary issues in learning and teaching.* London: Sage.

McNiff, J., and Whitehead, J., 2009. *Doing and writing action research.* London: Sage.

Moon, J., 2007. *Critical thinking: An exploration of theory and practice.* London: Routledge.

Munby, S., Phillips, P., and Collinson, R., 1989. *Assessing and recording achievement.* London: Blackwell.

Prensky, M., 2001. Digital natives, digital immigrants part 1. *On the Horizon,* 9 (5), 1–6.

Price, M., et al. 2012. *Assessment literacy: The foundation for improving student learning.* ASKe, Oxford Centre for Staff and Learning Development.

Richardson, W. 2010. *Blogs, wikis, podcasts and other powerful tools for classrooms.* London: Sage.

Roberts, G., et al. 2005. *Reflective learning, future thinking: digital repositories, e-portfolios, informal learning and ubiquitous computing* [online]. Research Seminar at ALT Spring Conference 2005 in association with ILTA and SURF, 1 April 2005, Dublin Institute of Technology. Available from: http://www.alt.ac.uk/docs/ALT_SURF_ILTA_white_paper_2005.pdf [Accessed 15 July 2017].

Schon, D., 1983. *The reflective practitioner: How professionals think in action.* New York: Basic Books.

Solomon, J., 1987. New thoughts on teacher education. *Oxford Review of Education,* 13 (3), 267–274.

Stefani, L., Mason, R., and Pegler, C., 2007. *The educational potential of e-portfolios: Supporting personal development and reflective learning.* London: Routledge.

Stenberg, K., 2010. Identity work as a tool for promoting the professional development of student teachers. *Reflective Practice,* 11 (3), 331–346.

Stenhouse, L., 1975. *An introduction to curriculum research and development.* London: Heinemann.

Tapscott, D., 1999. Educating the net generation. *Educational Leadership,* 56 (5), 6–11.

Towler, L., and Broadfoot, P., 1992. Self-assessment in the primary school. *Educational Review,* 44 (2), 137–151.

Vernazza, C., et al., 2011. Introduction of an e-portfolio in clinical dentistry: staff and student views. *European Journal of Dental Education,* 15 (1), 36– 41.

Vygotsky, L., 1978. *Mind and society: the development of higher psychological processes.* 1st ed. London: Harvard University Press.

Wenger, E., 2009. A social theory of learning. *Contemporary Theories of Learning: Learning Theorists...in their Own Words,* 209–218.

Zwozdiak-Myers, P., 2012. *The teacher's reflective practice handbook: Becoming an extended professional through capturing evidence-informed practice.* London: Routledge.

Index

A levels 140
abstraction 16, 18, 20
acceptable use policies (AUPs) 120, 126–127, 164, 190
access: bring your own device 188; digital citizenship 67, 68; digital equity 70; online resources 126; permissions 135; tablets 184–185, 192; video data 213, 214
accessibility 8
accountability 213, 219
action research 224, 226
activity theory 31–33
adoption of technology 106, 107, 186
advertising 4, 118, 200–201
affordances 7–8, 9, 23, 100, 104, 155
agency 66
aggressive aspects of online activity 119
agile learning 81, 83, 90
Ainscow, M. 167
Alexander, J. 173
algorithms 16, 17, 18, 20, 39, 139
Allen, A. 57
Allen, A. 81–96
Allen, R. 81–96
Alterio, M. 227, 230
ambiguity, tolerance of 143, 144
Anderson, M. 108
Android 160, 161
animation 98, 104
annotation 101, 164
anonymity 64, 115
anxiety 57, 59
apprenticeship model 147
apps 90, 97; bring your own device 184; creation of 161; e-safety 116, 117; iPad 182; limited functionality 160; professional development 105, 107,

191; tablets 155, 183, 188, 190, 191; updates 161; *see also* software
architecture 83
Argyris, C. 223
artefacts 34, 47, 145, 147, 229, 230
artificial intelligence 133–134
ASE *see* Association for Science Education
assessment 15, 43–51, 74; DigiLit framework 109; dynamic 86; political debate 10; tablets 183; unique contribution 124; video 209–210, 212–213, 215–219, 220; Voki 100; *see also* peer assessment; summative assessment
assistive technologies 170–171
Association for Science Education (ASE) 108
attainment 6, 185, 201, 219–220, 225
attitudes 5, 28, 33, 34, 65, 89
Audain, J. 181–194
AUPs *see* acceptable use policies
autism 170
automaticity 8
autonomy 46
avatars 100

backing up 162
Baird, D.E. 199
Bandura, A. 224
Barefoot Computing 20, 139–140
Barnes, J. 27–42
Barnett, A. 63–78
Barrett, P.F. 84
barriers to technology use 5
Bates, J. 27
Beauchamp, G. 182, 183
Bebo 45

Becta 157, 158, 170
Beetham, H. 65
behaviourism 14
Beland, L.P. 185
beliefs 28, 33, 35, 65, 67–68
Belshaw, D. 66–67, 120, 147
Berners-Lee, T. 97, 111
Berry, G. 22
Berry, L.F. 171
BESA see British Education Suppliers
    Association
Beyer, S. 57
bias 172–173
Bijker, W.E. 9
bilingual children 170
Bingimlas, K.A. 5
Bird, J. 155
Black Girls Code 174
Blackberry 160
Blackmon, S. 173
Blackwell, A.F. 20
blogs 102–103, 105–106, 107, 110,
    196, 228–229, 230
Boulton, H. 223–233
boyd, d. 64, 65, 198
Bradshaw, P. 43–51, 114–136
Brennan, K. 139
bricolage 102
bring your own device (BYOD) 121,
    153–166, 184, 188–189, 190, 214
British Computer Society 39
British Education Suppliers Association
    (BESA) 156, 182, 188
British Values 75
Broadfoot, P. 224, 227
Brockbank, A. 224
Brownlow, S. 55
Bubbl.us 102
'buddy' system 36
budgets 184, 189; see also funding
bulletin boards 155
bullying 119, 198; see also cyberbullying
Burbules, N.C. 6, 9
Burden, K. 183, 185, 187
Burke, Q. 174–175
Burrett, M. 107
BYOD see bring your own device
Byron report (2008) 117–119
Byron, T. 197, 199

CAA see computer-assisted assessment
CAL see computer-assisted learning

Caldwell, H. 155, 230
Callister Jr, T.A. 6, 9
capacity 8
career advisers 56–57, 59
career decision-making 55, 56
Carr, W. 223, 224
CAS see Computing At School
Casey, A. 216–217
CEBE see Coalition for Evidence-Based
    Education
CEOP see Child Exploitation and
    Online Protection
Certificate of Personal Effectiveness 48
Chandler, D. 6
change 5, 82, 114, 181
character education 68
CHAT see Cultural Historical Activity
    Theory
Child Exploitation and Online
    Protection (CEOP) 115, 116,
    118, 121
Childnet 121, 123
Church, L. 20
Churches, A. 48
civic responsibility 67
Clark, T. 156
classroom design 84
classroom management 155, 227
classroom observation 35
'Click Clever, Click Safe Code' 118, 120
Cline, T. 167
cloud computing 123–124, 126, 214;
    bring your own device 188; flipped
    learning 82; mobile devices 162;
    reflective practice 228; safeguarding
    91, 92–93; video data 211
Coalition for Evidence-Based Education
    (CEBE) 159
codes of conduct/behaviour 34, 210,
    211–212
coding 17–18, 22, 39, 137, 145
collaboration 8, 18; collaborative tools
    47; computational thinking 143,
    144; DigiLit framework 110; digital
    citizenship 75; flipped learning 89,
    90; MirandaNet Fellowship 85–86;
    online communities 204; robotics
    147; video use 210; Web 2.0
    technologies 97, 98–101, 104, 111;
    wikis 229–230; zone of proximal
    development 225
The College Board 141, 144, 145, 149

College of Teaching 106
commercial aspects of online activity 118–119, 200–201
Common Sense Media (CSM) 67, 68, 77
communal constructivism 104, 105
communication 8; assistive technologies 170; computational thinking 143; DigiLit framework 110; digitally mediated 67; e-safety 115, 116
communities of practice 105, 224, 228, 231
community structures 34
competence 5, 15
competitiveness 54
computational participation 174–175
computational thinking 15, 19–21, 39; creativity 137–138, 141–142, 149; curriculum changes 43, 52, 53, 137; definition of 138–139; learner characteristics 143–144; programming 17, 18, 145
computer-assisted assessment (CAA) 15
computer-assisted learning (CAL) 14
computer science 16, 22, 37, 39; computational participation 175; computational thinking 21, 138–139, 140; curriculum changes 15, 137; digital citizenship 74; programming 17, 18
Computer Science Teachers Association (CSTA) 139, 143–144
computing 14, 15–23, 39, 63; app creation 161; computational thinking 139–140; creativity 137, 141–142, 149; female participation 52–62; inclusive pedagogies 174–175; learner perceptions 46; pedagogical approaches 146–149; see also information and communication technology
Computing At School (CAS) 15–16, 21, 39, 55, 108, 137, 140, 174
concept maps 102
concepts 29
confidence 5, 15; bring your own device 163; computational thinking 143, 144; female participation in computing 57, 59; positive ICT experiences 58; social media 196
connectionism 105
connectivism 85, 146

Conole, G. 8
constraints 8
constructionism 14, 18, 19, 145, 147–148, 224
constructivism 14, 19, 146; mobile learning 104; Web 2.0 technologies 97, 98, 105, 111; wikis 230
content creation 86, 98, 155, 183, 200
content pedagogic knowledge (CPK) 17–18
continuing professional development (CPD) 22, 107–108, 110, 111, 156, 158, 163; see also professional development
contradictions 32–33
Cooper, J. 57
copyright 63, 67, 109, 117, 124–125, 127, 128
CorkBoardIt 229
counter-terrorism 122–123
coursework 47, 48
CPD see continuing professional development
CPK see content pedagogic knowledge
Craft, A. 147
Creative Commons 109, 125, 128
creativity 137–138, 141–142, 149; blogs 230; definition of 138; flipped learning 89; learner characteristics 143–144; learner perceptions 44, 46, 48, 49; positive ICT experiences 58; reflective practice 224; Third Millennium Learning schools 89; tinkering 141, 142; Web 2.0 technologies 98
credibility 114–115
critical theory 10
critical thinking 123
criticality 67, 68–69
cross-curricular competence 28–29, 30
crowdsourcing 69
Csizmadia, A. 137–152
CSM see Common Sense Media
CSTA see Computer Science Teachers Association
Cuban, L. 4
cultural context 10
Cultural Historical Activity Theory (CHAT) 32, 33, 35
cultural practices 28
cultures 68, 73, 75, 167, 169
curiosity 144, 145

curriculum 16, 28–31; changes to the 14–15, 21–23, 32, 38–39, 43, 44, 52, 53, 63, 137; computational thinking 19, 139–140; criticism of the 53; digital literacy 64; female participation in computing 54, 58; implementation 28; learner perceptions 44–45, 46; organisation of the 40; policy development 27–28; political debate 10; thinking skills 37; video feedback 218–219
cyberbullying 66, 67, 75, 117, 119, 191, 198
Cych, L. 97–113

Dalton, T. 181–194
damage 162, 190
Dann, C. 209–222
data: computational thinking 139; data mining 92; data protection 92–93, 120–121; misuse of 128–132; ownership of 124, 162, 214; storage of video data 211, 212–215; see also files; information
databases 14, 45
Davidson, C.N. 86
Davis, K. 181
Day, C. 223
de Bono, E. 19
de Bruin, C. 172
debugging 17, 21
decomposition 18, 20
Dede, C. 144
departmental sets 184, 187
design and technology 23, 28
design issues 83–85
determinism: social 5–7, 9; technological 4–5, 10–11
Dewey, J. 148, 223
dialogical opportunities 68–69
DigiLit Leicester 109–110
digital citizenship 63–75, 78, 98, 120, 133; bring your own device 164; critical social media literacy 123; risk management 121–122; tablets 191
digital divide 63, 91, 168
digital equity 70
digital footprints 67, 117, 164
Digital Leader Network 108–109
digital literacy 15, 16, 20, 22, 39; bring your own device 164; constructive and creative components 147;

critical 133; definition of 70; digital citizenship 64–65, 66, 72; Facebook use 199; norms of conduct 120; professional development 109–111; reflective practice 228, 229; Web 2.0 technologies 98–103, 105
digital projectors 6–7
digital society 70
digital wisdom 70, 71–72, 74, 120, 123
Digitalme 78
Digizen 68, 77, 121
disabilities 167, 170, 171
distraction 184, 200, 201
diversity 8, 54, 55, 167, 174
Dolan, P. 146
Donaldson Review (2015) 39
Downes, S. 85
duty of care 126
Dyke, M. 8
dynamic assessment 86

'E-flection' 228
e-learning 68
e-Learning Strategy 15
e-safeguarding 91–93
e-safety 91–93, 114–122; bring your own device 164; DigiLit framework 110; Facebook 197–199, 204; policies 120–122; social media 196; three Cs framework 118–119; see also safety; security
Echoes project 170
Edge, D. 9
Edmodo 91
Education Endowment Foundation (EEF) 6, 159
Education Technology Action Group (ETAG) 188
educational spaces 83
Egenfeldt-Nielsen, S. 173
Elliott, J. 224
employers 22, 164
empowerment 65–66, 72, 75, 119, 120, 121–122
engagement 183–184
Engeström, Y. 31–32
engineering 54, 56
England 29, 30, 35, 38–39, 64, 170
English language 169
enquiry-based learning 89, 90
ePortfolios 228–229
equal opportunities 52–53

equity 70, 167, 188
Estyn 30, 39
ETAG *see* Education Technology Action
   Group
Etherpad 229, 230
ethics 67, 114–136, 162; digital
   citizenship 70, 73; mobile devices
   221; video use 209, 210–212; *see also*
   privacy; safety
ethnicity 167
EU Kids Online project 120, 172
evaluation 20, 29, 37, 109
Every Child Matters 20, 21
evidence 4, 44, 106, 157–158; reflective
   practice 228; video 212–213,
   215–216, 217–219
examinations 47, 48, 183; *see also*
   assessment
exclusion 167, 170–171, 175
exploration 18, 101
extra-curricular activities 174
extremism 122–123

Fab Lab movement 142
Facebook 45, 52, 65, 91, 98, 156,
   195–208
Facer, K. 168
fake websites 133
feedback: blogs 103, 230; DigiLit
   framework 109; reflective practice
   228, 230; self-assessment 227; Third
   Millennium Learning schools 89;
   video assessment 215–216, 217,
   218–220
Feenberg, A. 6, 10
Fenn, J. 186
Ferri, B.A. 171
Fievez, A. 191
files 92, 124, 126, 128–129, 187, 214;
   see also data
filtering 126, 164, 172, 184
Fisher, A. 55–56
Fisher, M. 199
Flickr 45
flipped learning 82, 86, 87–91, 92,
   93–94
Florian, L. 174
Foley, A. 171
formative assessment 100, 215–217,
   218–219
forums 116
4oD 45

fragility 8
fraud 92, 135
Frederickson, N. 167
freedom of expression 68
Friedman, A. 183–184
friendships 57, 117
Friesen, N. 200–201
Fullan, M. 82, 191
functionality 160
funding 163; *see also* budgets
furniture 84
'futureproofing' 28

Galloway, J. 187, 190
gaming 47, 57, 133; e-safety 116, 118;
   English as an additional language
   170; gender differences 56; inclusive
   172; iPads 191; online distortion
   of values 134; sexism and racism in
   172–173
Garcia, E. 183–184
Gardner, H. 181
Gatewood, R. 55
GCSEs 48, 53, 137; computational
   thinking 140; employers' needs 22;
   female participation in computing 54;
   learner perceptions 43, 46
geek culture 55–56
gender 9, 22, 52–62, 167
geo-tagging 135
Gershenfeld, N. 142
Ghezzi, C. 22
Gibson, J. 7
girls 22, 52–62
Glogster 102
GoAnimate 98
Goldberg, D.T. 86
Google Drive 98, 106, 162
Google RISE 174
Goto, E. 181–194
Gove, M. 23, 44
Gowan, M. 55
Green, H. 200
Greenfield report (2002) 54
Greenhow, C. 202
groups 117
Gupta, N. 201
Guskey, T.R. 225

habits of mind 66
Habler, B. 156, 158
Hall, E. 147

Hammond, M. 8
Hannon, C. 200
hardware 34, 48
Harel, I. 147
Hattie, J. 90
Heinrich, P. 183, 184–185, 189, 190, 191
Hennessy, S. 156, 158, 159
Heppell, S. 44–45, 181
'high-stakes' assessment 43, 47, 49, 212
higher order skills 29, 37, 39, 89, 99, 111
Hill, V. 78
Hillier, E. 182, 183
Hind, E. 146
Hobbs, R. 66
Hodges, H. 56
Hole in the Wall project 87
home experiences 57, 58, 59, 185
homework 104, 185
Honeyford, G. 230
Hramiak, A. 223, 227, 228
Hudson, T. 227
humanistic approach 74
Hundred Word Challenge 108
Hynes, P. 153–166
hype 4, 17
hypothesis testing 29

IBI Group 83
ICO see Information Commissioner's Office
ICT see information and communication technology
ICT across the curriculum (ICTAC) 15
ICTmagic 107
identification information 92, 93
identity: development 65, 75; identity fraud or theft 135; multiple identities 125; online identity protection 64, 110, 117; professional 229; self-expression 67
iLeaders 183
images: acceptable use policies 126; bring your own device 164; copyright 125; modelling by teachers 127, 128; Web 2.0 technologies 102; see also photos
imagination 138, 141, 144
immediacy 8
implementation 28, 184, 186–189
inclusion 167–177, 185
individual needs 170–172

individualised teaching 174
inequality 168–169, 172, 175
informal learning 46, 48, 49, 86, 182–183
information: gathering 101–102, 201; profiles 116; sharing 115, 118, 135, 146, 197, 198, 200, 201; tablets 183; see also data; personal details
information and communication technology (ICT) 16, 28–31; curriculum changes 14, 21–22, 38–39, 43, 44, 63; female participation 52, 54, 55; learner perceptions 43–49; policy development 27–28; practices 28; tablets 182, 185; teaching of 31–38; see also computing; technology
Information Commissioner's Office (ICO) 92, 120
information literacy 67
information search 75, 82, 99, 109
information technology (IT) 15, 16, 53; female participation 54, 58–59; policy development 27; practices 28
innovation 141, 149, 186
inspections 28
Inspire project 110
Instagram 98, 196
institutional context 10
instrumentalist view 5–6
integration 171
intellectual property rights (IPR) 67, 124–125, 128, 162
interactive whiteboards 7, 18, 186
interactivity 8, 181
International Society for Technology in Education (ISTE) 139, 143–144
Internet: bring your own device 154, 160, 184, 188; children's use of the 200; DigiLit framework 109; digital divide 168; digital equity 70; digital literacy 70; ethical challenges 126; flipped learning 82; mobile technologies 117; network infrastructure 189–190; participation gap 168–169; participatory learning 86; Prevent strategy 123; reflective practice 228; safety 74, 114–122; tablets 183, 184–185, 188; Web 2.0 technologies 97; see also social media; websites

iPads 4, 10, 171, 182–185, 187, 189, 191
iPlayer 45
IPR *see* intellectual property rights
Irwin, J.D. 201
ISTE *see* International Society for Technology in Education
IT *see* information technology
iTunes 161

Joint Information Systems Committee (JISC) 64, 65, 75, 83, 229
Jones, B. 216–217
Jones, K.S. 52
Jones, R. 108
Jones, S. 157, 159
Junco, R. 201

Kacetl, J. 92
Kafai, Y.B. 174–175
Karsenti, T. 191
Kemmis, S. 223, 224
Kennewell, S. 7–8, 27–42
key concepts 29, 37
Key Stage 1 23
Key Stage 2 17
Key Stage 3 18, 21, 29–30, 35–36, 64, 140
Key Stage 4 18, 43, 44, 140
Kidsmart 121
kindergarten approach 147–149
knowledge 31, 45, 68; co-construction of 98, 111; collaborative knowledge creation 85–86; communal constructivism 104; content pedagogic 17–18; digital equity 70; higher order 29; MirandaMod 69; positive ICT experiences 58; reflective practice 226
Konstantinidis, A. 195–208
Kordaki, M. 57

Lai, E. 190
language 34
language issues 169, 170
laptops 160, 185
Lautenschlager, G. 55
Le Velle, L. 159
learner-centred approaches: agile learning 81; assessment 48; mobile technologies 103–104; Web 2.0 technologies 101, 103, 104, 111

learner perceptions 43–49
learning 14, 19, 33–34, 38; activity theory 32–33; agile 81, 83, 90; assessment for 216; blogs 103; bring your own device 156–159, 163–164; connectivism 146; constructionism 148; Facebook 199–200, 202–203, 204; flipped 82, 86, 87–91, 92, 93–94; inclusion 172, 175; learner perceptions 44, 45; learning culture 182–183; 'learning gap' 31; learning spaces 81–96; mobile 103, 104, 153; pedagogical tools 39; reflective practice 223, 225–226; rhizomatic 85, 86; self-organised learning environments 87, 146; tablets 182–186, 192; traditional 81, 90; video feedback 218–219
Leask, M. 104, 156
Lee, M. 162–163
LEGO 147
Lesson Study Groups 106
Levins, M. 162–163
licenses 109, 125, 128
Light, J. 171, 225
liminal space 86
Lino 101–102
Livingstone, S. 120
location tagging 135
lockdown of devices 161
logical reasoning 18, 20
LOGO 14
London Mobile Learning Group 87
Lowe, S. 200–201
Lynch, J. 10

MacKenzie, D. 9
Madge, C. 91
Mahara 229
maintenance issues 190
Make 142–143
Maker Movement 141, 142–143, 146, 148
Mallen, G. 216
Malone, T.W. 21
managed learning environments (MLEs) 15
Mapping Education Specialist knowHow (MESH) 106, 159
Maresova, J. 92
Margolis, J. 55–56
Martin, L. 142

massive open online courses
(MOOCs) 85
'masterclasses' 35–36, 37
mathematics 18, 53
Mazuch, R. 83–84
Mazur, E. 88
McFarlane, A. 86, 91–92, 185
McGhie-Richmond, D.R. 172
McGill, I. 224
McMahon, M. 225
McNaughton, D. 171
McNeal, R. 78
McNiff, J. 224
McTaggart, M. 187, 190
MDM see mobile device management
mechanistic approach 74
media 4, 55, 57, 59
Mee, A. 28
MESH see Mapping Education Specialist
knowHow
messaging apps 116
metacognition 32, 36, 37, 38, 90,
144, 225
Metzger, M. 114
Millwood, R. 45
Milter, R.E. 90
mind maps 102, 183
MindMeister 102
mindset 65, 75
Minecraft 78
MirandaMod 69
MirandaNet Fellowship 69, 85–86
misuse of data 128–132
Mitra, Sugata 48, 87, 146
MLEs see managed learning
environments
mobile device management (MDM) 121
mobile phones 185, 200, 209, 218; see
also smartphones
mobile technologies 18, 47, 124, 172,
217; defending the use of 159–
163; flipped learning 88; funding
possibilities 163; increase in use 221;
location tagging 135; mobile device
management 121; nature of learning
182–186; participatory learning
86; personalisation 117; reflective
practice 228; ubiquity of 87, 181;
video capture 209–210, 211, 215;
Web 2.0 technologies 98, 103–105;
see also bring your own device;
smartphones; tablets

modelling 127–128
monopolisation 8
Montessori, M. 142
MOOCs see massive open online
courses
Moon, J. 225
Mossberger, K. 78
motivation 14, 35, 38; assessment 46;
avatars 100; self-assessment 227; Web
2.0 technologies 98
Mr. Benny 111
Mull, B. 88
Muller, D.A. 203
multimedia 14; annotation 101; e-safety
117; mobile devices 158; reflective
practice 230, 231; tablets 104,
183–184
multimodality 8, 102, 155, 172
multitasking 201
Munby, S. 224, 227
Murphy, R. 185
music 23
MySpace 45
myths 4

Naace Third Millennium Learning
Award 88–89
National Advisory Committee on
Creative and Cultural Education
(NACCCE) 138, 141
national curriculum 15, 19, 21–23,
28–31, 34, 38–39; digital literacy 64;
female participation in computing
54; policy development 27–28;
programming 17; thinking skills 37;
see also curriculum
National Education Network (NEN) 93
Naughton, J. 45
Nees, M.A. 171
negative attitudes 5
negative effects of technology 4
NEN see National Education Network
netizens 68
networks 63–64, 67, 189–190; see also
personal learning networks; social
networking
neutrality 5–6, 7, 11
non-linearity 8
Norman, D. 7
norms 66, 67, 70, 120, 199
Northampton University 110–111
November, A. 88, 133

observation 35
OECD *see* Organisation for Economic Cooperation and Development
Ofsted 30, 118, 121, 122, 188
Ohler, J. 68
Oliver, M. 8
one-to-one (1:1) provision 105, 184, 185, 186, 187–188; bring your own device 160, 161–162, 163, 165; individual needs 172; user responsibility 190
online communities 204
online identity protection 64, 110, 117
open licenses 109
Open University 85
Oppenheimer, T. 4
Organisation for Economic Cooperation and Development (OECD) 6, 48, 82, 83, 169, 209
organisational structures 34
Ormerod, M.B. 53
out-of-school computer use 48–49, 57–58, 59, 91, 202
ownership of data 124, 162, 214

Padlet 69, 229, 230
Papert, S. 14, 19, 147, 148, 149
parents: bring your own device 163; e-safety 93; engagement with 88, 89, 191; gender stereotypes 56, 59; positive ICT experiences 58; tablets 187–188, 191
participation: computational 174–175; participation gap 168–169, 174
participative tools 47, 110
passwords 120, 121, 134, 211
pattern identification 20
Pau, R. 52–62
Payton, M. 63–78
Pea, R. 103
PebblePad 229
pedagogy 15, 19, 82; change in 32; content pedagogic knowledge 17–18; disruption to 219; flipped learning 88; inclusive 174–175; knowing your own 220; need for new pedagogies 74; pedagogical tools 37–38, 39–40; political debate 10; rhizomatic learning 85; variation in pedagogical practice 31
Pedagoo 108
peer assessment 47–48, 49, 99, 100, 101, 109

peer group influences 57
peer support 204
peer teaching 36, 38
permissions 115, 116, 117, 135
personal details 92, 115, 118, 120, 134, 198
personal learning networks (PLNs) 85, 88, 92, 94, 110
personalisation 46, 117, 147; blogs 103; bring your own device 162–163, 188; iPads 182; tablets 161, 187, 188
phablets 153
photos 101, 104, 117, 183, 203; *see also* images
physical education (PE) 216–217
physical space 83–84, 148–149
physics 53
Piaget, J. 14, 19
Pim, C. 170
Pinch, T.J. 9
Pinterest 108
Pinto, T. 93
Pixton 98
plagiarism 128
playful kindergarten approach 147–149
PLNs *see* personal learning networks
podcasts 88, 164, 183
policy 27–28, 34, 131; acceptable use policies 120, 126–127, 164, 190; safety 120–122; video use 210
political context 9–10, 63
pornography 119, 120, 198
portfolios 228–229
posters 102, 104
Powell, M. 168
power relationships 10
Powerpoint 45
Pratt, J. 53
prejudice 172–173
presentations 45
Preston, C. 63–78, 81–96
Prevent strategy 68, 122–123
Price, M. 227
PrimaryPad 98–100
privacy 116, 127, 134–135; cloud storage 214; digital citizenship 64, 67; Facebook 199; learning spaces 91, 92; video 212
problem solving 36, 37–38, 39, 48; computational participation 175; computational thinking 138, 139; learner perceptions 47, 49; positive

ICT experiences 58; reflective practice 227; Third Millennium Learning schools 89
processes 29, 37
professional development 22, 40; bring your own device 156, 158, 163; ePortfolios 228–229; personal learning networks 85; Prevent strategy 123; reflective practice 223, 225–226; tablets 190–191; Web 2.0 technologies 105–108, 109–111
professional values 125–127
profiles 116, 197, 198
programming 16–17, 20–21, 37, 145, 149; app creation 161; computational thinking 19; content pedagogic knowledge 17–18; creativity 137; curriculum changes 14, 43, 52, 53
progress 185, 213, 217
project work 49
projectors 6–7
propaganda 123
provisionality 8
pupil premium 163

QR codes 164
QuadBlogging 108
Qualifications and Curriculum Authority (QCA) 138

racial segregation 65
racism 119, 172–173
radicalisation 68, 122–123
Ramona, S. 78
range 8
Raskino, M. 186
Raza, A. 68
Redpath, T. 10
reflection 8, 223–233; digital citizenship 68–69; teachers 34, 35, 37, 223–227; technologies 227, 228–230, 231; Web 2.0 98
Regional Broadband Consortia 93
Renshaw, S. 110
reporting 127
representation 173, 175
reputation 67
research 18–19, 106; action research 224, 226; bring your own device 156–159; ethics 132–133
resilience 90, 119, 144, 145
resistance to change 5

Resnick, M. 137, 139, 141, 142, 144–145, 147–149
responsibility 117
return on investment 54
'revenge effects' 6
rhizomatic learning 85, 86
Ribble, M. 64, 67, 68, 78
Richardson, T. 209–222
Richardson, W. 229–230
rights and responsibilities 66, 67
risk 8, 119, 120; cloud storage 214; Facebook 197–199, 204; managing 121–122; video feedback 218; see also safety
roaming sets of tablets 184, 187
Robelia, B. 202
Roberts Review (2006) 138
Robinson, K. 141
robotics 147
Rogers, E.M. 106, 111, 186
role models 55, 58, 59
roles 34
Rosenbaum, E. 141, 142, 144–145, 147–149
routines 29, 37
Royal Academy for Engineering 39
Royal Society 15, 16, 19, 22, 39
rules 34

Saeli, M. 18
safeguarding 91–93, 116
safety 67, 74, 91–93, 114–122; bring your own device 164; DigiLit framework 110; Facebook 197–199, 204; flipped learning 82; inclusion 172; policies 120–122, 190; social media 196; three Cs framework 118–119; see also security
Sanders, J. 56
Savage, M. 63–78, 137–152
scaffolding 38, 99, 226
Schmidt, E. 15
Schön, D. 223–224
School Maker Faires 142–143
science 18, 53, 54
science, technology, engineering and mathematics (STEM) 56
Scoop.it 196
SCOT see Social Construction of Technology
Scratch 147, 174
ScratchEd 145

screencasting 183
Scully, R.P. 146
security 67, 82, 91–93, 120–121, 126, 134, 211; *see also* safety
self-assessment 109, 224, 226, 227
self-efficacy 57, 224
self-expression 67, 68
self image 67
self-organised learning environments (SOLEs) 87, 94, 146
self-regulating learning systems 48
Selwyn, N. 63–64, 168
'sense-sensitive design' 83–84
Sex Discrimination Act (1975) 52
sexism 172–173
sexual aspects of online activity 119, 197–198
sharing: DigiLit framework 109; files 128–129; information 115, 118, 135, 146, 197, 198, 200, 201; mobile devices 162; wikis 230
Sharpe, R. 65
Sharples, M. 103
Shelton, C. 3–13, 167–177
Sheppard, D. 187, 189
Shulman, L.S. 17–18
Siemens, G. 85, 91, 146
Singh, S. 57–58
SketchUp 98
skills: digital literacy 65; female participation in computing 54; higher order 29, 37, 39, 89, 99, 111; metacognitive 37, 38; online 203; reflective practice 226; social 170; Web 2.0 technologies 98
Skype 45, 69, 116
SLTchat 107
smartphones 104, 105, 117, 156; *see also* mobile phones
Snapchat 98
Social Construction of Technology (SCOT) 9–10
social constructivism 97, 98, 104, 105, 111, 146; *see also* constructivism
social context 9–10, 74
social determinism 5–7, 9
social informatics 74
social justice 67
social media 18, 45, 65–66, 86, 91, 196; critical literacy 123; DigiLit framework 110; employers 164; knowledge sharing 146; MirandaMod 69; Prevent Duty 68; professional development 108, 111, 156; as tool for learning 202; Web 2.0 technologies 105; *see also* Facebook; Twitter
social networking 57–58, 68, 97, 98, 196; DigiLit framework 110; digital citizenship 75; e-safety 114–117, 118; iPads 191; modelling by teachers 127–128; permissions 135; research 132–133
social skills 170
society 9, 58, 59; digital 70; networked 63–64
socio-economic status 168–169, 172
Socratic teaching 88
software 14, 20, 34, 39, 45; inclusive 172; licensing 125, 128; problem solving 36, 37; social network platforms 117; updates 161; video editing 214; Web 2.0 technologies 98; *see also* apps
SOLEs *see* self-organised learning environments
Solomon, J. 223
South West Grid for Learning (SWGfL) 67
spam 118
Specht, M. 181
special educational needs (SEN) 167, 170–171
specialists 16, 30, 36, 37
speed 8
SpicyNodes 102
spreadsheets 14, 18, 39, 45, 53
Squire, K. 173
Staksrud, E. 198
Stefani, L. 227
STEM subjects 56
Stenhouse, L. 224
stereotypes 55–56, 59, 172–173
Stevenson Report (1997) 15
Stinson, J.E. 90
Stone, A. 56
storage of data 92–93, 211, 212–215; *see also* cloud computing
stories, multimedia 104
storyboards 98
strangers 115
subject choices 53
summative assessment 47–48, 100, 215–217, 218–219

SuperJanet 93
surveillance 8, 135
SWGfL *see* South West Grid for
   Learning
Swidenbank, R. 22–23

tablets 7, 104, 105, 160–162, 181–194;
   apps for teaching with 155;
   implementation models 186–189;
   nature of learning 182–186;
   personalisation 117; research on
   156–157, 158; video capture 209;
   Web 2.0 technologies 98; *see also*
   mobile technologies
Tapscott, D. 47
teacher training 7–8, 75, 121–122, 123
Teacher Training Resource Bank
   (TTRB) 158
teachers: ability to use technology
   87; activity theory 33; adoption
   of technology by 186; barriers
   to technology use 5; bring your
   own device 154, 155, 158, 163;
   computational thinking 140;
   computing 16, 22; content
   pedagogic knowledge 17–18; data
   protection 121; digital citizenship
   75; digital networks 67; e-safety
   121–122; ethical use of technology
   131; Facebook used as a tool for
   learning 202–203; flipped learning
   87–91; influence on female
   participation 56–57, 59; modelling
   practice 127–128; older 209;
   positive ICT experiences 58; Prevent
   duty 68, 122–123; professional
   values 125–127; reflective practice
   223–227; research on the teaching of
   ICT 31, 34–38; roles 34; supported
   by students 182; tablets 190–191;
   teaching styles 17; traditional
   learning 81; video use 210,
   215–216, 217–218, 220; Web 2.0
   technologies 105–111; Welsh ICT
   curriculum 30; *see also* professional
   development
TeachMeets 106, 108
technical support 5, 189
techniques 29, 37
technology: affordances 7–8, 23; claims
   and counterclaims about 3–4, 10–11;
   ethical challenges 114; evidence
on effectiveness 157–158; flipped
   learning 91; inclusion 167–177;
   learner perceptions 48–49; reflective
   practice 227, 228–230, 231; social
   and political aspects 9–10; social
   determinism 5–7, 9; teachers' ability
   to use 87; technological determinism
   4–5, 10–11; ubiquity of 82; UN
   report 175; Web 2.0 technologies
   97–113; *see also* computing;
   information and communication
   technology; Internet; mobile
   technologies
'technopositivist ideology' 4
TED talks 142, 143
Tenderfoot 140
Tenner, E. 6
terrorism 122–123
text messaging 116
theft 190
thinking skills 19, 37, 89, 99, 111
Thinkuknow 77–78, 121
Third Millennium Learning schools
   88–89, 90
Thomas, T. 57
three Cs framework 118–119
time: curriculum organisation 40; lack of
   5; reflective practice 225
tinkering 141, 142, 145, 147–149
Tolbert, C. 78
Toneva, K. 102–103, 104
tools 34; digital society 70; online 83;
   participative and collaborative 47;
   pedagogical 37–38, 39–40
ToonDoo 98
Towler, L. 224, 227
Townsend, G. 55
traditional learning 81, 90
training, lack of 5
translational research 159
Traxler, J. 103, 189, 190
Trowler, P. 27
trust 133, 204, 210–211
'Trust Me' resource 123
Tsagala, E. 57
TTRB *see* Teacher Training Resource
   Bank
Tumblr 196
Twining, P. 182
Twitter 69, 91, 98, 196; professional
   development 156; teachers on 106,
   107–108; Twitterstorms 65–66

UK Council for Child Internet Safety (UKCCIS) 118
UKEdChat 107
ultrabooks 153
uncertainty 8, 153
United Nations (UN) 175
updates 161
user-generated content 86, 97, 98

values 10, 23; British 75; digital citizenship 65, 67–68, 70; e-safety 119; flipped learning 89; inclusive 167; online distortion of 134; policy implementation 28; professional 125–127
Vernazza, C. 229
video 209–222; blogs 230; bring your own device 164; e-safety 117; editing 183, 214; ethics 210–212; Facebook 195, 203; flipped learning 88, 90; reflective practice 228; SpicyNodes 102; storage implications 212–215; tablets 104; video sharing sites 97; VoiceThread 101
violent content 119, 120, 134, 172
Virgin Media Business 87
virtual learning environments (VLEs) 15, 36, 86; bring your own device 164; design of 84–85; flipped learning 82; Web 2.0 technologies 99, 100, 102
virtual reality 7, 133–134
visible learning 90–91, 92, 94, 155
visual concept maps 102
Vitruvian principles 83, 84
VLEs see virtual learning environments
voice 47–48, 49, 120
VoiceThread 98, 101
Voki 100–101
Vygotsky, L. 32, 219–220, 225, 230

Wajcman, J. 9
Wales 29–31, 35, 37, 39

Warschauer, M. 168
Weaver, K. 57
Web 2.0 technologies 97–113, 195, 196, 200
Webb, M. 31, 32
webcams 116
websites: bring your own device 160; creating 104; design 83; filtering 126; inclusive 172; knowledge sharing 146; language issues 169; veracity 133; see also Internet; social media
Weller, M. 91
whiteboards 7, 18, 155, 186
Whitehead, J. 224
Whitten, A. 20
Whyte, J. 53
Wikipedia 115, 133
wikis 99, 110, 228–230
Williams, L. 97–113
Williams, R. 9
Willis, M. 220
Wilson, A. 138
Wing, J. 19, 138–139, 140, 145
Winner, L. 10
wireless technology 154, 162, 189–190
Wisconsin Task Force on Arts and Creativity in Education 143, 144
wisdom 70, 71–72, 74, 86, 93, 120, 123
Wolak, J. 197
Wood, C. 31
Woollard, J. 14–26, 43
word processing 14, 39, 45, 53, 100
workshops 35–36, 37
writing 98–100, 101, 108, 183; see also blogs

Younie, S. 93, 97–113, 114–136, 153–166, 186
YouTube 45, 106, 133, 183

zone of proximal development 219, 225, 230
Zwozdiak-Myers, P. 226